Landscape
Modeling

Landscape Modeling

Digital Techniques for Landscape Visualization

Stephen M. Ervin

Hope H. Hasbrouck

McGraw-Hill

New York Chicago San Francisco Lisbon London Madrid Mexico City Milan
New Delhi San Juan Seoul Singapore Sydney Toronto

McGraw-Hill

A Division of The ***McGraw·Hill*** *Companies*

Cataloging-in-Publication Data is on file with the Library of Congress

1234567890 VNH/VNH 0987654321
P/N 0-07-135746-7
ISBN 0-07-135745-9

The sponsoring editor for this book was Wendy Lochner, the editing supervisor was Steven Melvin, and the production supervisor was Sherri Souffrance.
Von Hoffmann Press was printer and binder.

McGraw-Hill books are available at special quantity discounts to use as premiums and sales promotions, or for use in corporate training programs. For more information, please write to the Director of Special Sales, McGraw-Hill, 2 Penn Plaza, New York, NY 10121-2298. Or contact your local bookstore.

This book is printed on recycled, acid-free paper containing a minimum of 50% recycled, de-inked fiber.

Contents

Chapter 1: Landscape Modeling

Chapter 2: Landform

Chapter 3: Vegetation

Chapter 4: Water

Chapter 5: Atmosphere

Chapter 6: Synthesis

Preface

This book has taken a seemingly long time to come to fruition, but is a chronicle of a discipline still in its infancy. Both the authors have been modeling the landscape for years, it seems, but it has really only been twenty years; Stephen Ervin made his first digital landscape model in 1980, on computer punchcards; since the 1990s, Hope Hasbrouck has led dozens of graduate students and several professional projects through the process. In those years, the hardware and software we have had to work with have undergone exponential changes. What we can rather easily do now is really quite incredible, technologically, compared to what we both started with.

And even what our predecessors and colleagues were doing thirty and forty years ago, in the 1960s and 1970s, on far more rudimentary equipment, had very similar goals: to produce images (usually, but more generally, models and representations), in the process of design inquiry and communication, as part of teaching and doing landscape architecture and landscape planning. We have never been involved in this endeavor purely for art's sake, though we have seen and made some beautiful things, in their own right, along the way. Modeling, as we have learned, and tried to teach, and emphasize in this book, is a value-laden, technically dependent but ultimately concept-motivated activity. There are no perfect or best models; rather there are nearly infinitely many different ways of representing almost anything. Choosing between the options, and combining and using them in different ways, is a design act of the highest order.

Both the authors were trained as "traditional" architects and landscape architects, versed in pen and pencil representational techniques. We have both evolved along with computing and information technology, to a position of not replacing, but augmenting and building upon, our original drawing and communications skills. In creating this book, we have used dozens of different computer programs on several different computers and operating systems – any we could get our hands on – to see what we could learn from, or do with, them.

This book has been a joint venture, from its conception to production. As with any combined effort, some division of labor has been obvious and essential. Most of the text was written by Ervin; Hasbrouck provided the graphic narrative, layout, tutorials, and most of the modeling and illustrations, especially of the "University Commons" project used throughout the book. But we remain jointly, and solely, responsible for any errors or omissions.

We hope the book serves both as a reference into an already large, but largely uncollected, body of work, and also a stimulus for new inventions and applications in landscape modeling – for which there is still a lot of room.

Cambridge, Massachusetts 2001

Acknowledgments

Thanks to:

• Our colleagues, collaborators, teachers and students, far too numerous to itemize each and every one, but especially: Emlyn Altman, Pierre Belanger, Mirka Benes, Rick Casteel, Amy Cupples-Rubbiano, John Danahy, David Diethelm, Nick Dines, Alex Duval, Mike Flaxman, Aaron Fleisher, Mark Gionet, George Hargreaves, Chuck Harris, Gary Hilderbrand, Rodney Hoinkes, David Hulse, Mark Klopfer, Eckart Lange, Mark Lindhult, James Lord, Alistair Macintosh, Kaki Martin, Miho Mazereeuw, Malcolm McCullough, Anne McGhee, Adrian Mendoza, Arancha Muñoz, Bruce MacDougall, Andreas Muhar, Doug Olson, Peter Petschek, Madis Pihlak, Alan Shearer, Stephen Sheppard, Carl Steinitz, Letitia Tormay, Christian Tschumi, Joe Volpe, Mark von Wodtke, John Paul Weesner, Curt Westergard, Caroline Westort, and others

• Others we don't know so well, but who have provided valuable information, illustrations or other contributions, including: Chuck Clarke at Evans and Sutherland (RapidSite); Urs Frei at University of Zurich Remote Sensing Laboratories; Dennis at DigArts; Jamie Kurtz at 3D Nature (WCS); Stephane Gourgot at JMG Graphics (AMAP); Bojanna Bosanac and Pjer Zanchi of Onyx Software (TreePro); Brett Casebolt at Natural Graphics; Christopher Seeger; Midori Kitagawa deLeon, Greg Schmidt, and others at Texas A&M Forest Simulation Lab; Karin Egger at Bodenkultur University Vienna; Olli Pekka Saastamoinen; Paul Bourke at Swinburne University; Kevin Woolley of Genesis software; David Ebert for fractal cloud images; Igor Borovikov at Animatek; Andreas Ögren at Blueberry3D; C. Soler for plant growth images and movies; Damian Sainsbury; Francoise Rossi at Geo-Metricks; Jessica Hodgins at Georgia Institute of Technology; staff at Hargreaves Associates; staff at Peter Walker and Partners; staff at Martha Schwartz Associates; Mary Daniels, Alex Reiskind, and Anne Whiteside from the Visual Resources at the Harvard Univsersity Loeb Library; and others

• Those who have blazed parts of the path before us, including but not limited to Ivan Sutherland, Alvy Ray Smith, Loren Carpenter, Premeslaw Prusinkiewicz, F. Kenton Musgrave, Benoit Mandelbrot, Jack Dangermond, and others

• Our editor Wendy Lochner and the team at McGraw-Hill who encouraged the book, and tolerated delays, demands, and digressions

• Our parents, families, and friends, who also encouraged, supported, and tolerated a project that took far longer and far more out of us than any of us ever guessed it would

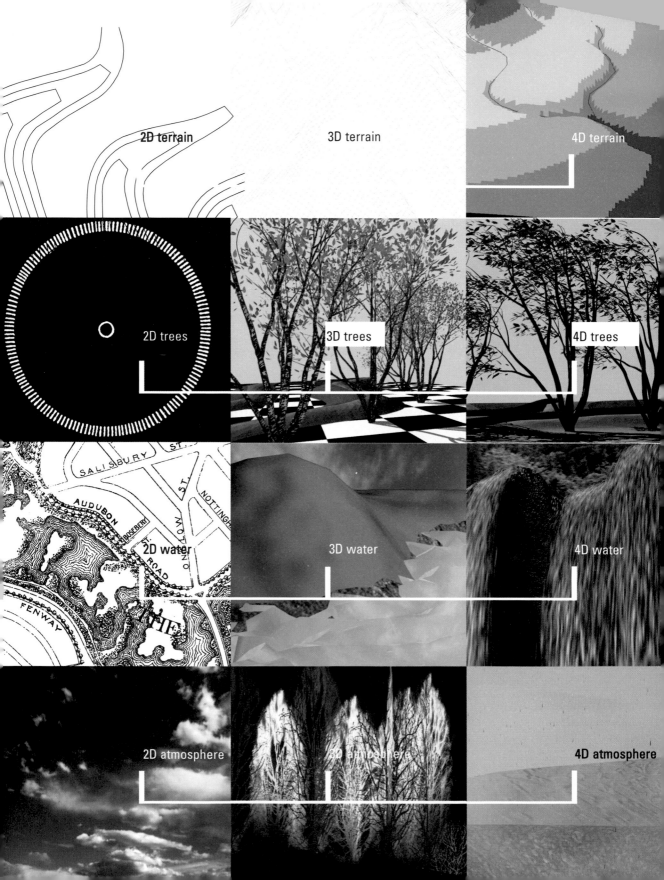

2D terrain

3D terrain

4D terrain

2D trees

3D trees

4D trees

2D water

3D water

4D water

2D atmosphere

3D atmosphere

4D atmosphere

Landscape Modeling 1

1.1 Introduction to Landscape Modeling

This book is about modeling the landscape, and so it has both an action-oriented purpose – *modeling* – and an object-oriented one – *landscape*. Modeling simply means making representations, such as drawings, paintings, and cardboard mock-ups; or, more specifically, using digital computers and computer software to organize information in the form of numbers or bits, then creating images on a computer screen or printed on paper; or creating a series of images to form an animation; or even producing a three-dimensional artifact, such as a physical model created by a numerically controlled machine. Modeling by computer is similar in some ways to drawing or painting with pencil or brush, but is quite radically different in other ways – the differences are mostly what this book is about.

Landscape means the natural world, in which we live, garden, work, and build, including both natural systems such as plants and weather, and also built systems, such as roads and cities. Though we may sometimes speak of "the landscape," that is misleading, as there are many different landscapes in this world, and many different perceptions of them. In this text, "the landscape" is used in the same spirit as when we speak of "the human race," meaning to focus on the commonalities and shared attributes, but without ignoring or demeaning the variety and individuality to be found within it.

Four essential elements of the landscape – *landform, plants, water,* and the *atmosphere* – are the focus of this book. The first three are the traditional palette

1

of landscape architects, and are the essential components of the natural world, without people or buildings. Of course, in the real world that we live in, the landscape includes structures of all kinds, including buildings and bridges and cars, and a wide variety of animals whose activities are vital to the function and look of the landscape. There is a vast literature on using computers to model buildings and structures, using Computer Aided Design (CAD) software, and while this book assumes some familiarity with those ideas, it does not focus on making models of buildings.

Landscape elements are different enough from most buildings and machines – rarely square or flat or simple or small, often curved and fuzzy and complex and large – that while many of the same basic digital tools are used in modeling the landscape, their application requires different techniques, and often a different frame of mind, as well. Landscapes usually combine the four major elements in a myriad of ways, both in nature and when designed and built by humans in many forms including gardens, parks, building sites and urban plazas. This book is motivated by a desire to share techniques for using CAD modeling and rendering tools, combining them with Geographic Information Systems (GIS), and tapping the power of computing to help landscape planners, designers and modelers expand their representational repertoire, as well as start to grapple with the complexity and dynamics inherent in the landscape.

Figure 1.1
The landscape of the Fens, in Boston, by landscape architect Frederick Law Olmsted, bridge by H.H. Richardson. Most landscapes are made up of varying proportions of landform, including rocks, vegetation, structures, water, atmosphere, and animals, including people.

1.1.1 Reasons for Modeling

There are many reasons why people need or want to make models of landscapes and landscape elements, and there are many ways of doing so. Modelers include landscape architects, garden designers, architects, planners, engineers, illustrators, scene designers, and others who are engaged in synthetic design processes. Some modelers make models so as to portray landscapes as "scenery" like classical landscape paintings do, or to be used as backgrounds, much like stage sets, or environments for computer games. In quite another vein, scientists and planners may seek to model landscapes and landscape processes so as to be able to simulate or understand them, exploring scientific hypotheses, or measuring aspects of quantitative simulations, such as soil erosion, hydrologic process, or vegetative succession.

In between, combining art and science, landscape architects and other environmental designers make models of landscapes for the same reasons models are made in all design disciplines: it is easier, faster, often safer, and more responsible, to experiment and try out alternatives with "stand-in" representations, rather than with the "real thing." A landscape architect comparing alternative planting plans – one-, two-, or three-abreast rows of shade trees, for example – can look to the real world for some examples of each, and so good designers do keep libraries of examples and references garnered from their own and others experiences and observations. To actually try out several different schemes, *in situ*,

Figure 1.2
"Texas Redbuds"
Landscape painting by A.R. McTee c.1950
Here as in all landscapes, landform, vegetation, and water combine to create a sense of place.
The landscape painter's eye is focused on composition, texture, color, and light.

3

though, is complicated almost to the point of impossibility. Comparing growth patterns over time, or visual effects in different light conditions, could take literally years.

Sketches, models, computer renderings, and other representations, however, can be made relatively quickly, and with infinite subtle variations. How good these representations are in helping designers choose between alternatives becomes a question of the detailed characteristics of the representation used – the media, the techniques, the levels of abstraction and realism, and so on. There are no "perfect" or neutral representations; rather, there are a number of important decisions to be made in choosing and making a representation for a specific purpose, and a set of conventions on the one hand, which have become established as appropriate and recognizable (the "artists rendering" of proposed buildings, for example, or the diagrammatic cross-section), and on the other hand, an expansive realm for invention and variety in representations. All models are imperfect, containing simplifications and abstractions, even perhaps distortions. Choosing and using modeling techniques appropriate to the task, is an essential part of using modeling in design.

Making digital models, as with any representation-making, will always have to be informed by professional judgment and possibly social context, and will always be an act of "abstraction" and simplification. There are many ways of model-making and many kinds of models. Choosing the right model(s) for a given purpose, whether political and public, or personal and private, is an important part of the overall modeling process. This book is most concerned with model making as part of a design conception and communication process, with a heavy emphasis on the visual, and to a lesser extent, the analytical properties of landscape models.

An important note: sometimes, models are made as part of a larger decision-making process, in which the models are used to further analysis and discussion, leading to a decision which may have far-reaching and real-world consequences, such as costs, visual impacts, environmental impacts, or even health and safety implications. In such cases, naturally, the validity of any model used – how well it actually represents the qualities of the real thing or event it is standing in for – is critical. Models of environmental impacts, and systems that have health or safety implications, need to be fully informed by scientific and engineering knowledge, and probably developed slowly, incrementally, and with full processes of open review and validation. Models used to determine visual impacts may seem less severe in their requirements, but not to the one person or community whose view is changed forever, and for the worse, by some action or design. There is a growing literature on the art and science of visual simulation, taking into account important considerations of human perception, psychology, and culture, as well as statistically valid techniques for performing and interpreting visual preference surveys. The scope of these important matters is well beyond the present book. Similarly, the complexities of scientific landscape modeling –

Figure 1.3
*Multiple represen-
tations:
a. Photograph of a
view down an
allee of trees in a
garden outside of
Rome, Italy.
b. A black-and-
white "sketch"
made by image
processing filter
operations.
c. A computer-
generated view of
a 3-D model.*

ecological, hydrological, air-pollution modeling, and others – are not covered, except in passing reference, in this book.

The emphasis throughout this book is on digital methods of visualization, and the necessary abstraction they entail. Some of the techniques presented are based on physics and natural properties; some are based purely on human perception. Most of the examples come from the domain of landscape architecture, which is equally concerned with the ecological and functional aspects of landscape, and with the visual, aesthetic, and formal.

Throughout the second and third chapters, many of the techniques for modeling will be presented with reference to a specific landscape project: the design by Hargreaves and Associates for a campus plaza, called University Commons, at the University of Cincinnati. This project was chosen because of its formal elegance and because it is typical of many designed landscapes in its artful combinations of landform, vegetation, water, and human circulation systems (paths and paving). The project demonstrates very well a variety of techniques for forming terrain into beautiful and functional sculptural landforms, and for integrating those with tree plantings and groundcovers, as well as path systems, drainage, and lighting. The project has the advantage of having been designed at least in part with digital tools, and built (in 1998 and 1999) so that photographs and construction details are available.

Other real and built projects, as well as imaginary landscapes, are also used as examples in subsequent chapters. In all cases, the goal is to use these examples to highlight the essential characteristics of landscape, to show exemplary landscape design and planning, and to demonstrate useful and appropriate techniques for digital modeling and visualization.

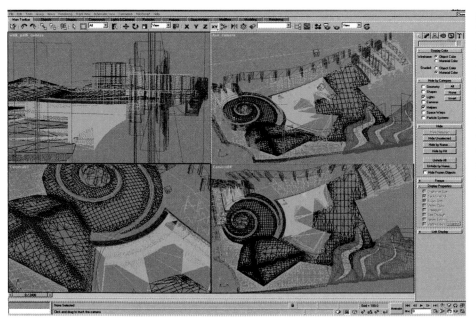

Figure 1.4
Wireframe representation of the University Commons Model in 3D Studio Max. The abstract colored lines on a computer screen are indicators of landscape elements.

Figure 1.5
A view across raked gravel into the pine forest, and stream with stone bridge, at the Ginka-kuji temple, Kyoto, Japan. Photograph courtesy of Christian Tschumi.

Figure 1.6
The "Blue Steps" at Naumkeag, a composition of trees, shrubs, landforms, structures, and water by landscape architect Fletcher Steele.

1.1.2 Dimensions of Modeling

The "real world" in which we operate, the alternative worlds designed by landscape architects and urban planners, and even the imaginary worlds imagined by computer games designers or stage-set creators, is usually thought of as being three-dimensional (3D) – occupying the spatial dimensions X (width), Y (breadth), and Z (height, or depth). This conventional coordinate system, attributed to Euclid and Descartes, enables detailed descriptions of solid geometry, and is the underpinning of all Computer Aided Design (CAD) and Geographic Information Systems (GIS) representations. At the same time, the most common representations used, certainly for centuries and still today, are only two-dimensional (2D), such as maps, plans, images on flat paper, or computer screens. The art and science of perspective projection, representing three dimensions in only two, has been developed by painters, first three or four hundred years ago, and more recently by computer scientists in the last thirty or forty years.

In cartography, or geographic science, mathematical methods of *projection* have been developed also, for the purposes of converting the spherical reality of the earth's globe to a flat paper representation (map). Much has been written about cartographic projections, and their role in both conveying and misrepresenting the truth. It is an established principle in all map projections that in converting from a sphere to a flat plane, some aspect of "truth" must be distorted: No projection of a sphere can accurately maintain both shape and area, for example, and all map projections can be classified as maintaining one or the other (or of compromising, and distorting both). The common *Mercator projection*, for example, preserves shape and compass bearings, at the expense of distorting area (so that the polar regions and Greenland are distorted to appear far larger than they really are). But the first characteristic of this projection made it invaluable for ocean navigation, simplifying the task of charting a course using only a compass and straightedge, and so was the preferred map projection for years. Using a satellite image to analyze characteristics of the earth's surface, however, counting total area of tropical forest, or arctic ice, requires the opposite characteristics (shape and bearings aren't so important as accurate and equal areas), and so satellite images used for natural resources analysis are ordinarily presented in an equal-area projection.

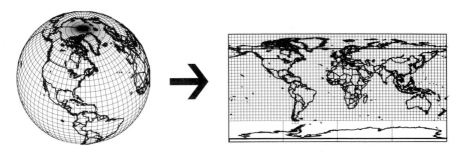

Figure 1.7
Cartographic projection forces a spherical surface to a rectangle, necessarily distorting it in the process.

These examples, specific to cartographic and GIS concerns, vividly illustrate a more general principle of representation that is central to all modeling enterprises: That is, no representation is true or perfect, all contain errors, omission, abstractions, simplifications, points-of-view, and exaggerations, and that far from damning all representations therefore as flawed, this is exactly what makes them valuable and useful, but to be carefully chosen amongst and deployed. Landscape modelers, as much as painters or scientists, navigators or cartographers, make choices about representations, based on their purposes and their resources (time, talent, ink, computer power, etc). Throughout this book, these aspects of representation will be highlighted: their suitability to purposes, their resource requirements, their limitations and capabilities.

Furthermore, even the best 3D models of our worlds are inadequate, as they fail to capture the fourth dimension of time, and change. Perhaps simple shapes, and even more complex ones, like buildings or mechanical pieces like gears, can be usefully represented as static and isolated, frozen in an abstract mathematical description; but landscapes, and other complex structures, like organisms and societies, do move and grow and change – they exist in at least one more dimension. Scientists and artists have attempted to handle the needs of representing time in various ways, by labeling one axis of a 2D graph as time, for example, or making a series of paintings or images, side by side, representing similar spatial situations at different times (the four seasons, for example, or night and day). The invention of cinema (as celluloid movies, or subsequently as television and digital computer animations), brought the fourth dimension of time closer to hand, and opened new avenues for explorations of representation. Time-lapse photography, for example, at the micro-scale of flower petals opening, or sun-shadows progressing, or computer animations at the macro-scale of glacial or geologic events, are invaluable in visualizing and communicating natural dynamic processes. Computer models which enable "walkthroughs," whether precanned or user-guided and interactive, also take advantage of time change to help explain and explore.

This book emphasizes the two-dimensional representations which are derived from three- four- and even more- dimensional descriptions. The accompanying CD-ROM more vividly and directly illustrates a range of time-based or dynamic representations (animations and procedural models).

Figure 1.8 *Three frames from an animated walkthough of the historic Park Würlitz, near Dessau, Germany.*
Courtesy of the Institut für Neue Medien, Frankfurt, Germany.

It is worth noting that digital media have one major difference and advantage over the hand tools often used for representation: computers are programmable. Whereas all the hand tools typically used for drawing and painting depend upon the hand of the designer, or modeler, computers and their peripherals can be autonomous, can be programmed to perform work (still under the guidance, but not the direct manipulation, of a person). This characteristic is what gives rise to the advantages of automation, and of procedural operations, in which repetitive, including repetition with variation, tasks can be given over to the machines. These include drawing every line in a hachure pattern, or tracing every ray of light to determine shadows in a 3D scene, automatically generating variations and permutations 2D and 3D forms, and a host of other activities, which are invaluable to both design conception and representation.

A second advantage of a digital model over an analog one is that it's relatively easy, or at least possible, to translate into other forms, and thereby perform other analyses or make other representations. A single robust 3D model can be used to make an infinite number of perspective views, with variations in frame and viewpoint for example. Or a 3D model may be able to be analyzed numerically, to compute the volume and mass of objects, for example, or the amount of cut and fill between two terrain models. This mutability of format and view is useful and powerful. (It may also introduce new non-trivial problems, unique to the digital domain, such as conversion between one file format and another, but these are all susceptible to work-arounds and engineering solutions over time.)

Figure 1.9
Complex forms created by procedural operations (e.g., spiral twisting) and combinations of simple elements (in this case, stacking and decreasing size).

1.1.3 Techniques for Digital Modeling

The rest of this chapter is a summary review of basic computer modeling and computer graphics terms, tools, and concepts. Readers who are intimately familiar with 2D, 3D, and 4D modeling may skip ahead to the next chapter which starts the landscape-specific treatment, but since terms that are used throughout the rest of the book are introduced and defined, this summary is recommended for all. It is not intended to be a comprehensive review, for which a good reference text on computer graphics or digital media should be consulted. It assumes a general level of knowledge about computers, and such terms as memory, disk space, processor speed, and a beginning-to-intermediate level of knowledge with 2D and 3D modeling and rendering software in general. Although step-by-step tutorials are provided for many of the topics in the next four chapters, they are not software- or platform-specific.

Note that while the capabilities of modeling software are discussed in detail, there is no mention of any specific commercial programs or brand-names of software in the text. The available systems, their names, and capabilities are too numerous, and change too rapidly! A listing of some of the current systems that are available in Summer 2000, can be found in the appendix and much more information, including links to the World Wide Web and sample files, on the accompanying CD-ROM. (Most example illustrations throughout the book will identify in their caption which software was used to create them, where relevant.)

The rest of this section is organized in a framework used in each of the subsequent chapters, progressing from simpler (2D) to more complex (3D, procedural, 4D) topics.

Figure 1.10

Computer model of the Department of Housing and Urban Development in Washington D.C. HUD Plaza Improvements, Martha Schwartz, Inc.

Courtesy Martha Schwartz, Inc.

1.2 Two-Dimensional Models

The most common models we know of in the design world are 2D: drawings, photographs, maps, plans, sections, projections, et al. In analog representations, much of the power and variety comes from the diverse media, ranging from rough paper to mylar to photographic film, and the tools, including cameras, bristle brushes, technical pens, felt tip markers, and others. The science of computer graphics and the related technologies of digital printing have not supplanted these – especially in such ergonomic matters as portability, ease of use and reliability – but have offered surrogates for almost all of them.

Computers with appropriate software and hardware can simulate (the results of) ink-brush painting, photographic darkroom effects, and technical line drawings with relative ease. However, digital media are far more restricted in their essential elements. All these computer systems use binary numeric representations at their core, and almost all generate 2D graphics with pixels, or dots of color or light. These lowest common denominators have much to do with the effects that are capable of being generated, and the kinds of tools and operations that are available. The lowest common denominators for all modeling and rendering systems include *coordinate systems* and *pixels*.

1.2.1 Coordinate Systems

Positions in 2D space, whether on paper, the surface of the earth, or a computer display screen, can be described by a pair of numbers, representing distance along two orthogonal axes, whose crossing is labeled the origin, and has a value of zero on each axis. In the Cartesian system, these coordinates are typically called x for the horizontal, or width dimensions, and y for the vertical, or height dimensions. On a spherical surface, like the earth, they are called longitude and latitude; in a two dimensional image used as a texture they are sometimes called u and v, or s and t. Two dimensional coordinates can also use the *polar system*, in which any position has an angle and a distance from the origin; these are sometimes encountered in landscape work, as in the descriptions of land surveys, for example.

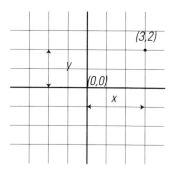

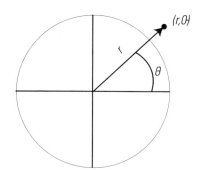

Figure 1.11
a. Cartesian coordinate axes; each point is represented as an (x,y) pair.
b. Polar coordinates; each point is represented as (distance, angle) or (r, Ø) from the origin.

Coordinate values may be either *real numbers* (values with a decimal point and some number of decimal places, like 3.14159, sometimes called *floating point*), in the case of infinitely subdividable space, such as real world measurements; or *integers* (values with no decimal point, like 0, 1, 2, 3, sometimes called *whole numbers*), in the case of discrete spaces, such as the elements in a grid or array. In the latter case they may also be identified as *rows* (horizontal) and *columns* (vertical).

Typically, coordinate values increase in one direction away from the origin, and decrease in the opposite direction, so that positive *x*-values are to the right, or east, negative ones to the left; positive *y*-values are "up," or north, on a flat piece of paper, and negative ones are "down." (There is already some confusion, since "up" and "down" may also refer to the third *Z* dimension.) Also, on a printed page, or computer display screen, rows and columns often have their origin in the upper left corner, so that increasing row values go "down".

Most of the time, it is clear what is meant by the various coordinate axes, but it is always worth checking, especially when results seem to be coming out upside down or backwards! Almost any good computer graphics reference text will have further discussion of coordinate systems, and details on the so-called "right-hand rule" for determining which direction is positive on various axes, by convention.

1.2.2 Map Coordinates

In the special case of map coordinates, indicating positions on the earth's surface (or any sphere, such as a planet or moon), there are two additional considerations: *units* and *projections*.

Latitude and longitude are not normally given negative values, rather they are identified by the hemisphere: north (positive) or south (negative) for latitude, east (positive) and west (negative) for longitude. Also, these systems, being spherical, are in units of *degrees*, rather than distance, and are often subdivided into

Figure 1.12

Three coordinate systems shown on USGS topographic quad sheet: Geographic (longitude and latitude), UTM (in meters), and State Plane System (in feet).

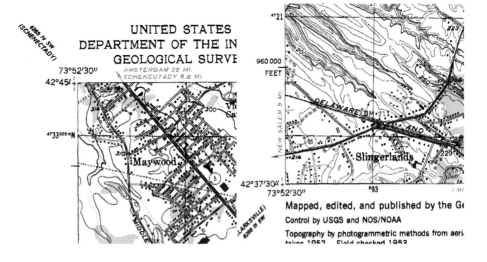

13

minutes (1/60th of a degree) and *seconds* (1/60th of a minute). In this system, degrees and minutes must be integers, and usually seconds are integers as well; but seconds may sometimes be represented with a decimal point and an arbitrary number of decimal places. Alternatively, units of degrees may be reported as *decimal degrees* (70.5 degrees = 70 degrees, 30 minutes, e.g.) These units are most often found in surveying and cartography, so many GIS systems provide tools for converting between them.

Finally, coordinates on a spherical surface that are measured in distance, rather than degrees, are subject to a process of conversion from latitude and longitude called *map projection*, in which the curved surface is flattened out, and in so doing, slightly distorted. There are many mathematically defined projection systems, and all flat maps use one or another, with names such as *Universal Transverse Mercator* or *Lambert conformal*, etc. A detailed discussion of projections is well beyond the scope of this book, for which a good GIS or cartography reference should be consulted. What's most important to know about projections is that coordinates in two different projections will not match up, or put another way, the same numerical values in two different projection systems do not refer to the same spot on the earth. Again, GIS software is usually equipped with tools to manage and convert between projections. For landscape modelers, who may be working with map data, it's important to make sure that all data, which may be from different sources, such as maps, surveyors, landscape architects, and engineers, are in the same coordinate system and the same map projection, if they are to line up in the final model.

  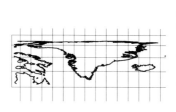

Figure 1.13
Three different projections of the land mass of Greenland: Mercator, Geographic and Peters projection.

1.2.3 Pixels and Color Space

Whereas the input data for landscape modelers may come in a variety of projections, units and systems, the output is much simpler – almost always a *raster array* of "picture elements," or *pixels*, which make up an image on a computer screen (or printed page). Pixels are usually measured by rows and columns, and the spacing between them, in dots per inch, or *dpi* (also measured as *dot pitch*, which is the actual distance between pixels on a display device). Pixels, and display screens, may also have an *aspect ratio*, which is the ratio of width to height. A perfectly square screen with pixels equidistant in both directions would have an aspect ratio of 1.0; most actual display devices and pixels are slightly elongated in the y-axis, so the aspect ratio is slightly less than 1.0. All computer graphics, whether line drawings or photographic images, are represented in pixels. The total number of pixels, for a display screen, or the dpi of a printed image, are sometimes referred to as the *resolution* of the display or image. Most computer screens are around 1000 by 1000 pixels (for *one megapixel* resolution), and between 72 dpi and 100 dpi. Printed images are often around 600 dpi or more for ordinary laser printers, and 2000 dpi or more for high quality printing.

A pixel that has only two possible colors, black or white, corresponds to a single *bit* in computer memory. A pixel with *full-color* corresponds to 24 or 32 bits, or 3 or 4 *bytes* of computer memory. On a color display screen, these values are represented as separate values for Red, Green, and Blue (or *RGB*) light intensities, each with a value from 0 to 255 (eight bits), for a total range of over 4 billion different colors. On a printed page, the pixel is represented by combinations of inks, with separate values for Cyan, Magenta, Yellow, and Black (or *CMYK*). The same numeric values in RGB and CMYK will represent different colors to the human eye. Many simpler images are represented by the use of a *color lookup table* (or *CLUT*), which stores a table of generally only 256 or 1024 different colors that are combined to produce the final image. A full treatment of color theory, perception, and digital color representation is beyond the present scope, and a good reference on image processing or color printing should be consulted.

Figure 1.14
a. 24-bit (full RGB) color.
b. 8-bit (indexed) color.
c. 8-bit gray scale.
d. 1-bit (mono-chrome) image.

A pixel may correspond to a point in a 2D or 3D model, but because of scale variations, a pixel may also represent far more than that. In a satellite image, for example, a single pixel may represent an area of 30m x 30m on the ground; or in a perspective view, a distant tree in the background may be reduced to a single pixel. In general, pixels are the final output result; 2D and 3D modeling works with more mathematical coordinates and constructs, which only become pixels when rendered to a screen.

1.2.4 Points, Lines, Polygons, and Curves

All 2D and 3D geometric models are composed of some combination of:
- *points* or *vertices* (zero dimensional objects, with position only)
- straight *lines* or *edges* (1D objects, defined by any two points, and having length)
- *polygons* or *faces* (2D objects, defined by three or more intersecting lines, having area)

These can be organized and represented in a hierarchical way, so that polygons are made of lines which are made of points which have 2D (or 3D) coordinates. In a geometric figure, 2D or 3D, the connectivity of lines connecting points and creating polygonal surfaces, or faces, is called the *topology* of the model. Without a record of the connectivity, points and lines are just so much spaghetti. With carefully regulated and enforced topological relationships, all

Figure 1.15
A typical site plan, constructed in a CAD or GIS system.
Street lines, parcels, and building footprints are polygons composed of line segments; building centroids and other spot features are represented as points.

kinds of additional properties such as "inside" and "outside," can be calculated. These are essential for most computer modeling.

Elaborating slightly on this foundation, curved lines and curved polygons may be added in; although any curve can be approximated by a series of short straight lines, (or on screen, by a series of pixels), curves such as circular and parabolic arcs, or *polynomial spline curves*, or curved areas such circles or ellipses, may be represented in a purely mathematical way (with a center point and radius, for example).

Each modeling program has its own proprietary, internal way of representing these and other elements and their combinations. There are some efforts at standardized representations for transferring between programs, such as the *IGES* (International Graphics Exchange Standard) format or the *DLG* (Digital Line Graph) format of the USGS. The simpler a shape, or drawing, the more likely it is to be converted without modification from one system to another; the more it has complex curves or other elements such as text, color, and fills, the more likely there is to be loss of information when converting.

Figure 1.16

Data tables from a GIS system showing the features – points, lines, and polygons – illustrated in the image at left.

Each row represents one item, each column is some attribute about the item, including its geometry (the X,Y,Z coordinates, which are hidden in this case), and other nongraphic attributes.

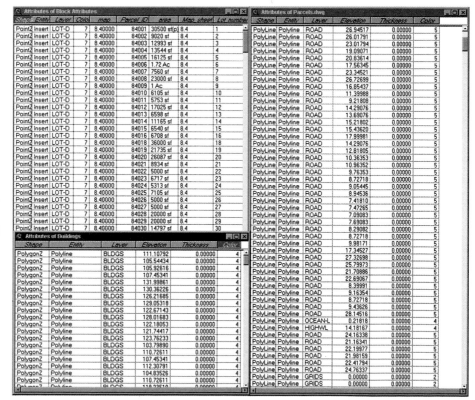

1.3 Three-Dimensional Models

Whereas 2D models are described in 2D *planar* space, 3D models occupy a *volume* of space. A third axis, usually called *Z*, is orthogonal to the first two, and each point has three coordinates, expressed as a *triple (x,y,z)*. This mathematical description encompasses what we think of as the geometry of the real world, in which things have width, depth, and height, and corollary properties such as volume, mass, and centroid. Among three dimensional objects, there is an important distinction in computer modeling: between pure *surfaces*, which may exist in three dimensional space, and are more than a single flat plane, but are mathematically infinitely thin, having only a front side and a back; and *solids*, which have thickness, and an interior and exterior. As an example, 4 points in space may be connected to form a surface (a curved *hyperbolic paraboloid*) or a solid (a *tetrahedron*).

1.3.1 Surfaces

Surfaces are created by many modeling systems by default, since they are easier to represent and manipulate than solids. A simple planar object, such as a rectangle, or circular disk, is usually only a surface. For rendering purposes, it is necessary to determine the *surface* norma*l*, a vector that is perpendicular to the face of the surface; this vector determines which direction a surface is facing. In some systems, it may be necessary to explicitly compute these, or to force the object to have two sides visible; otherwise, one face of the surface may be invisible to the rendering system.

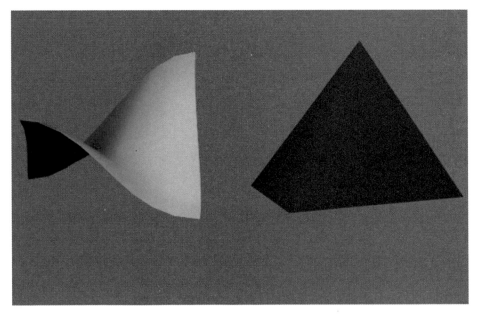

Figure 1.17
The same four points may define a surface (a quadratic patch) or a solid (a tetrahedron).

1.3.2 Solid Models

Solids are more complex than surfaces, since they have thickness and other attributes, but this makes them more robust for some modeling purposes. (They can be sliced through, for example, and their mass or center of gravity can be computed.) The simplest solids are created by just extruding a 2D polygon by some amount (sometimes called *2.5D*); others are created by sweeping or revolving a profile; and more complex ones can be created by using various modeling tools. Most modeling software offer a selection of geometric primitives including cubes, spheres, cylinders, and cones which can be parametrically varied to produce a wide variety of shapes alone and in combination.

Curved and complex solid objects such as found in nature (landform and plants, for example) are more difficult to create, and often require procedural methods of generation and combination. Suitably small triangular faces and cylinders can be combined to approximate more complex forms. Some modeling systems may offer *metaballs*, blobby objects created by aggregating spheres together and filling in the space between them with mathematically controlled curved surfaces.

Figure 1.18

Image of a 3D solid model of the Villa Rotunda, by Palladio.
As with too many architectural models, it is floating in a void, with no landscape elements to ground it.

1.4 Operations in 3D Modeling

Building solid models, or surface representations, can be a process requiring primarily eye-hand coordination, using various primitives in the modeling software to build up a complete model, mostly by mouse-clicks and menu selections. But many real world environments have systems and regularities about them, including repetitive elements, grids, or other rules of alignment, which can make computer modeling especially appropriate and facilitate accurate constructions. Grid snaps, duplications, controlled offsets, and regular arrays are operations offered by all modeling software which can be used to create landscape elements that actually form space and give design form to the composition.

1.4.1 Organization: Repetition, Combination, et al.

Linear repetition, specifying a spacing between and a total number of elements, can be used to create an allee of trees, or rows of lamp posts along a street; regular rectangular arrays and circular arrays may organize shrubs or stone bollards. The overuse of strict geometry and symmetry leads to static, overly formal compositions, but some organizing systems and regularity can give a controlled, navigable sense to landscape designs.

The simple act of using vertical elements to create "walls" in the landscape, or overhead trellises and canopies for "ceilings," and variations in groundcover and pavement, can help to delineate "rooms" and create spaces in the landscape.

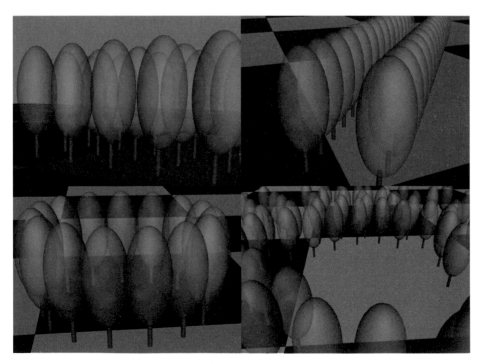

Figure 1.19

Simple lollipop trees combined in various ways to create space-forming enclosures:
a. rectangular array, or bosque;
b. a double row, or allee;
c. a circular bosque;
d. a clearing in a thicket.

The simplest forms of combination in most modeling systems include grouping, linking separate elements together such that they can be moved, resized, and given attributes as a single object, or *group*. Some systems have hierarchical grouping, so that several subgroups can be combined into one overall group, to several levels. This capability is useful for building up assemblies of elements, such as creating a fence out of multiple separate pickets and rails, for example. Such hierarchical groupings can also be used to implement a form of dynamic linkage, called *inverse kinematics*, so that when one element moves, other attached elements move too, but possibly with modifications, such as a hand which remains attached to and moves with an arm, but also has additional motions itself (and similarly attached subassemblies, such as fingers). These linkages can be very powerful for making dynamic and interactive models.

1.4.2 Boolean Operations: Intersection, Difference, Union, et al.

Simple grouping causes subelements to be treated as one, but does not actually fuse the elements together – they can always be ungrouped. An additional set of modifiers are available in some modeling systems, which enable the so-called *boolean* operations of intersection, union, and difference. (These are named after George Boole, the French mathematician and logician, who described the logical operations *and* and *or*, first as operations on sets, and then as the primitive operators in binary arithmetic, which is the theoretical basis on which all digital computers operate.)

Figure 1.20
Boolean operations. The brown cylinder (A) and grey rectangular solids (B) are combined to create:
A minus B = ("Lincoln log" form);
B minus A = (blocks with cylindrical notches cut out);
and
A intersects B = (the small brown cylindrical "chips" from the log).

The boolean operator *and* creates all the elements that are in each of two or more sets; in solid modeling, it is used to deliver the solid of *intersection* between two other solids. (It is empty if they don't touch at all, may be only a point or line if they are literally only touching, and is otherwise a solid object.) The other operator, *or*, is used in solid modeling to create the *union*, or set of all points that are in either one of one or more other objects. This is similar to making a group, but has the difference that it creates a single object. The other logical operation commonly used is *difference*, which returns the solid left after taking one object away from another. For example, drilling a hole through a solid can be performed by taking the difference between the object and a cylinder of suitable size and orientation. In landscape modeling, boolean operations are most often used to create special landforms, such as tunnels or bridges; unions and hierarchical dynamic linkages may be used in modeling vegetation.

1.4.3 Procedural Operations and Scripting

The combining operations, grouping, and boolean operations give a great deal of power to modeling, but still require hand-control of every individual step. In many modeling systems, you can gain even greater power for automation of tasks and creation of complex models, by using a built-in scripting, macro, or programming language. Sometimes a general purpose programming language such as *C*, *Basic*, or *Lisp* can be used to control the modeling environment, sometimes a unique proprietary programming language is required. In any case, the basic elements of programming – assigning variable names and values, using arithmetic, trigonometric, and other operations and functions, conditional control with some kind of "if-then" statements, and some form of controlled repetition – are all available in some form or other. Writing programs, or scripts, or macros (which are all equivalent terms), can be very helpful in generating variations, where several variables are given values to create, for example, stairs with varying numbers of steps, and varying riser and tread dimensions, or more complex forms, such as branching trees or eroded landscapes. Simple programs are usually easy to get started with; more elaborate programs may require study, effort, and reference to a good text on programming.

```
for (int x = 0; x < imageWidth; x++) {
    int         rgb            = imagePixels[i];
    while (j < MAX_EVENTS && x > eventIndex[j]) {
        j++;
    }
    int divisor = eventDivisor[j];
    if (divisor != DAYLIGHT) {
        int        alpha  = rgb & 0xFF000000;
        int        red    = (rgb & 0x00FF0000) >> 16;
        int        green  = (rgb & 0x0000FF00) >> 8;
        int        blue   = (rgb & 0x000000FF);
        Color.RGBtoHSB(red, green, blue, hsb);
```

Figure 1.21
A fragment of a program in the JAVA language, which calculates and displays colors for a sunrise simulation.

1.5 Rendering

The process of creating a 2D image from a 3D model is called *rendering*. Some modeling software has rendering integrated into it; some software is for rendering only, taking input in various standard formats. In all cases, a virtual camera is located somewhere in 3D space, looking at the model, and an image is created onto a picture plane located in virtual space between the camera and the model elements. The projection of the image may be perspective, or it may be one of the orthographic projections, such as a plan, elevation, or axonometric. Some rendering systems enable you to specify camera lens characteristics, such as focal length; this is useful when you are trying to match a 3D computer model with real world photographs. The size of the image is specified in pixels, width and height, and the basic process of rendering is to determine what color each pixel in the image should be. A wide variety of rendering algorithms exist, and this has been an area of research and invention in computer graphics for many years.

1.5.1 Ray-tracing

Many rendering systems, especially those that seek to create "realistic" images, use some form of *ray-tracing*. In ray-tracing, a three-dimensional vector, or *ray*, is simulated as if it were passing from the camera, through each pixel of the picture plane, and into the volume of the 3D model. When the ray intersects an object, the pixel's color value is set to whatever color the object is, modified by the presence of lights, and shadows, and surface texture characteristics such as bumpiness, or shininess, etc. Ray-tracing is particularly effective at modeling reflectivity, transparency, and refraction, since the ray need not stop at the first object it hits, but can be continued on, bouncing through the 3D model, so that an object defined as a mirror, rather than creating pixels with its own color, will get its surface color from the next object hit, reflecting that object's color.

The depth of reflection, or how many times a ray is "bounced" in the 3D model determines how realistic optical effects (such as reflection or refraction) will be, how accurately shadows will be cast, and so on. Sometimes this parameter is user-controllable, sometimes not. A number of variations and refinements of ray-tracing have been developed, and have given rise to rendering systems with different capabilities and specialties. An advanced kind of rendering is called *radiosity-based*, in which not just multiple light rays are bounced around from object to object, but in fact every object's surface casts some light onto every other neighboring object. Radiosity can give very realistic and subtle renditions of lighting effects, especially with indirect light.

1.5.2 Multichannel Textures

Images are the end result of modeling and rendering, but they may also be used as inputs, as well. A digital image – created by a digital camera, or a scanner, for example – can be manipulated using image processing software to change pixel colors, scale and change resolution, apply filters and special effects, and so on. These images can also be used as textures, applied to objects in a 3D model, to give color and other surface attributes to geometric objects.

The simplest surface that a 3D object can have in a rendered image is a single color. Every object has some default color, often gray – or else the object would be invisible when rendered. Colors are specified in the modeling system usually in RGB values; when rendered, the image can be saved with CMYK colors.

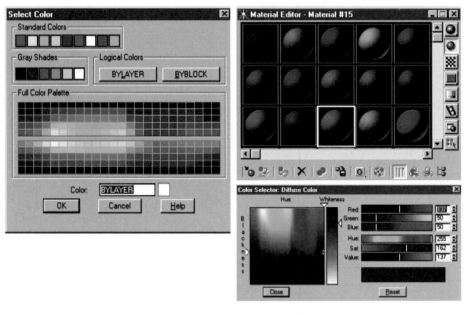

Figure 1.22

A typical "color picker" from a CAD, modeling, or rendering program, shows colors and shades along with corresponding RGB and CMYK values. From AutoCAD.

Beyond simple color, objects in a 3D rendered scene can have a wide range of surface attributes. These include roughness, reflectivity, transparency, and others. Transparency information may be encoded directly into a color image in a separate layer, often called the *alpha channel*. Any digital image can be used as a *decal*, or *image map*, pasted onto, or repetitively tiled over, the surface of an object. Choosing size and repetition (tiling) parameters makes a big difference with image maps, especially in landscapes where objects may be in the foreground, midground, or background, and in most cases this involves visual judgement as much as any hard and fast rules. Some systems may use *MIP-maps*, which encode textures at varying levels of detail, so that more information and less distortion can be presented in the foreground, and less complex (and so less memory-intensive) textures used in the background where they are less visible.

Figure 1.23
a. 3D models of primitive solid objects: cube, sphere, cylinder, cone, pyramid, torus, and plane.
b. Simple solid colors applied, with no lighting (only ambient light).
c. Various textures and effects applied and rendered with ray-tracing: brick texture on cube, reflective surface on sphere, wood texture on cylinder, transparent blue on cone, bumpy surface on pyramid, chrome reflectivity on torus, and bitmap of a leaf on the plane.

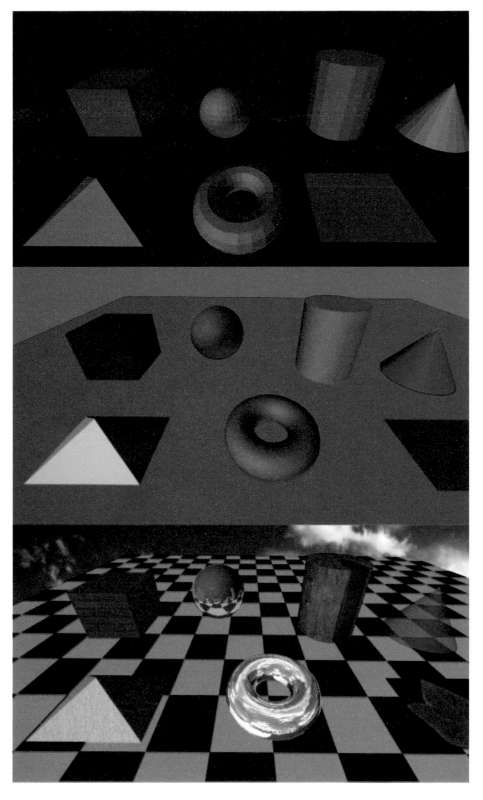

1.5.3 Procedural Textures

Some simple repeating textures, like bricks in a running bond, or complex textures like the veins of marble, or puffs of smoke, can be procedurally generated by computer, without any need for a photographic image. These procedural textures are usually generated based on a small number of input variables, or *parameters*. Some systems may provide a mechanism for writing your own procedural textures. Such procedural textures are sometimes called *shaders*, and many have been developed for the advanced rendering system known as "RenderMan," which is available both in commercial packaged form, and as an open-source specification, so that some free or public-domain software can use its formats.

Procedural shaders are especially effective in creating surfaces with random or organic effects, and for dynamic, animated textures, such as water, fire, smoke, and clouds.

1.6 Presentation

The end goal of most modeling is to create a presentation, either of an image or several images, an animation with many images, or sometimes a 3D artifact such as a computer generated cardboard or resin model. (The technology of computer aided manufacturing or *CAD/CAM*, is beyond the scope of this text, but many of the 3D modeling techniques are relevant to the preparation of files for computer controlled fabrication machines.) For images, the content is most important, but presentation is important too.

Beyond the objects – their location, size, and detailed geometry – and their associated attributes, such as color and texture, which are interpreted by the rendering system, two aspects of presentation make a huge difference in the final product: *lighting* (including the effect of *shadows*) and the choice of *frame* and *viewpoint*. (The final presentation medium, whether paper, or on-screen animation, etc., is important too; see Chapter 6 for more on media and viewpoints for landscape models.)

1.6.1 Lighting and Shadows

All renderers are sensitive to the lighting conditions on the model, and all recognize at least two distinct kinds of light: *ambient* light, which is directionless, overall illumination; and *directional* light, which has location, intensity, and beam properties, such as the parallel rays of sunlight, or the cone shaped beam of an electric spotlight. Often, multiple light sources must be placed in a scene to provide the illumination and emphasis desired .

Shadows are the inverse of lighting, and also serve to add depth and atmosphere to renderings. Strong shadows are created by direct light, whether originating from sunlight or from artificial fixtures. Indirect light, as on a hazy day, produces only very weak shadows, or none at all.

Shadow casting is a computationally expensive operation, and so it is often foregone, especially in quick studies or animations, where rendering time is an important consideration. There are several short-cut methods of casting approximate shadows, such as *shadow maps* which can also be used. (See Chapter 5 for more on lighting and shadows in the landscape.)

Figure 1.24
Photograph of a golf course landscape; gray clouds and indirect light contribute to luminous colors, few shadows.

Figure 1.25
The effect of various frames on an image.

a. Landscape (5:3)
b. Portrait (3:5)
c. Square (1:1)
d. Panorama (4:1)

1.6.2 Camera Frame and Viewpoint

Framing a picture is an essential part of the composition process. Choosing between landscape mode (a rectangle with a longer horizontal axis), portrait mode (a longer vertical axis), or even a perfect square, is a first step. Many landscape images naturally look best in a landscape format. Historically, one aspect ratio has dominated computer-generated visualizations: the 4:3 ratio of most computer display screens (640 x 480 pixels in early models, 1024 x 768 or 1600 x 1200 more recently). This rectangle still is not really very elongated, and so some landscape representations have tended for even more extreme aspect ratios, such as 8:3, so that two frames fit vertically in a standard computer window. The advent of high definition digital television (*HDTV*) has brought its new standard aspect ratio of 16:9 (nearly 2:1) into regular use, a format more suited to landscape scenes (and large movie screens). See Chapter 6 for more on frames and viewpoints in landscape modeling.

1.7 Calculations from 2D and 3D Models

One benefit of making digital landscape models, beyond the range of visualization and presentation options, is that the database created may be used for additional analytical and calculation purposes. In addition, other existing digital data base information can be incorporated and used to inform and shape the model.

1.7.1 Database Models

Although 2D and 3D models are composed primarily of the graphic and geometric primitives surveyed above, they are usually organized by the software into a database including higher level aggregations, including groups of elements as named *objects*. These objects may have attributes, such as color, which are stored in the application's file, but in some systems you may also be able to link to attribute information stored in external files. A geometric file of a forest, for example, may include each tree's position as a 3D spot location, matched to a terrain model's elevation, but information about species, and size, and other characteristics such as age, or potential harvest dates, may be stored in a separate database file. When the two are linked, the rendering system might be able to make use of this additional database information to create appropriate tree textures, or densities, etc.

Conversely, other programs might be able to read the information from a 3D model file, and extract information for useful calculations. For example, two terrain models, one describing existing and another showing proposed conditions, can be used to determine the total difference in volume, or cut-and-fill requirements, between the two models.

In order for these database linkages to be made, specific rigorous conditions usually have to be met, governing the format of the files and of the individual data items in them. Often, data conversion and cleaning are required, as well as careful management of file names and directory structures, but the results can be extremely valuable in extending the uses of the model.

1.7.2 GIS-Based Analysis

For landscape modelers, a common source of data and potential database linkage is *Geographic Information Systems (GIS)* software. These are often the original source for much terrain data, and for information about landuses and landcovers such as buildings, vegetation, and water. GIS databases are usually organized with a distinct separation between geometric information, such as positions and elevations, and other attributes, such as color, cost, ownership, etc. These can be used to inform and extend landscape models. Sometimes, making invisible attributes, such as cost or ownership, visible, as by coloring or shading, is a powerful way of adding communicative power to landscape visualizations. Most GIS software represents data in either raster format (as pixels, for example, in a satellite image), or in vector format (as lines and polygons, such as in a map of land parcels and streets in an urban area). Common image processing software, or CAD editing software, can sometimes be used to edit and modify these GIS data, but care must be taken not to disrupt any database relationships, or topological connectivity, maintained by the GIS system.

Figure 1.26
Visualization of two alternative scenarios for land-use growth and change. Images at top are derived from GIS data in maps shown below.
Courtesy of David Hulse, The Institute for a Sustainable Envonment, University of Oregon. Images by David Diethelm.

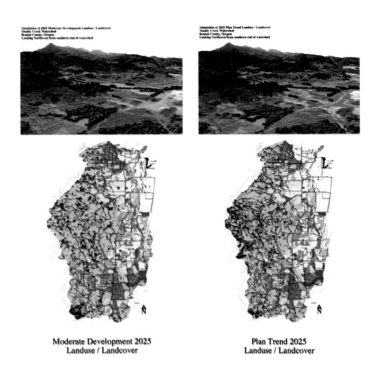

Moderate Development 2025
Landuse / Landcover

Plan Trend 2025
Landuse / Landcover

1.8 Dynamics: 4D Models

Although 3D models of landscape are mostly what this book is about, they fail to capture an essential characteristic of landscapes: that they are dynamic. They change over time, daily and seasonally. Our perception of them is often in motion, as we walk or travel through. Using digital models gives us the opportunity to begin to represent these dynamics in ways which are impossible with traditional analog media, by adding the fourth dimension of *time* and creating animations and other dynamic 4D models.

1.8.1 Generation

One way that computer models can capture landscape dynamics is by using the power of procedural, or algorithmic, generation. Plant growth, for example, can be modeled by a computer program with rules about how buds, leaves, stems, and branches form. Then, to create a model of a plant at a particular stage of growth, the generative procedure can be given the desired age, and generate an appropriate model. Using generative procedures can be far more efficient and powerful than modeling "by hand," and makes possible the generation of variations based on some changing *parameters*. Often, this involves *programming*. Many modeling and rendering systems have some embedded programming language, or scripting or macro capability; sometimes it may be necessary to use a computer language such as *C* or *Java* to create the procedures. Although programming is not for everybody, sometimes it is the best way to achieve fine control, or to create dynamic effects, in your 3D models.

Figure 1.27
Two variants of recursive forms ("tree" and "mountain") generated by simple computer algorithms.
See the JavaTree and JavaMountain programs included on the attached CD-ROM.

1.8.2 Movement *Through*

The simplest kinds of dynamic effects to produce with typical 3D modeling software are *animations*, made by generating a series of still images, each with a slightly changed camera position and view. This results in an animation, or *digital movie*, which can be played back with appropriate software; at frame rates above about 15 frames/second or more, the human visual system blends these images together to create the illusion of motion.

These kinds of animations are often known as *walk-through*s, or *flyover*s, since they are best used to simulate the experience of walking through, or flying over, a landscape. Creating an effective walk-through requires a good, robust 3D model which has enough detail to support a walk through it, and some attention to the choreography of the camera path. Often, camera paths are assigned to a smooth continuous spline curve, which simulates the motion of a professional movie camera on a well-oiled dolly, but not usually the way people really walk. Moving through the landscape is a process with stops and starts, obstacles and subtle changes in grade and eye-level. Eye-level animations should ordinarily be made following a path which touches the ground at all times, to avoid an unrealistic floating feeling. Flyovers, which simulate a helicopter path over a landscape, can be effective for giving overview information, but are typically very detached and impersonal.

Animations, since they require between 15 and 30 frames/second, can generate extremely large file sizes. Many technical tricks including various compression techniques are in use and under development, and a good reference on digital animation techniques should be consulted for more details.

Figure 1.28

Diagram comparing a flyover animation with a flythrough animation. Both include a camera in two time positions and a path element.

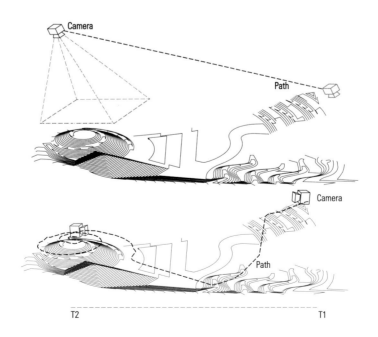

1.8.3 Movement *Of*

The same techniques used to animate camera paths can sometimes be used to animate the motion of other landscape elements. An artificial sunlight, for example, can be animated over a circular path through the sky, and so be used to generate an animation showing changing shadow patterns over the course of the day. In some animation systems, not only position, but all of an object's modeling parameters can be animated over time. In this way, geometric properties such as the diameter of a cylinder, or its length, or thickness can be animated, or non-geometric properties such as a color or texture can be changed over time.

Some modeling systems contain various special effects and deformations, such as ripples, or twists, and these too may be able to be animated. Changing the amplitude and frequency of a rippled waveform, for example, can be a useful way to animate waves on a water surface.

Figure 1.29 *Animated sunlight and ambient light – University Commons Model (see "uc-light.mov" on CD-ROM)*

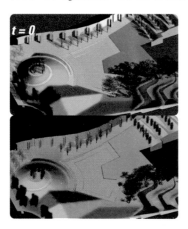

Figure 1.30 *Animated water surface (see "bluewave.mov" on CD-ROM.)*

1.8.4 Interaction *With*

An important form of dynamics in landscapes is their dynamic interaction with observers, or participants, or computer-users. In the real landscape, if you sweep a branch out of your way, it moves, then springs back when you release it; if you press the lever on a gate handle, the gate opens. Using modern technology including hyperlinks, Java, and VRML, "active worlds" can be modeled digitally, which react in various ways when you "touch" them. Usually, this touching involves clicking a mouse somewhere on an image, or using a virtual pointer of some sort in a virtual 3D world. The result can be anything from jumping to another page on a website, or another node in a virtual model, to *haptic* force-feedback from the model transmitted back to the user through some mechanical interface. The details of VRML and haptic interfaces are well beyond the scope of this book, but some of the modeling techniques herein can be used to make the virtual worlds and landscapes within which these interactions can happen.

Figure 1.31

An interactive World Wide Web page, using hyperlinks, or "hot links" on a map to provide educational information about the Allegheny River Watershed. Courtesy of Suzy Meyer, Image-Earth, Inc.

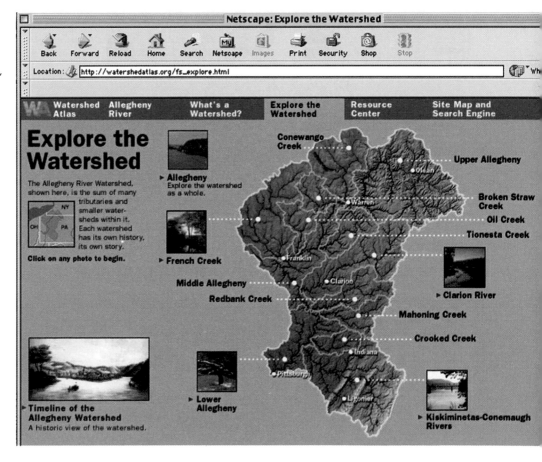

1.9 A Brief History of Computer Graphics in Landscape Modeling

Digital landscape modeling, like all other digital techniques, is really less than 40 years old. Many of the techniques presented throughout this book have been developed over that time by researchers, programmers, and practicioners in academia, computer science, the military, the entertainment industries, and the disciplines of architecture and landscape architecture.

Many computer graphics techniques can be traced back to Ivan Sutherland's original work at MIT, in the 1960s, which demonstrated the possibility and value of a graphical user interface for CAD. Sutherland went on to make major contributions to visualization technology and flight simulation software; today, the company Evans & Sutherland is the maker of landscape visualization software, among many other products.

The late 1960s and early 1970s also saw the development of GIS at several places around the world, but notably at Harvard University's Graduate School of Design, where Professor Carl Steinitz oversaw a series of projects in computer-aided landscape planning and design, some of which are directly responsible for today's GIS software and capabilities.

In the late 1970s, the United States Forest Service, one of the largest employers of landscape architects and planners, developed techniques for visualization of large-area landscapes and forests which are still in use.

Up until that time, computers were mostly large and expensive equipment only owned and used by universities or large agencies. In the late 1970s and early 1980s the development of personal microcomputers, including the Apple, the Commodore, and the IBM PC, introduced a whole new era of computer graphics development. Small firms and individuals could afford these computers, and new programs for CAD and GIS proliferated. The graphics and computing capabilities of these computers were relatively primitive compared to modern standards, but the possibilities they opened up were seized upon by many disciplines.

Throughout the 1980s and 1990s hobbyists and researchers avidly explored these technical possibilities. Many reported on their work at the annual Special Interest Group for Computer Graphics (SIGGRAPH) meetings of the Association for Computing Machinery (ACM). These ACM SIGGRAPH meetings became the standard venue for reporting on new developments in computer graphics, and many seminal efforts at digital modeling and visualization of terrain, vegetation, water, and atmospheric effects were first documented in SIGGRAPH proceedings.

In the last 10 years, a number of commercial software companies have incorporated and elaborated upon those developements, so that today built-in techniques for modeling and visualizing landscape elements are included in a number of commercial modeling and rendering programs. (For a listing of some of these, see the Software Appendix at the end of this book.)

Figure 1.32

a. GIS map of the DELMARVA study. area, printed on impact matrix line printer, c. 1966. Courtesy of Carl Steinitz.

b. Monochrome green-on-black 3D perspective, created on an Apple][+ computer, c. 1980. Courtesy of Stephen Ervin.

c. Detail of a tree planting, in an early version of AutoCAD, c. 1984. Courtesy of Art Kulak.

d. Pen plotter drawing of landform, c. 1985. Courtesy of Steve Estrada.

e. Color 3D plot of forest, from the "Perspective Plot" program, c. 1979. Courtesy of the US Forest Service.

f. Deschutes National Forest. Mt. Bachelor Visual Assessment. US Forest Service, Office of the Landscape Architect. Printed on pen plotter c. 1979. Courtesy of the US Forest Service.

1.10 Summary

Landscape modeling depends upon basic computer graphics, 3D modeling, and GIS software techniques and conventions, but as the next four chapters show, requires attention to the specific challenges of modeling landscape elements: landform, vegetation, water, and atmosphere. As with all representations, landscape models can span a broad range of styles, presentation media, and ranges of realism from "photographic" to impressionistic and highly abstract. Choosing and using the right level of abstraction, and the appropriate medium for presentation and communication, requires both technical knowledge of the media, and professional design judgement. This book attempts to provide the former, only time and experience can inculcate the latter.

Chapter Matrix Picture Credits [Facing Page 1]

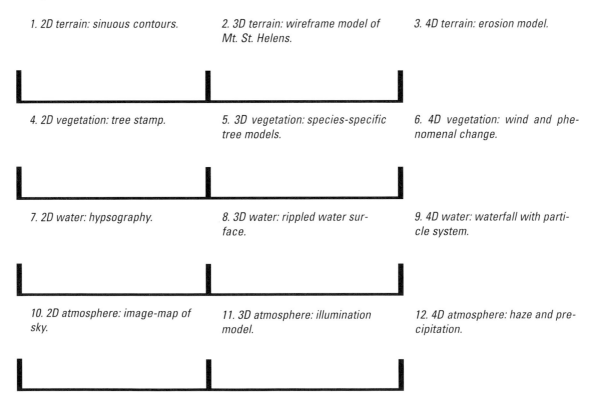

1. 2D terrain: sinuous contours.

2. 3D terrain: wireframe model of Mt. St. Helens.

3. 4D terrain: erosion model.

4. 2D vegetation: tree stamp.

5. 3D vegetation: species-specific tree models.

6. 4D vegetation: wind and phenomenal change.

7. 2D water: hypsography.

8. 3D water: rippled water surface.

9. 4D water: waterfall with particle system.

10. 2D atmosphere: image-map of sky.

11. 3D atmosphere: illumination model.

12. 4D atmosphere: haze and precipitation.

References

Ashford, Janet, and John Odam. *Getting Started with 3D: A Designer's Guide to 3D Graphics Illustration*. Berkeley, CA: Peachpit Press, 1998.

Foley, James D., and Andries Van Dam. *Computer Graphics, Principles and Practice, 2nd edition*. Reading, MA: Addison-Wesley, 1992.

Laurini, Robert, and Derek Thompson. *Fundamentals of Spatial Information Systems*. London, England: Academic Press, Harcourt Brace & Co, 1992.

Mitchell, William J., and Malcolm McCullough. *Digital Design Media, 2nd edition*. New York, NY: Van Nostrand Reinhold, 1995.

Mitchell, William J., Robin Liggett, and Thomas Kvan. *The Art of Computer Graphics Programming: A Structured Introduction for Architects and Designers*. New York, NY: Van Nostrand Reinhold, 1987.

Motloch, John L. *Introduction to Landscape Design*. New York, NY: Van Nostrand Reinhold, 1991.

Sullivan, Chip. *Drawing the Landscape*. New York, NY: Van Nostrand Reinhold, 1995.

VonWodtke, Mark. *Design with Digital Tools: Using New Media Creatively*. New York, NY: McGraw-Hill, 1999.

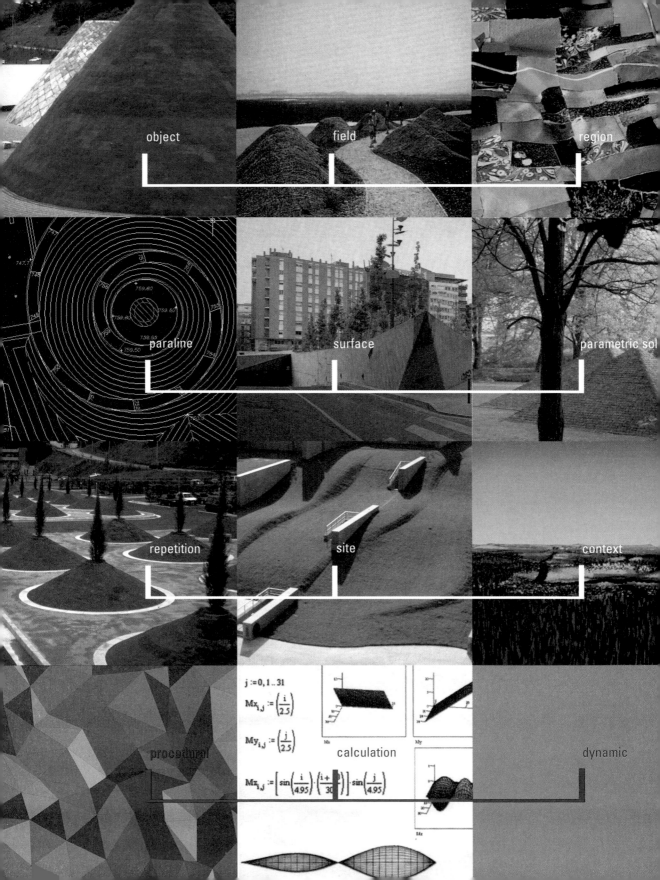

Landform 2

2.1 Introduction

Landform, or terrain, is the basis of any landscape, forming the (roughly) horizontal foundation upon which all else is arrayed. Landform is made up of various underlying geological substrates, with diverse surface coverings: exposed rocks, sand, gravel, synthetic paving, grass, leaf litter, and so on. Usually, we don't see the constituent material directly, but rather the covering – often vegetation – that forms the surface. The underlying material, however, gives characteristic shape and texture to landform, influencing the way natural forms occur, and how built structures and surfaces will appear and behave.

Landform is rarely seen in the foreground, except when the viewer is explicitly looking down (at a path, or road, for example), or in the case of exposed rocks or boulders. Instead, the shape of landform is revealed by objects or textures upon it. In the natural landscape, hills, valleys, and plateaus are subtle, with low slopes and gentle undulations. These features are most vividly seen under special lighting conditions: long shadows and oblique lighting emphasizing the curves and surfaces of the terrain. More dramatic landforms, such as steep mountains and cliffs, are typically perceived only in the background, or when confronted head-on as by a mountain climber. In landscape visualizations, distant landform provides the context within and against which other landscape elements are perceived; and the mid- and foreground structural base upon which other elements sit.

This chapter describes the basic forms that terrain can take in the landscape:

INTERNAL REPRESENTATION

EXTERNAL REPRESENTATION	2D representation paraline drawings	3D representation surfaces		
		polygon/plane	ruled surface	grid mesh
wireframe				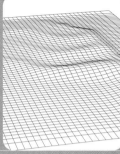
simple color			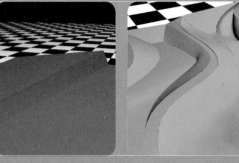	
texture maps diffuse map				
multi-channel /procedural				

41

as discrete terrain objects, as a site-scale continuous field, and as all-encompassing regional context. This chapter also illustrates the three most important forms of digital representation of terrain: two-dimensional paraline drawings, three-dimensional surface models, and three-dimensional solid models. It explores the space-forming and design uses of landform, again as objects, fields, or context, and concludes with some information on procedural or algorithmic terrain, examples of calculations based on terrain models, such as slope analysis, and describes aspects of dynamic or animated terrain models.

2.2 Two-Dimensional Representations

For landscape architects and others making 2D schematic drawings (plans), a stylized conventional form of representing landscapes by spot elevations and contour lines is used. These are often the base data from which a digital model is created. Surveyors capture spot elevations, and use mathematical formulae to interpolate the elevation, shape, and location of contour lines. These curved, closed, nonintersecting lines trace the imaginary beach line that would be formed by water at various elevations (e.g., every foot, or every 10 meters) but are rarely ever seen in the real landscape (except at water bodies, of course, and in other special landscapes such as rice paddies).

Contour lines also convey a variety of 3D formations by recognizable 2D patterns – valleys and ditches, for example, by repeated series of nested c-shapes, which can also represent linear mounds, or berms, depending upon the absolute value of the elevations of the lines. When projected into 3D, in a wire frame perspective, for example, contour representations may be almost unreadable, especially without hidden lines removed. When projected onto a shaded surface, however, their presence, though not realistic, can aid in understanding shapes and slopes.

Cross sections, also extensively used by design professionals, are similar to contours, but are produced by taking vertical, rather than horizontal slices through the landform. Rarely experienced in nature, cross sections can be very vivid for portraying three-dimensional relationships such as visibility and enclosure.

2.2.1 Spot Elevations

Most land surveyors produce data on landform by recording spot elevations at irregular intervals, attempting usually to capture important features in the landscape: high points, low points, centerlines of ridges and valleys, top and bottom elevations of walls, elevations at the base of notable trees and structures, etc. Often each such point is identified by a unique label. These spot elevations represent the basic data structure from which most other terrain data is constructed. Elevation data may be gathered by other methods as well, including remote

Figure 2.1

Partial plan of the spiral landform as seen on previous page. The surface is expressed as spot elevations. Each point is labeled with a number that corresponds to the point table inset. University Commons, Hargreaves Associates (1998-1999).

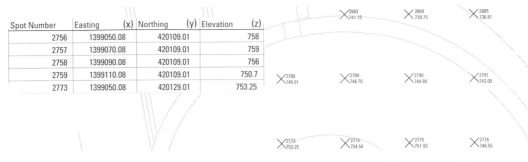

Spot Number	Easting (x)	Northing (y)	Elevation (z)
2756	1399050.08	420109.01	758
2757	1399070.08	420109.01	759
2758	1399090.08	420109.01	756
2759	1399110.08	420109.01	750.7
2773	1399050.08	420129.01	753.25

sensing by aircraft and satellites, and ortho-photo interpretation from pairs of aerial photographs.

Each spot elevation data point consists of three values: x, y, and z coordinates, and so a set of spot elevations can be represented as a table with three columns, X, Y, and Z. These are often originally measured relative to some arbitrary fixed point, or *datum*, which is assumed to have values (0, 0, 0) and may be measured in feet or meters (or other units). When the location and elevation of the datum are known relative to some larger measurement system, such as latitude and longitude for location, and mean sea level for elevation, then the spot elevations can be transformed to absolute values in that system, and so can be located in their geographic context. Such values are called *geo-referenced*.

Figure 2.2

Conic landform with spiral path, represented as a paraline drawing with contours and spot elevations. Screen capture of AutoCAD R14. University Commons, Hargreaves Associates (1998-1999).

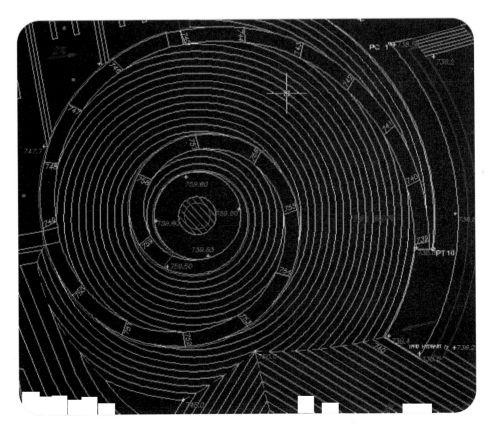

TECHNICAL NOTE: PROJECTIONS

Geo-referencing information depends on both units of measurement (feet, meters, miles, etc.) and a *projection system*, which converts spherical coordinates on the earth's surface to rectangular (*x,y*) coordinates in a Cartesian system. *Latitude* and *longitude* are a spherical coordinate system, based on 360 degrees of longitude in the equatorial circle, with an arbitrary 0, located at the meridian passing through the royal observatory at Greenwich, England, and conventionally measured in *degrees*, *minutes* (1/60 of a degree), and *seconds* (1/60 of a minute). Because of the nature of the sphere, in which lines of longitude converge into a point at either pole, one degree of longitude represents a distance ranging from approximately 300 miles at the equator of the earth, to zero at the pole, and so is an inconvenient unit for measurement of distances. Consequently, most geographical *x,y* measurements are converted into some planar grid system, by means of a mathematical *projection*.

One such grid system is the *Universal Transverse Mercator* (UTM) system widely used by the federal and military agencies of the United States, and covering the entire globe. In the UTM system, the sphere is divided into 60 *zones*, 6 degrees of longitude wide, and a mathematical transformation converts degrees of longitude and latitude into meters from an arbitrary origin. Other grid systems are in use in different countries, and in the United States, each state has a unique State Plane Grid system mandated for construction work in that state. Each such grid system has an associated (0, 0) point and a projection, as well as some parameters used in the mathematical formula for that projection.

For projects involving relatively small areas of terrain, grid systems, projections, and parameters are of little concern, and local, relative measurements may be perfectly satisfactory. For larger projects, involving landform that may cross territorial boundaries, or for which data comes from multiple different sources, careful attention to projection data, and possibly conversion from one system into another, are an absolute necessity. Most commercial Geographic Information Systems (GIS) software have programs or modules for performing projection conversions. It's also important to note the difference between feet and meters; the UTM system and others are based on meters, whereas local survey data may often be in feet, especially elevation data. A final note for large projects: most projection systems mathematically reduce the spherical surface of the earth to a flat plane, inevitably introducing some distortion. For simple horizontal measurements this is usually acceptable, but in certain visualization tasks, the distortion may be unacceptable. On a flat plane, a small object may still be visible at a very great distance away; on the earth, however, distant objects appear to drop below the horizon at some distance away. (In clear weather, on a flat sea, that distance is about thirty miles for a 10' tall object; or a ratio of about 1 foot in 3 miles, or or .1m in 1 km). Consequently, in questions of visibility of objects at great distances, such as in visualization of transmission towers over a distance of several miles, great care must be taken to verify that the curvature of the earth has been accommodated in your data, and in your software.

Figure 2.3
*Map showing dif-
ferences in regis-
tration produced
by two different
projection systems
– the UTM system,
in meters, and the
Massachusetts
State Plane sys-
tem in feet – over
an area of about
30km x 40km.
The misregistra-
tion can be as
much as 1 kilome-
ter near the edges
of the study area.*

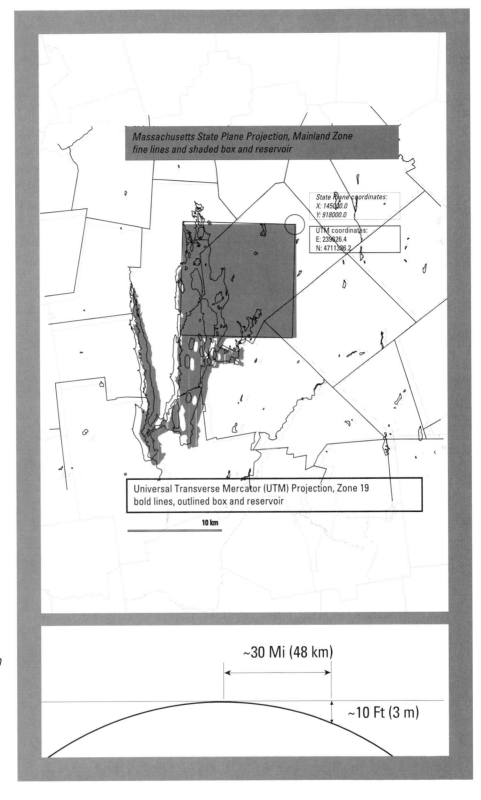

Massachusetts State Plane Projection, Mainland Zone
fine lines and shaded box and reservoir

State Plane coordinates:
X: 145000.0
Y: 918000.0

UTM coordinates:
E: 239626.4
N: 4711386.2

Universal Transverse Mercator (UTM) Projection, Zone 19
bold lines, outlined box and reservoir

10 km

Figure 2.4
*The curvature of
the earth, about 10
ft. in 30 miles
(or about 1 meter
in 15 kilometers).*

~30 Mi (48 km)

~10 Ft (3 m)

2.2.2 Contours

The most common form of representation of terrain at the site scale by professionals is the contour plan: a series of curved lines, each with a specified elevation, set at a fixed vertical contour interval apart, representing lines of equal elevation (isolines). The contour interval may vary from a few inches, or fractions of a foot, for detailed construction plans or very flat areas, to tens of meters for larger scale maps and more mountainous terrain. Contour plans may also incorporate spot elevations, especially at high points and low points, whose elevation would not otherwise be conveyed by the contours. These data-sets are often derived from spot elevations for existing terrain, or produced by landscape architects and engineers for new proposed surfaces. Contours may also be obtained from USGS Topographic maps, and other data sources such as local or state highway engineering departments. Although they are a conventional 2D representation, contours can be hard to understand except by trained professionals, and when projected into three dimensions, tend to yield just so much "spaghetti."

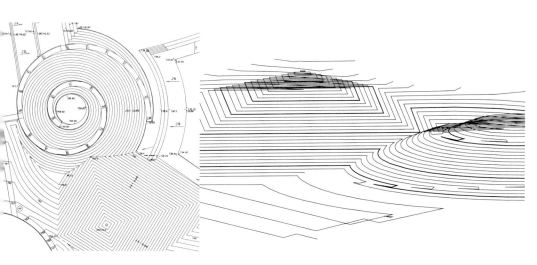

Figure 2.5
Partial 2D contour plan at spiral mound and pyramid landform represented with both 2D and 3D contour lines (polylines). University Commons, Hargreaves Associates (1998-1999).

Most of the time, contours will be used to create three-dimensional surfaces, solids or grids, as described in sections 2.3.1 and 2.3.2. It is important to note that in order to be useful for model building, contour lines in a CAD drawing must have their elevation value explicitly set – not just indicated by nearby text on the drawing, for example. Each line entity must have explicit z-coordinates associated with it. For many purposes, also, it is important for the lines to be joined up together into one continuous object (called a polyline in some systems). Finally, the lines may need to be explicitly closed when describing a closed contour. These requirements vary in their strictness from modeling system to system, so some experimentation is sometimes required. As a rule, explicit z-values, and continuous lines, explicitly closed when appropriate, are required of all 2D contour plans used to create a digital terrain model.

Although contour lines represented digitally are just connected series of spot elevations, and they can be simplified into a tabular table of spot elevations, with x-, y-, z- coordinates for some operations, for other operations the topological connectivity of point to point may be important, and can be used in the formation of the final surface or solid.

Figure 2.6
Note the precise linear contours of the pyramid landform in contrast to the curvilinear forms of the freeform berms.
University Commons, Hargreaves Associates (1998-1999).

Traditionally, hand drawn contour lines have been produced with the aid of french curves and other drawing tools to produce aesthetically pleasing smooth curves, even though the actual landform may not be formed into those same curves. In many CAD systems, or when produced by various automated engineering software, contour lines are produced without the use of spline curves, or other smoothing, and so have an angular or segmented look.

When contours have been produced with the use of spline curves, or other smoothing operations, the results when converting into 3D surfaces and solids may not be predictable or controllable, so it is usually better to resample these mathematical curves and replace them with specific points and short straight line segments. In the end, in most models, it is just these 3D points that will be used to form the terrain surface, and not the 2D curves. (However, surfaces and solids may be formed directly with the use of 3D splines and other curves.)

Figure 2.7
Sinuous contours produced with smooth curves, and straight-line approximations of them.

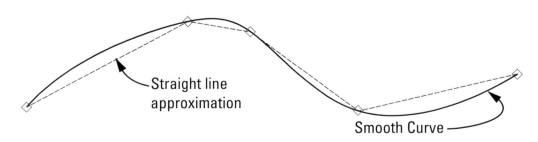

Straight line approximation

Smooth Curve

2.2.3 Cross Sections

Contour lines are limited to representing surfaces which are continuous in two dimensions, in which no vertical, overhanging, undercut, or multilayered conditions can be adequately represented (except by confusing graphic techniques such as dotted lines, etc.) Consequently, especially for site scale design, cross-sectional drawings of terrain conditions are also often used. Contours are in fact themselves cross sections, taken horizontally; most other cross sections are taken vertically, at specified locations, to reveal a side-cut view. (Terrain is rarely represented by real side views, or elevations, such as are used for the sides of buildings, etc., because terrain usually has few or no vertical faces).

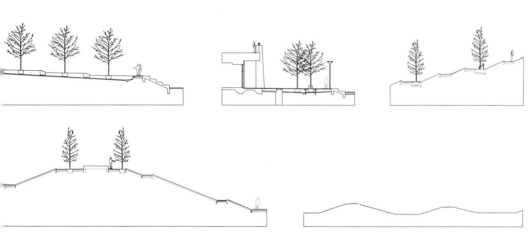

Figure 2.8
Series of cross sections cutting through the variety of landform and plaza conditions. University Commons, Hargreaves Associates (1998-1999).

Cross-sectional drawings can be valuable for the generation of terrain surface and solid models by using a sweep operation, or by continuously joining up, or morphing between, a series of cross sections. This technique is especially useful for linear landform features, such as roadways, or drainage channels, in which cross sections are given at regular intervals along a path, or centerline.

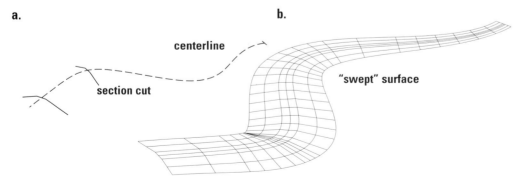

a.

centerline

section cut

b.

"swept" surface

Figure 2.9
a. Section cuts of a free form berm with a centerline. b. The section cuts can be "swept" along the center-line to produce a three dimensional berm. The resulting geometric object can be either a ruled or NURB surface.

2.3 Three-Dimensional Terrain

The various representations and tools described in the previous sections were designed to transform the sinuous, massive, and solid aspects of real terrain into 2D data structures for analog representations on paper. With a digital model, you can represent terrain in its three-dimensional complexity and then generate either 2D or 3D visual representations for analysis or presentation. The following sections will explore the variety of 3D data structures that can be employed for the creation of a three-dimensional digital terrain model. Although real terrain is massive and solid, with depth and volume, the starting point for most representation is to treat the ground as a surface.

Figure 2.10
Access to North Entrance, Plaza de la Constitucion de Girona. Giron, Spain, 1983-1993. The office of Elias Torres & Martinez LaPena.

2.3.1 Surfaces

A surface is a mathematical, infinitely thin object, with two sides, so that in a 3D view you can go beneath, and see the back side. Mathematically, a surface can be characterized as a set of points (x,y,z) such that $z = f(x,y)$; that is, at each location (x,y) seen from above, there is only a single z-value, or elevation. Terrain surfaces may be simple or complex, flat or rolling, shallow or steep. In the real landscape, landforms are constrained in their shapes and slopes by real-world physical criteria such as the geologic makeup of the soil, the climate, vegetative covering, and other ecological concerns. In most digital models, these constraints do not automatically apply, but should be considered if the terrain being represented is to be subject to real-world influences.

Figure 2.11
Typical surface:
a. From above.
b. From below.

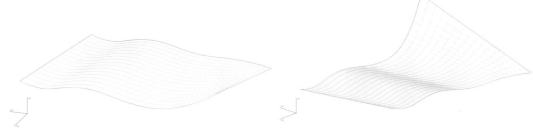

2.3.1.1 Simple Planes

The simplest landform of all is just a flat plane; the next more complex is a tilted plane, representing a sloping hillside. At least this minimum landform is required for modeling a landscape, and provides a surface which can be used to locate other features, such as trees or buildings, and on which those features can cast shadows. Often, to make sure that surface objects appear to be sitting upon the terrain, they are created with their base elevation just below the elevation of the terrain surface, or plane, so that they are truly embedded in the surface.

Figure 2.12
a. Simple surface plane parallel to the construction plane.
b. Simple surface plane sloped at 30 degrees from the construction plane.

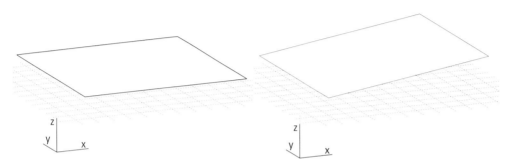

In the landscape, designers often organize the floor surface into a series of sloping flat planes, designed to drain water away from use areas (doorways, steps) and into drainage collectors (structural ones such as catch basins and grills, or open drainage courses such as ditches and ponds). This process of designing the land surface is called grading, and in professional practice is communicated in a grading plan, showing spot elevations, desired slopes, and possibly contour lines. In interior spaces, in buildings, floors may in fact be quite level; in outdoor areas, in the landscape, truly level areas are uncommon, as they will form puddles and pools of water. Surfaces for human use (walking, playing, parking) generally have gentle slopes between 0.5% (half a foot elevation change over one hundred feet of distance) and 10% (one foot elevation change over ten feet). In simple visualization models, level surfaces may provide an acceptable approximation; if real grading data is being used as a basis for modeling, there will doubtless be multiple gently sloping surfaces.

Most natural landforms are far more complex than just tilted planes, but at high levels of abstraction, may be modeled as a series of intersecting planes, their intersection lines forming ridges and valleys. In nature, the valleys are where water will run, ridges will define the watersheds which create catchment areas (or watersheds). Local depressions of low slope are where water will collect and form pools and lakes. In steep valleys the water will run a relatively straight course, modified by the component materials of the geologic substrate. In large flat low sloping areas, running water will meander, forming sinuous s-shaped curves.

2.3.1.2 Grid Mesh

While contour lines have appealing graphic qualities in 2D, they are a somewhat complicated data structure to store digitally, as the data file must contain information about the connectivity of each point to its two neighbors, keep track of multiple lines, each with its own z-value, and so on. A far simpler, and therefore more common data structure for a digital elevation model – especially for large areas, such as the statewide and national coverage provided by the United States Geological Survey (USGS) – is a *raster grid*: a rectangular array of numbers, each representing the elevation (z) value of the land at each point (x,y) located on a regular grid. This form of digital elevation model (*DEM*, or *DTM* for digital terrain model) can be found at varying (coarse) resolutions for most areas of the world, from a variety of sources. (See the section on data sources on the accompanying CD-ROM.)

The simplest visualization of a raster grid data set is a fish net grid, made by drawing lines from the center of each grid cell to its four rectangular neighbors. In this case, each line is simple and straight, but note that each quadrilateral face made from four lines may not be a simple plane – it's far more likely, in fact, to be a curved surface like a *hyperbolic paraboloid*. This fact has important ramifications in rendering, since no single surface normal vector exists, and the surface cannot be simply shaded. As a *wire frame* representation, however, this form is simple, straightforward, and usually effective, especially with hidden faces removed and hidden lines removed.

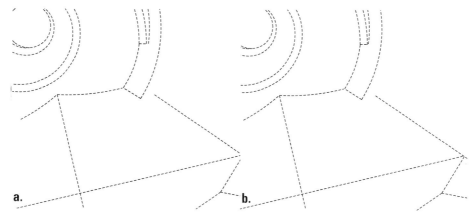

Figure 2.13

a. The plan on the left shows a grid mesh surface with a resolution of 20'.
b. The plan on the right shows a grid mesh surface with a resolution of 5'. Consider what detail is maintained with the higher resolution at the cost of efficiency.

The most important variable decision to make for these models is the size of the grid cell. If the grid size is too small, the file size may get enormous, rendering time will increase, and the resulting image may be too dense with lines. If too large a cell size is used, the surface may appear too coarse.

In addition to the raw grid of elevation values, some information must ordinarily be supplied locating the data in a geo-referenced system and specifying projection parameters and other information such as grid spacing. These values

a.

b.

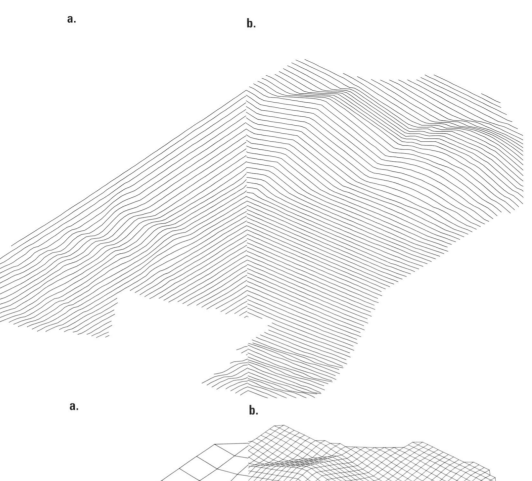

Figure 2.14
This set of images illustrates two of the ways in which a surface generated through draped polylines can be represented.
a. M direction polylines.
b. N direction polylines.
University Commons, Hargreaves Associates (1998-1999).

a.

b.

Figure 2.15
This set of images illustrates in a three-dimensional view the same surface represented with a 20 ' and a 5' polyface mesh grid.
University Commons, Hargreaves Associates (1998-1999).

are usually located at the beginning of the data file, or in a separate *header* file. One format for distribution of raster elevation data, and associated land-cover information, is the *Geo-TIFF* file format, a variant of the TIFF image file format which also contains the georeferencing information. A number of other conventions, some specific to particular software, are in use, and often, conversion may have to be made between them.

TECHNICAL NOTE: GRID MESH

In grid mesh files, it is important to distinguish between numbers stored in *Integer* or *Floating Point* formats. Integer values, with no decimal point, are more compact in storage and quicker for computers to calculate with, but are inherently less precise (a value of 1.5 must be represented as either 1, or 2). In terrain with steep slopes and high variability (mountainous terrain, for example) integer data values may acceptable. Floating Point values, with a decimal point and some specified amount of precision (numbers to the right of the decimal point), consume more space, making larger data files (each value may have to be written out with all decimal places, as 1.000000, 1.500000, etc.), and are more complex and time consuming for computers to operate on.

In areas of low slope and low variability, where, for example, there may be less than 0.5 meters in elevation difference between adjacent points, this representation is more desirable. Often, conversion to integer format in these sorts of landforms will result in a visible "stairstep" artifact when viewed obliquely. One obvious workaround, if integer values are required for some reason, is to reduce the spatial resolution, measuring in centimeters, e.g., instead of meters. Obviously, this may also result in larger data sets and larger file sizes. The Geo-Tiff format, for example, is limited to conveying elevation information in integer values, whose magnitude is limited by the byte size, or *tonal resolution* (8-bit, 16-bit, 24-bit, etc.). Floating Point values must be conveyed in a special binary file format, for which no generic standards are used, and which vary from software application to application.

Note also that some DEM data formats may use some special reserved

Integer Values:			Floating Point Values:		
514	512	510	513.99	511.11	509.995
509	500	504	509.0	499.886	504.01
499	496	499	499.00	495.76	498.551
50	505	509	500.77	505.45	508.77
-999	-999	-999	NODATA	NODATA	NODATA

value, such as -9999, to indicate cells for which the elevation is "unknown" (technically, this is a value meaning "No Data"). Often these values lie outside of some bounding polygon, or rectangle, for which the elevation values are known. In rendering, and for analytical purposes, it is usually appropriate to ignore these values, by clipping around them, rather than to keep them in the data set.

An additional important consideration, for the purposes of accuracy, is whether the cell's elevation value is assumed to be at the center of the cell, or at one of its corners. The grid mesh is typically drawn from centers of cells, rather than corners (because this requires no additional interpolation of intermediate values). Thus from a data set with m rows and n columns, a grid will be drawn with m-1 rows by n-1 columns (or $mn - m - n + 1$ total cells), and a marginal area one-half grid cell wide all around will not be represented in the wire frame mesh. (So, for example, an aerial photograph or other texture draped over the mesh will overlap the mesh at all edges.) And since data for the elevation of points just outside the mesh is unknown, errors of slope and orientation may be introduced at the edges. Consequently, it's important to make sure no areas or objects of real interest occur close to any edge of the digital terrain model, or put another way, that the model extend well beyond the areas of most interest or importance.

Note that in a wire-frame representation, in areas where the slope of the

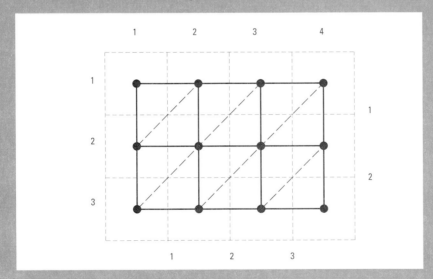

Figure 2.16
If the dots are at the center of the cell, the grid is 4 x 3; if the dots are the corners, it is only 3 x 2.

terrain is viewed obliquely, and there is a greater density of lines (or pixels, on a computer screen), the greater density results in a darkening of the region, and in areas where the faces are viewed more head-on, and there is less density of lines (or pixels), there is an corresponding lightness. This gives a sense of shading to the image so produced, but this shading has nothing to do with lighting, or light or shade, and is in fact quite artificial and may be even be misleading.

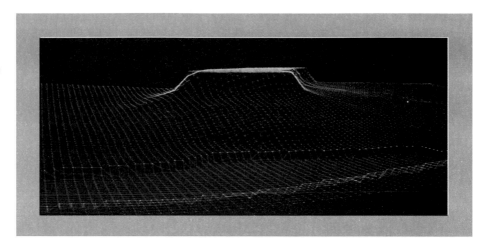

2.3.1.3 Ruled Surface

Another simple and direct method of generating a 3D surface model from contours is to create a *ruled surface*, generating 3D faces between adjacent pairs of contour lines. If each contour line is a 3D *isoline* (a polyline with a constant *z*-value), one simple approach consists of connecting each vertex point on the first line with an appropriate number of points on the second line, to form a series of quadrilaterals or triangles which together create a band of connected 3D faces. Since each point on each line is used in this method, there will be continuity across contour lines, and no gaps. The biggest trick to this method is determining, for each pair of lines, the appropriate number of points on the second

Figure 2.18
*a. Simple isolines or contours (polylines) from which the ruled surface will be derived.
b. Ruled surface as derived from the contours. This example makes explicit the risk involved with using the ruled surface. Consider carefully the resolution and density of the surface before generation. Note the gaps between the contour line and the ruled surface.*

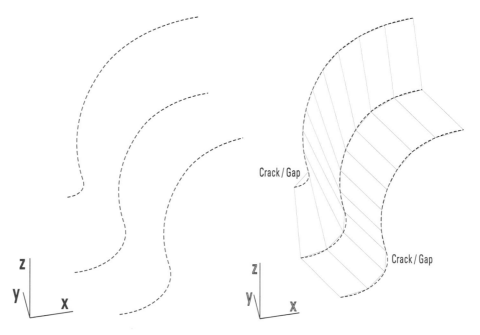

55

line to connect to each point on the first. If the number of points on each line happens to be identical, then the choice is simple and a series of rectangular, trapezoidal, or lozenge-shaped quadrilateral faces will be created. If the numbers are unequal, especially if they are greatly unequal, then a series of triangles will be created.

Some CAD modeling systems offer a ruled surface tool, which may make this option attractive for quick modeling. Note however that sometimes these tools subdivide each line into an equal number of shorter line segments, in order to make the quadrilateral connections described above, and some may slightly distort the exact geometry of the original lines. Furthermore, it may be a time-consuming process requiring the human operator to repetitively select each adjacent pair of contour lines, and apply the ruled surface tool. If the number of subdivisions chosen for one pair of lines is different from the number chosen for the next pair (for example, if the lines are getting shorter and a smaller number is appropriate, as in any cone-shaped, bowl, or mounded form), then there will be a gap, or spatial discontinuity, along one contour line where the faces from above do not exactly match the faces from below. Clearly, in this converging, or tapered condition, introducing triangles is appropriate and necessary.

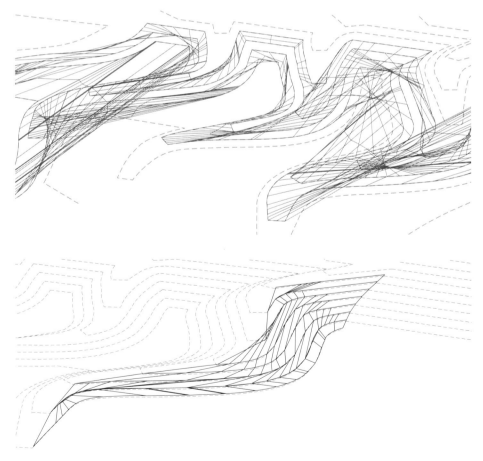

Figure 2.19
a. Using a ruled surface to generate a surface between the contours of a free form landform can produce unpredictable results.
b. One approach is to "break" the isolines at the ridges and breaklines, and then use the landform-specific contours as input for the ruled surface. Note the rectangular, trapezoidal, or lozenge-shaped quadrilateral faces.

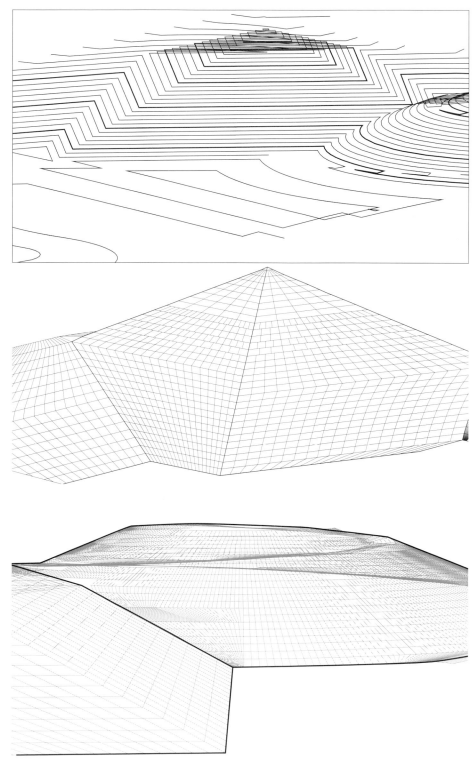

Figure 2.20
Ruled surfaces are suitable for representing either regular or geometric landforms.
a. An axonometric view of the pyramid and cone landforms as isolines/contours.
b. Those same landforms modeled with ruled surfaces. Note the differing density of the ruled surface and the crispness of the ridges.
University Commons, Hargreaves Associates (1998-1999).

RULED SURFACE

Objectives:

The objective of this tutorial is to demonstrate the procedure for generating a ruled surface. The tutorial begins with the basic inputs and the making of a simple ruled surface and concludes with an example of a ruled surface model at the project scale.

Input Items:

The type of input entities for the ruled surface varies according to the software package, but can be generated from any combination of the following: **point, line, polyline (open, or closed)**. Input entities should be at the appropriate z elevation. **Note:** Input entities must have similar topological directions.

Exception:

A ruled surface cannot be generated between an open and a closed polyline, or between two points.

RULED SURFACE ENTITY INPUTS

| 2 POLYLINES | 2 LINE SEGMENTS | 2 CLOSED POLYLINES | POINT & LINE | POINT & CLOSED POLYLINE | 2 CLOSED POLYLINES | POINT & FREEFORM POLYLINE |

▶ TOPOLOGICAL DIRECTION

1. Determine and set the resolution for the surface entity. The resolution can be set according to the dimension/length of the surface segment or by the number of divisions along the length of the input entity.

2. Activate the command and select the input entities in any order.

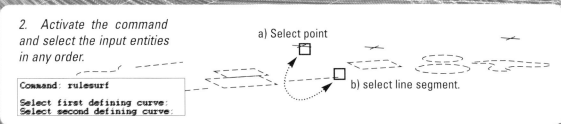

a) Select point

b) select line segment.

```
Command: rulesurf

Select first defining curve:
Select second defining curve:
```

Ruled Surface Variations

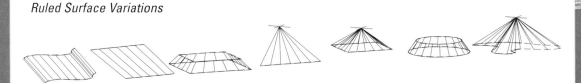

1. With the ridge and breaklines as a reference, the contours were generated as unique 2D polylines or line segments at the appropriate Z height or elevation.

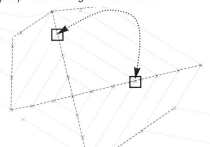

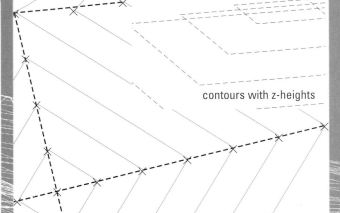

contours with z-heights

2. Using the ruled surface command, the input contours for the first contour interval were selected, and a surface generated.

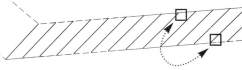

3. This was repeated for the remaining contour intervals, until the face of the pyramid was built. When that face was completed the other faces of the landform were built in a similar manner.

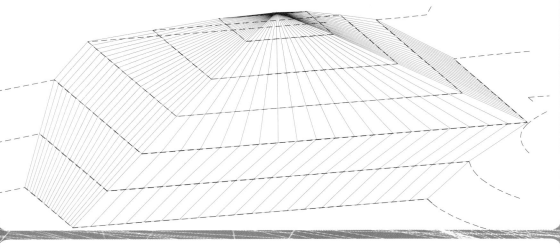

Notes:
1. An alternative to using contours is to use the section cuts as ruled surface inputs, therefore generating a horizontal rather than vertical ruled surface.
2. The ruled surface above divides each ruled surface into 20 equal intervals.
3. This surface data can now be exported for uses in a rendering application or to generated perspective views.

2.3.1.4 TIN – Triangulated Irregular Network

Although regular rectangular gridded meshes (*fishnets*) and ruled surfaces are conceptually simple and computationally efficient, they suffer from several drawbacks. For one, regularly spaced grids may be inefficient: the regular spacing between cells cannot be varied, and in areas of low or no relief, many redundant and repetitive points must still be entered, and in areas of high variation, important features may be missed if they do not fall directly on the regular grid spacing. In terrain with a range of relief, the smallest grid required to pick up detail in the areas of greatest relief must be used for the entire area. If a larger grid is chosen for economy's sake, then detail may be missed in local areas; for example, a peak, or high point, maybe located in between grid points, and so not measured or stored. Second, as noted above, the non-planar surfaces of the quadrilateral faces in a rectangular mesh present a problem to simple rendering algorithms, as no single surface normal vector can be found.

An alternative data structure which overcomes these obstacles, and offers some additional advantages, is the *Triangulated Irregular Network* (or TIN). In a TIN, irregularly spaced and located spot elevations are joined together into a continuous network of triangles, each point (*vertex*) is connected by lines (or *edges*) to at least three other points. There are several alternative methods for connecting up any set of more than three points into contiguous triangles, but the

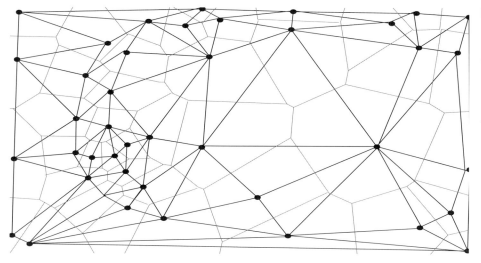

Figure 2.21
Illustration of Delaunay triangulation, in black, and its inverse, or "dual," a Voronoi tesselation, in gray.

most commonly used is the *Delaunay triangulation*, a method which attempts to assure a most efficient triangulation, connecting each point only to its nearest neighbors. (Technically, for any set of three points making a triangle, the circle defined by them should not contain any other points.)

Having triangles and irregularly spaced points overcomes both of the disadvantages of the fishnet mesh described above. Since there is no regular grid, data points need only be collected where there is variation in terrain. Over a large rel-

Figure 2.22
*Triangulated sur-
face without break
lines.
a. Plan view.
b. Axonometric
view.*

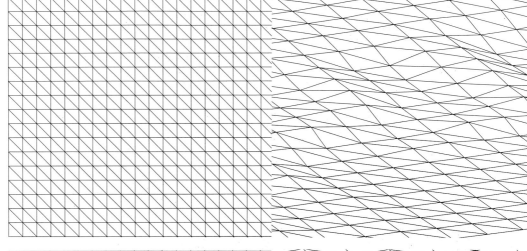

Figure 2.23
*Triangulated sur-
face with breakline
included.
a. Plan view.
b. Axonometric
view.*

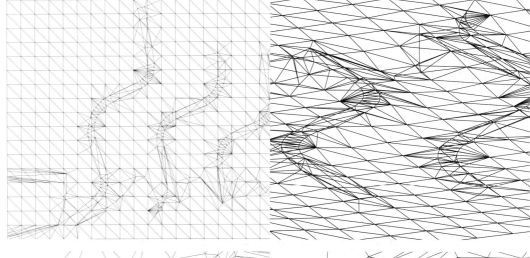

Figure 2.24
*Plan and axono-
metric view of a
TIN surface made
from contours.
a. Plan view.
b. Axonometric
view.*

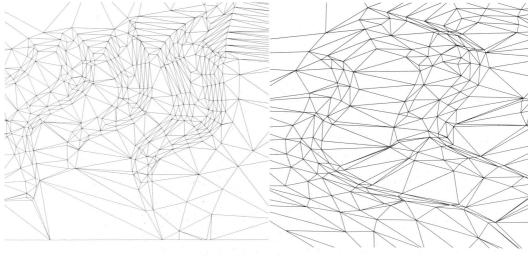

atively flat or low slope area, only a few points will serve to describe the form; in areas of greater relief and higher, changing slopes, more frequent points can be measured and stored. Furthermore, in this scheme, important points such as local high points and peaks, or low points, stream centerlines, etc., can be measured and incorporated into the model. These can be important hints to the software about how to break the surface, so that creases, or edges between triangles, are lined up with natural features such as streams and valleys, and triangular facets are not created that run crosswise to such features.

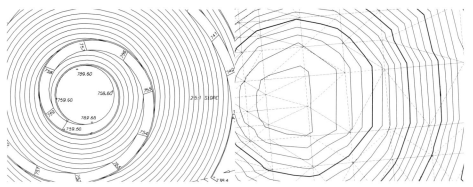

Figure 2.25
a. Contour plan of conical mound and path.
b. Plan of the same condition with contours generated from a TIN surface. The original TIN surface is shown in gray.

A TIN may be directly created from contour lines by simply treating each vertex point in the contour description as a spot elevation; then the resulting TIN will tend to contain all of the edges, or lines, from the contours, with bands of triangles running between them. Alternatively, a TIN may be created from either irregularly spaced, or regularly spaced, spot elevations, in which case a surface is first interpolated from the points, and then triangles created according to some controlling criteria, typically either the absolute total number of triangles, or some limit on the size of the smallest triangle , or both.

Since there are only triangles to be rendered, computing a single surface normal is simple, and so shading using *Lambert cosine shading* or some other simple shading technique is straightforward. In addition, since a single sloped triangle is guaranteed planar, it is simple to extract contour lines for any such triangle, and so it is easy to generate a contour plan from a TIN model. Sections also can be cut with certainty and ease. Since each triangular face has a simply calculated slope and orientation, making analytical slope and aspect maps is easy from the TIN. And since TINs can support arbitrarily small triangles, any modifications made to the surface, by moving faces, or adding other forms (such as mounds, sideslopes, berms) can be easily blended by patching in smaller triangles as needed.

TIN models, however, suffer from their own disadvantages. Most notably, the data structure required to describe the triangulation is relatively complex. Separate tables of points, lines, and faces must be maintained, with a complex system of pointers linking up points into lines (edges), and lines into triangles (faces). (Compare to the simple rectangular table of values required for a raster

DEM, as described previously.) The time required to initially compute a triangulation may also be great, for a large set of points.

When a TIN is transferred from one computer program to another, it is possible that the complex topological relationship between points will be lost, and each triangular face saved as a separate entity. This of course is inefficient, since each edge (except those at the periphery) will be transferred twice, once for each triangle of which it's a part. This is wasteful, but acceptable so long as there will be no further editing of the triangular mesh, as for example, if the final step is rendering only. However, if any further editing will be done, changing the elevation or location of any points, or introducing new triangles, then each change must be made carefully, with attention to making corresponding changes to every point or line that is involved (which for a vertex with many connections, may be a large number of affected triangles).

TECHNICAL NOTE: VRML Code for Triangular Irregular Network

The VRML language specification, at version 2.0, contains a clear specification and syntax for encoding the topology of TINs, and may be an attractive format for transferring between programs if the option is available. Using some other exchange formats, such as .DXF, often loses the topological connectivity, and represents every triangle separately, so many points are saved with all their 3 coordinates multiple times, which is grossly inefficient on a large TIN. In the VRML format, each point is entered only once, then a table of faces lists the three points used in each face just by its index number, which is much more efficient.

```
#VRML V2.0 utf8
# a simple TIN, with 4 points and 2 triangles
Group {
  children [
    Transform {
      rotation 1.0 0.0 0.0 0.0
      children [
        Shape
          geometry IndexedFaceSet {
          coord Coordinate {
            point [
                        0.0         0.0         0.0
                        100.0       0.0         50.0
                        100.0       100.0       0.0
                        0.0         100.0       75.0
            ]
          }
          normalPerVertex TRUE
          solid FALSE
          creaseAngle 0.5
          coordIndex [
              2,    0,    1, -1
              2,    3,    0, -1
          ]
        }
      }
    ]
  }
  ]
}
```

TIN — *Triangulated Irregular Network*

Objectives:

To create a TIN Surface representation of a topographic condition for visualization analysis, and calculation. This tutorial outlines the procedure for the generation of a TIN surface in a traditional CAD package with a civil engineering module, Like AutoDesk's Land Development Desktop. This procedure parallels surface generation in both ESRI's Arc View and ArcInfo.

Input Entity and Interface:

Points (x,y,z): *Spot Elevation. Zero dimensional entities with an elevation attribute or Z height/value. (Points can be used alone or in combination with contours.)*

Contours 2D or 3D: *Linear information that defines significant topographic features like a ridge, toe of slope, or the edges of pavement and curbs. (Use of breaklines is optional.)*

Breaklines: *Linear vector information with an elevation attribute or a vector entity with a constant Z height or elevation. (Contours can be used alone or in combination with point data.)*

Site Boundary: *Linear information that defines the limits of the surface to be built and analyzed. The boundary can often be associated with a project's "limit of work" or the site boundary. (Boundary information is required.)*

1. Initiate the process for defining the surface. Depending on the software application, this often entails launching the terrain analysis and generation module. In the AutoDesk Land Development Desktop it is the Terrain Model Explorer.

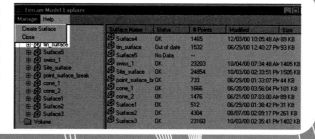

2. Define the Surface. Defining the surface can be associated with creating a database within which the topographic information will be entered and stored. The software application will ask you to name the surface or provide you with a default name.

3. Add Input Data. Now that you have named the surface and created the database, the software application expects you to identify and input the data you will use to represent the surface. You must enter either point or contour data or a combination of both, and a site boundary. Breaklines are optional but will ensure accurate representation of surfaces and detail. Entities for input can be selected directly or can be entered by specifying the layer upon which the data is located within the CAD file. When working with GIS, the user specifies the coverage or shape file name.

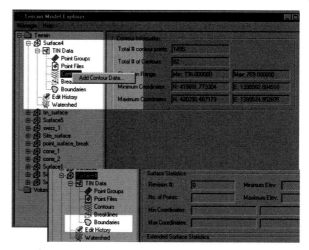

4. *Build the Surface.* This process associates the topographic data with the site boundary and breaklines information. The application determines the topological relationships among the entities and constructs a surface representation which is then stored within the file's internal database. When this process is completed there will be no physical entities visible in the applications graphic window. To see the surface you must request its display. If the surface has changed or you have either added or subtracted topographic data, the surface must be rebuilt. The changes are not recorded until the surface is "built" again.

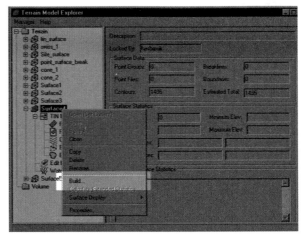

5. *Surface Display.* The surface representation resides within the database of the CAD file – display can be delivered to the user at any time and can be represented temporarily or result in the generation of physical entities.

6. *Temporary Display.* A temporary representation would be the delivery of a hidden line view to the monitor, typically a TIN. The surface representation can be screen captured and saved as a raster image. The usefulness of this representation type is limited.

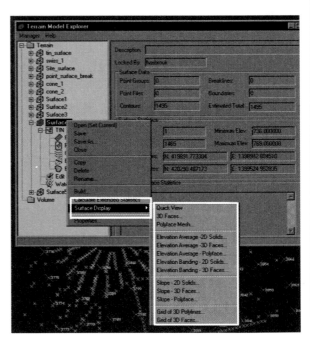

7. *Physical Entities.* For the generation of physical entities, the application will provide a series of entity types that facilitate either visualization or analysis. You can choose to generate 3DFaces, a Polyface Mesh, or 3D entities that either describe the surface, slope percentage, or elevation value. For slope percentage or elevation values the surface entities color attribute is used to differentiate between values. These three-dimensional entities can be exported to rendering applications for visualization or as underlays for the generation of three-dimensional views. Change does not occur dynamically if the surface data changes in any way. The surface definition must be rebuilt and the physical representation regenerated.

2.3.1.5 Parametric Surfaces: Patches and NURB Surfaces

The greatest disadvantage of TIN representations, other than their complex data structure, is their simple geometry and faceted nature. Truly smooth curves cannot be represented, except in approximation. In rendering, the sharp facets and plane faces of a TIN can be smoothed out, an important fact to remember. *Smooth shaded* renderings may be generated from faceted surfaces, by using interpolation in rendering to compute multiple intermediate angles between faceted surfaces, and generate an apparently smooth curve.

For modeling truly smooth curved surfaces, more advanced geometric modeling tools must be used, to create mathematically controlled curves and curved surfaces. There are a variety of mathematical techniques used to describe curves and curved surfaces, including *patches*, and *parametric surfaces* including *NURB* surfaces. All of these are characterized by using mathematical formulae to describe curves based on a small number of *control points*. These control points, whether in 2D as for creating contour lines, or 3D for surfaces, are the ones defined and manipulated in the modeling system; the curve or surface is created from them. In some systems, the curve or surface is constrained to pass through, or touch, the control points; in others, the curve or surface may lie some distance away from the control points.

Figure 2.26
NURB surface showing control points, curves, and surface mesh. Modeled in Rhino3D.

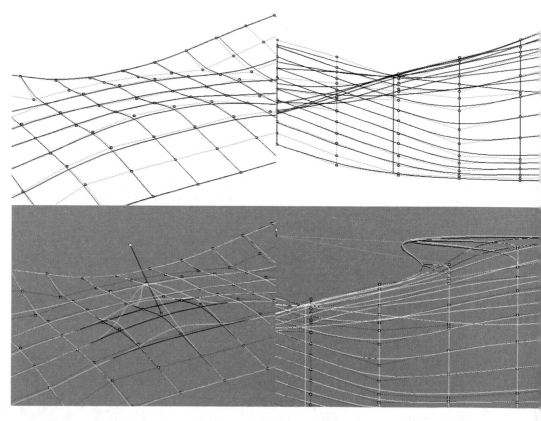

NURB SURFACE

Objective:

The objective of this tutorial is to demonstrate the procedure for generating a NURB surface. The tutorial will begin with the making of a simple swept NURB surface and conclude with an example at the project scale focusing on the representation of a designed topographic feature with a NURB surface.

Notes:

NURB entities can be derived from existing geometric entities (lines, polylines, b-splines, etc.). The advantage of the NURB surface is its predisposition to maintain smooth curvature and its potential for real-time manipulation. The NURB entity will appeal to anyone familiar with vertex-by-vertex manipulation of a ruled surface. The NURB surface entity consists of both a mesh and its control points. Real-time sculpting can be achieved through direct manipulation or spatial transformation of the control points. Control points can be manipulated individually or as groups. These actions do not yet mimic the real actions of digging or moving earth, but tools are currently under development that will help to make digital manipulations more like real-world sculpting.

Inputs:

Software applications and input entities will influence how the NURB surface is generated. The chart below compares procedures and input entities that can be used for the generation of continuous terrain surfaces. The tutorial will focus on the "Rail Sweeps" and the "Drape" approaches.

NURB Surface Type	Appropriateness for Terrain	Inputs	Notes:
Surface from corner points	Good	Snap to 3D Objects	Surface generation can be time consuming.
Surface from (2,3,4) Edge Curves	Very Good	Contours, Ridge & Breaklines	Suffers from the same awkwardness of the individual ruled surface objects.
Direct Generation (through corner inputs)	Good	Coordinate input through keyboard or graphical input	Best used for the modeling of simple planar surfaces. Can easily undergo geometric transformation (move, rotate, scale, shear).
Extrusion	Poor	Open or Closed Contours	Does not result in a continuous surface.
Loft	Not Recommended	Contours, Ridge & Breaklines can be used as inputs	
Surface from Curve Network	Not Recommended	A combination of Contours, Ridge and Breaklines	Problems will occur with sinuous contours of great length and complexity.
1 Rail Sweep	Good	Ridge & Breaklines	
2 Rail Sweep	Good	Ridge & Breaklines	
Revolve	Not Recommended	Axis of rotation and profile	
Patch	Not Recommended	Ridge & Breaklines and points.	
Drape	Excellent	Solid or surface objects.	The user draws a metaphorical NURB sheet over existing 3D objects. Mesh density and sheet size are determined by the user.
From Image Map as Height Field	Very Good	Gray scale image map	Requires a gray scale image, and prior knowledge of bitmap pixel values e.g., White =0 Black=255. Image resolution determines precision, while pixel values influence smoothness.
Surface from Point Grid	Very Good	Coordinate triplets (x,y,z) are input by the user sequentially or read directly from a point file.	User needs to determine best cell resolution. Works best when the application reads a text file of input points. This means that data can easily be exchanged between modeling applications (GIS, Rhino, Autodesk Land Development Desktop).

Generating a NURB surface through edge selection
Input entities:
2, 3, or 4 edge curves. The curves can be parametric or linear.

Overview:
Similar to the ruled surface command. You can use anywhere from 2 to 4 curves to define this type of NURB entity. In this example the edge curves happen to be contours. As with the ruled surface commands, results might be unpredictable with long sinuous curves; therefore strategically breaking the input contours at breaklines or ridges is strongly recommended.

Process:

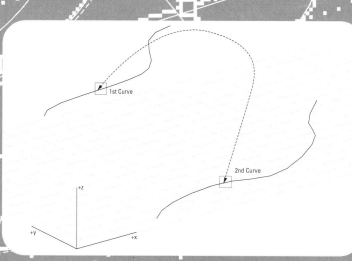

1. Invoke the "Surface from Edge Curves Command."
2. Select the edge curves.

3. The resolution of the resulting surface can be manipulated in relation to purpose, as well as real-time deformation through the manipulation of control points.

Generating a NURB surface through "Rail Surf"
The two Rail Surf commands are related to the family of sweep commands.

Input entities:
One section or profile that will be swept.
1 or 2 edge curves.

Overview:
The "rail surf" sweeps a geometric entity along one or between two edge curves. The act of sweeping defines a NURB surface between the two edge curves in the shape or profile of the swept entity.

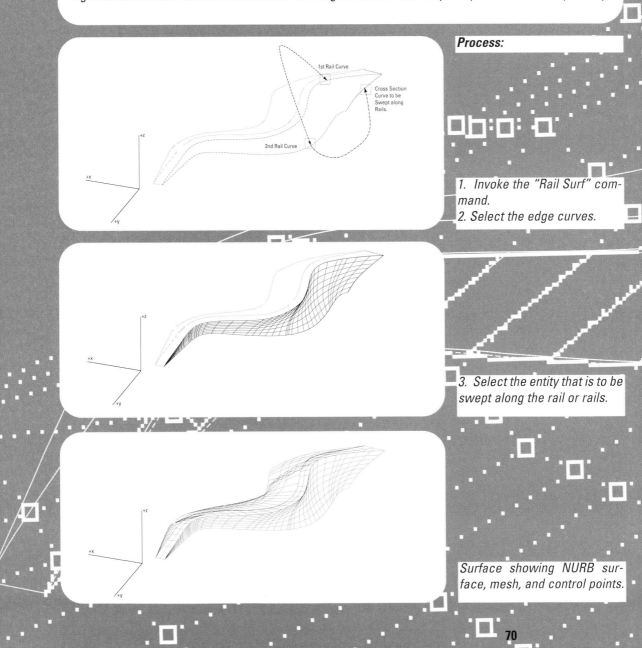

Process:

1. Invoke the "Rail Surf" command.
2. Select the edge curves.

3. Select the entity that is to be swept along the rail or rails.

Surface showing NURB surface, mesh, and control points.

Generating a NURB surface through "Drape"

Overview:
The drape command metaphorically "drapes" a NURB surface over a set of existing 3 dimensional entities. The action is similar to floating a bed sheet over several solid objects, revealing their outline forms, somewhat smoothed.

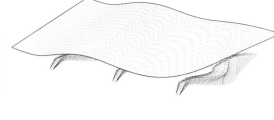

Input entities:
A set of existing 3-dimensional entities. The entities can be surfaces, or solids, or both.

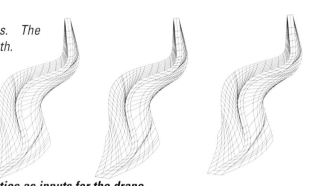

3D Entities as inputs for the drape.

Process:
1. Activate the drape command. Depending on the application you might be presented with a shaded view to illustrate the presence of surface or solid entities and to assist you in defining the limits of the new NURB surface.
2. Using the cursor, snap to the diagonal limits of the new surface. (This action is similar to defining a vector polygon.)

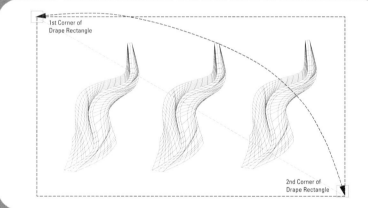

1st Corner of Drape Rectangle

2nd Corner of Drape Rectangle

3. The resolution of the resulting surface can be adjusted depending on its specifications or intended use. You will notice a smoothing between the slopes.

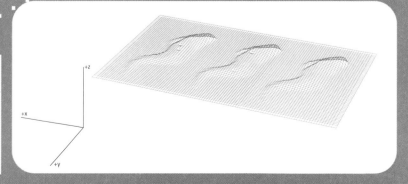

2.3.2 Three-Dimensional Solid Terrain

All of the previous section's representations are founded on a critical limiting assumption: that the terrain surface being modeled is a continuous surface, with no breaks, overhangs, holes, tunnels, bridges, etc. Mathematically, this means that for any x,y position, there is only one single z value. Such a surface is sometimes referred to as a *2.5D surface*, because although there is a third dimension, it is severely constrained by the first two (this term is also used sometimes to refer to extruded forms, which have a similar characteristic). Plains, fields, mountains, planes, and the surfaces of cones all meet this criterion. But in the real world, this limitation doesn't hold, and many interesting and important landforms are in fact not continuous surfaces. Real terrain, of course, is not just a "skin," but has substance and mass. These characteristics can best be modeled using a different representation – a *solid model*. Solid models are in principle more complex than surfaces, and may offer more possibilities, including analytical ones such as the ability to slice cross sections, or compute mass or centroid, for example.

Figure 2.27
a. Herbert Bayer (1900-1987) Mill Creek Canyon Earthworks, 1979-1982.
Courtesy of City of Kent, Washington Parks, Recreation and Community Services.
b. Harima Science Garden City, Hyogo Prefecture, Japan, 1993.
Courtesy of Peter Walker and Partners.

For these kinds of forms, the conventional representations so far discussed (contours, meshes, TINs, swept and NURB surfaces) are inadequate, and the entire realm of geometric 3D solid modeling must come into play, combining all of the above surface representations with other geometric solid models and boolean operations.

2.3.2.1 Parametric Solids

The simplest building blocks for a solid digital terrain are the geometric primitives: slabs, wedges, cones, pyramids, spheres, etc. The primitives can be used alone and in combination to form a terrain model. Few natural landforms mimic these platonic shapes exactly, but they are often employed in designed landscapes, as evidenced in the work of Martha Schwatz, Herb Bayer, Jaques Wirtz, and the office of Peter Walker and Partners.

In general, the ability to form earth into controlled shapes is limited by the composition of the earth's material – whether solid rock, gravel, or a mixture soil clay, sand, and silt – and the resultant characteristics, including angle of repose, erodability, bearing strength, and the designed objects shape. Without special construction techniques, earth-formed elements will not maintain the crisp angles of the geometric primitives. Time and phenomenal change will soften the angles forming smooth, parabolic, curved fillets and sinuous saddle forms.

Figure 2.28
This computer generated image, by Rick Casteel shows the hemi-spherical turf mounds encircled by undulating park benches.
Martha Schwartz, Inc., General Services Administration, NY, NY, 1996. Courtesy Martha Schwartz, Inc.

Figure 2.29
These pyramids, considered as "land art," were used as a grand unifying device that march diago-nally through a park surrounded by abundant vege-tation.
Jaques Wirts, Parc Cogels-Pyramids and Trees. Schoten, Belgium, 1976-1978.

1/2 sphere

cone

geometric primitives

pyramid

slab

PARAMETRIC SOLIDS

Objective:

The objective of this tutorial is to demonstrate the procedure for generating a parametric solid object. The tutorial will illustrate the generation of a parametric solid through both direct generation and derivative actions. The approach to making a solid geometric primitive varies according the software application, but most applications allow you to create a solid entity by selecting an object from a list of primitives or through generative actions like extrude and revolve.

Direct Generation of a Parametric Solid Entity:

Inputs:

There are no entity inputs, just coordinates and parameters. Depending upon the type of entity, you will be required to input coordinate triplets (x,y,z) and the parameters that contribute to the definition of the object. You can respond to the request for inputs by either typing with the keyboard or snapping to points within the graphics window. The chart below outlines the typical inputs required for the creation of parametric solids.

Overview:

Parametric solid entities are defined through the selection of an entity from a menu or interface and directly generating the object through the input of parameters.

Solid Entity Type	Typical Inputs	Variation
Box	Corner to Corner and Height	Center, Height, Length
Sphere	Center Point,(Radius or Diameter)	
Cylindar	Center Point (Radius or Diameter) and Height	
Cone	Center Point (Radius or Diameter) and Height	
Wedge	Corner, Length, Width and Height	
Torus	Center Point, Tube Radius, Torus Radius	Center point Tube Radius, Torus Diameter

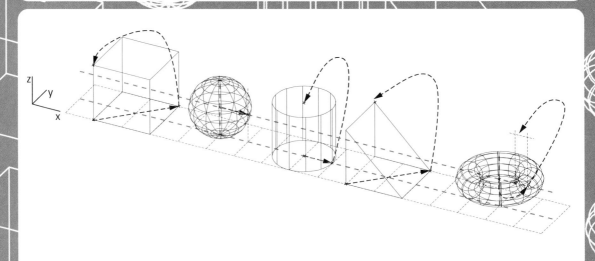

Derivative Actions: SWEEP

Inputs:
Closed polylines or polygons.

Overview:
Solid objects generated through derivative actions require you to act upon two-dimensional entities. In order to define the solid volume an input entity and the path of extrusion is required. The path of extrusion can be either implicit or explicit. A path is implicit when invoking the extrude command because the entity is being swept perpendicular to the construction plane. An explicit condition is when a geometrical entity (line, polyline, spline) is used to define the path of the sweep operation. In most situations the input entities can be transformed through tapering while performing the command.

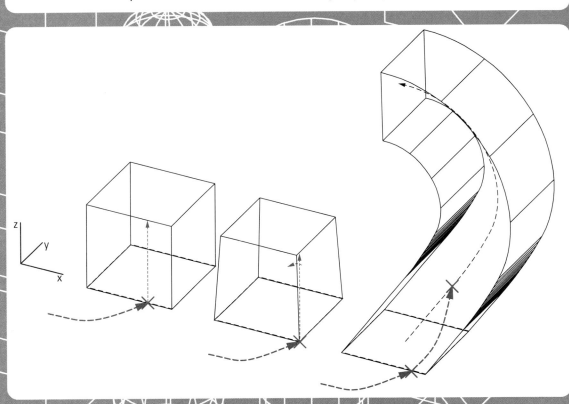

Process:
Simple Extrusion
1. Invoke the extrude command.
2. Select the entity to be extruded.
3. Specify the height.

Process:
Extrude & Taper
1. Invoke the extrude command.
2. Select the entity to be extruded.
3. Specify the height.
4. Specify the angle of taper.

Process:
Extrude Along Path
1. Invoke the extrude command.
2. Select the entity to be extruded.
3. Select the path that will be used for the extrusion.

Derivative Actions: REVOLVE

Overview:
When revolving a two-dimensional entity in order to create a solid object you must determine the axis of rotation and the degree of revolution.

Inputs:
Spline, line, or polyline. Entities to be revolved should be closed.

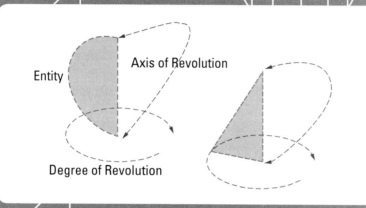

Process:
1. Invoke the Revolve Command.
2. Specify the axis of revolution.
3. Select the entity to be revolved.
4. Specify the degree of revolution.

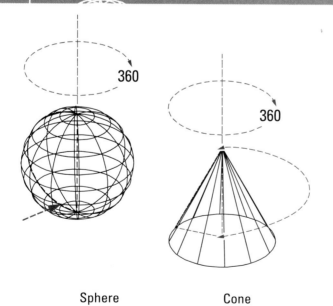

2.3.2.2 Stepped Contours ("Pancake" Models)

Most landforms are not simple planes or solids, and a more irregular modeling technique is required. Perhaps the simplest and most direct method of generating a 3D solid model from contours is to extrude contour lines, in a vertical direction, by an amount equal to the contour interval, creating a stack of polygonal solids, akin to a stack of pancakes, or a "layer cake."

Figure 2.30
Pancakes and layer cakes along with a wireframe and rendered stepped contour model.

When the vertical distance is too great, this technique introduces an objectionable stair step look into the result, which is difficult to overcome using simple rendering techniques. (In analog models, using the same technique of cutting out and stacking layers of cardboard, cork, or styrofoam, for example, a smoothing layer of clay, plaster, or other material can be used to smooth out the steps between layers. A similar digital approach is hard to come by.) Nonetheless, when the contour interval is relatively small compared to the extent of the model, the visual effect can be quite acceptable, and for certain conditions, such as in amphitheatres and other structural landforms, the effect can be even the most appropriate.

Figure 2.31
Analog stepped contour model, produced by Letitia Tormay, is flanked by a wireframe and rendered view. The visual comparisons here clearly show the derivation of the digital form from the traditional analog model form. Both model forms share similar functionality, limitations, and visual behaviors.

SOLID STEPPED CONTOUR MODEL

Objectives:

To present a method for generating a stepped contour model by extruding a set of closed two-dimensional contour lines. This type of model results in a series of unique solid objects that when viewed together represent a stepped terrain surface.

Inputs:

Two-dimensional closed polylines or splines preferably with a Z height of zero (Z=0).

Process:

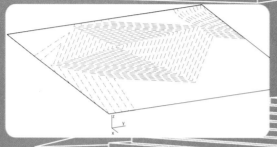

1. Determine the elevation of the model's ground plane. In most situations a Z height of zero is preferable. (Z=0)

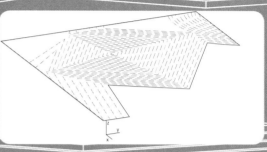

2. Make sure that all of the contour intervals are closed.

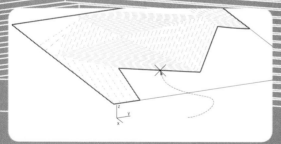

3. Invoke the EXTRUDE command.
4. Select the contour interval that you wish to extrude.

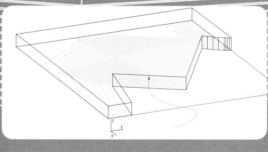

5. Specify the height of the extrusion. If the boundary height is zero, the height of the extrusion should equal that of the contour interval. (Extrude height = contour interval.)

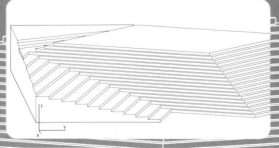

6. Repeat for all other contour intervals.

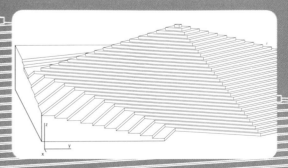

78

2.3.2.3 Boolean Operations

Surfaces, simple solids, and solids formed from surfaces, all share a similar characteristic: they represent continuous surfaces, without gaps, holes, or overhangs, and are sufficient for the majority of topographic models. But in more complex situations, especially as architectural buildings and other features (bridges, tunnels, et al.) come in to the model, an expanded range of 3D modeling tools will be required. These tools facilitate modeling the intersections between the continuous topographic surface and built structures as well as the anomalies of tunnels, caves, and retained walls.

The geometric solid boolean operations of union, intersection, and subtraction, enable the modeling of cut-outs or holes and the combinatorial landscape forms that constitute the topographic medium. CAD modeling software that supports boolean operations will typically only do so with solids, and so any surface representations must first be converted to solids. Boolean operations require two solids on which to act and some operations are order-sensitive. (Just as in normal arithmetic, the subtract operation is not transitive: $a - b \neq b - a$.) So where the union operator, who welds two solids together, is not order sensitive, subtraction is.

The boolean operation of subtraction can be used to model the pool as seen in the project from Peter Walker and Partners pictured below. The geometric shape of the pool is "subtracted" from the solid landform. The modeling of a tunnel also capitalizes on the subtraction operation. First the base landform is selected, then an appropriate shape (a cylinder, e.g., or a cylinder cut in half longitudinally) is subtracted from it.

Figure 2.32
a. Circular pool structures in a field of turf and crushed stone.
b. Detail of pool structure.
Harima Science Garden City, Hyogo Prefecture, Japan, 1993.
Courtesy of Peter Walker and Partners.

BOOLEAN OPERATIONS

Objective:

To illustrate the use of boolean operations in the representation of a designed land-scape condition. The example will use both the subtraction and intersection func-tions to model the pool structures as seen in the project example by Peter Walker and Partners. Keep in mind, layer and object management is integral to success.

Inputs:

Parametric Solid Objects – on unique layers according to type or function.
1 Solid Plinth – extruded rectangle (ground plane).
3 Solid Cylinders – geometric primitive (pool volume).
3 Smaller Cylinders – geometric primitives (water volume).

Overview:

This process has three parts.
Part 1: Subtract the pool volume from the ground plane.
[designed ground plane = ground plane – pool volume]
Part 2: Subtract the water volume from the pool volume in order to determine the edge and boundary material of the pool. **[pool boundary = pool volume – water volume]**
Part 3: Find the intersection between the ground plane and the pool objects so that the pool objects will be flush with the ground plane. **[pool object = intersection (ground plane, pool boundary)]**

Results:

1 Solid rectilinear object with pool volume as void (designed ground plane).
3 Solid cylinders with water volume as void (pool object)

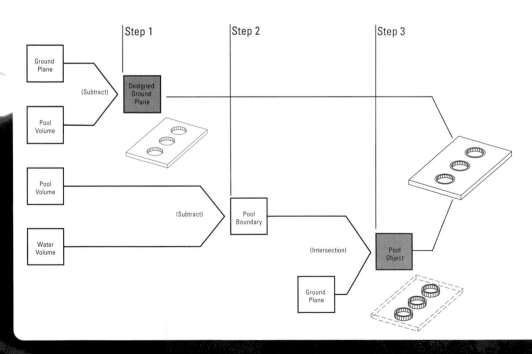

80

Part 1: [Designed Object = Ground Plane – Pool Volume]

1. Invoke the "subtraction" command.
2. Select the object that you want to subtract from – the ground plane.
3. Select the object that you want to subtract – the pool volume.
4. Repeat for the remaining pool volumes.

Result = Designed ground plane.

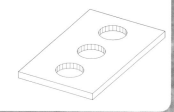

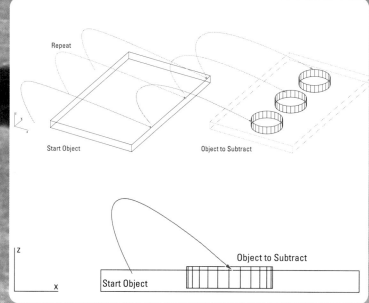

Part 2: [Pool Boundary = Pool Volume – Water Volume]

1. Turn off the "Designed object layer."
2. Define a new layer called "pool boundary" and make it the current or active layer.
3. Invoke the "subtraction" command.
4. Select the object that you want to subtract from – the pool volume object.
5. Select the object that you want to subtract – the water volume object.
6. Repeat for the remaining pools.

Result = Pool boundaries.

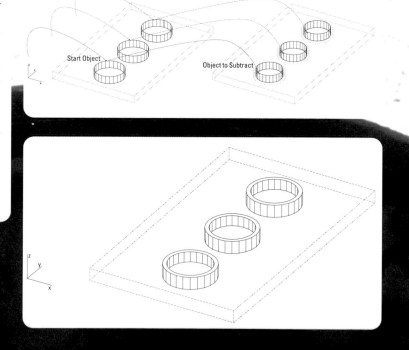

Part 3: [Pool Object = Intersection (Ground Plane, Pool Boundary)]

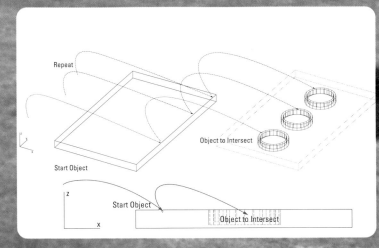

Repeat

Start Object

Object to Intersect

Start Object

Object to Intersect

z

x

1. Define a new layer called "pool object" and make it the current or active layer.
2. Invoke the Intersection command.
3. Select the "start" object – the ground plane.
4. Select the object that you want to intersect with the ground plane – the pool boundary.
5. Repeat for remaining pools. Result = Pool objects.

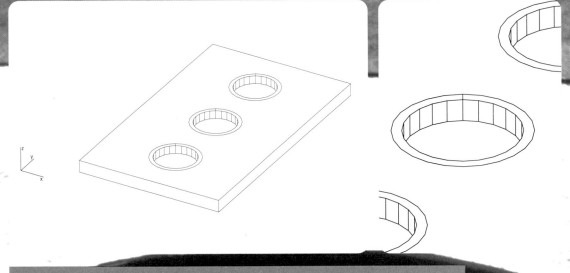

TECHNICAL NOTE: BOOLEAN OPERATIONS

The solid resulting from some boolean operations (especially subtraction and intersection) sometimes can no longer be represented by simple contours or surface model, and may be represented internally in a unique format, so it may not be transportable between one software package and another. Also, some boolean operations may generate "ill-formed" solids in which all surface normal vectors have not been computed, or may be incorrect, etc. Often some cleanup operation must be applied to solids generated from boolean or other combinatorial operations to correct these defects before they can be reliably rendered.

2.3.2.4 Rocks

While the emphasis for most landform modeling is the surface characteristic required as a base for other landscape elements, sometimes the underlying geological base manifests as rocks visible on the surface, as objects. Whether giant *glacial erratics* (boulders left behind by ancient glacial processes), or small rounded stones found in a riverbed, rock objects offer some challenges for modeling, which reiterate in microscale the techniques presented so far for landform in general. That is, rocks may be modeled as geometric primitives (spheres, egg-shapes, crystalline forms); solids constructed by ruled surfaces; grid-meshed or triangulated solids.

Some surface rocks may be exposed bedrock, in which case they may be modeled, by mesh or TIN, along with the surrounding terrain, and differentiated only by surface texture and color. In other cases, apparent rock objects may be modeled as lumps in the terrain, perhaps constructed by boolean union operations, rather than as separate solid objects.

When solid objects are called for, the techniques for generating them may be several. You can start with a solid primitive, such as sphere or rectangle, then deform and extend it through a series of operations, either by *tweaking* (moving slightly) vertices of the object, or boolean operations, depending upon the software and the desired effect.

Rocks may also be generated algorithmically. A computer program for generating, and deforming the vertices of a multifaceted solid can be used. See the TIN-Solid generating program on the accompanying CD-ROM, for example.

Texture mapping of rock faces is an important part of the overall modeling and rendering process (see Section 2.4).

Figure 2.33
a. Individual rocks with photographic rock textures. Modeled after Peter Walker's Tanner Fountain at Harvard University in Cambridge, Massachusetts. Modeled in Rhino3D software; rendered in 3DStudioMax.
b. *Tanner Fountain, Harvard University.* Courtesy of Peter Walker and Partners.

2.4 Operations on Terrain: Space Forming, Design Approaches

In the creation of space, architectural or landscape, landform may play several roles, ranging from subtle, supporting base to central, sculptural object. Landscape architects and earthworks artists have explored the use of earth as a sculptural material; these earthworks sculptures tend to be large in scale and undulating in form. Crisper, more vertical surfaces are possible at smaller scales by the addition of architectural reinforcing elements such as retaining walls. Compositional techniques such as repetition, variation, rhythm, juxtaposition, and layering can all be used with earth forms, and terrain objects including stones and boulders, just as painting or architecture manipulate other materials.

At the other extreme, landform masses can be used to form spaces, just as walls and floors do in architectural spaces. The various technical and artistic moves that can be used to form space with landform include berms, terraces, cuts, steps, and ramps. Studying the work of landscape architects is a good way to become familiar with some of these space forming uses of landform.

Figure 2.34
Harima Science Garden City Hyogo Prefecture, Japan, Peter Walker and Partners.
Courtesy of Peter Walker and Partners.

2.5 Textures on Landform

For visualization purposes, after the underlying surface, or solid form, has been given dimension and shape, the surface texture must be applied. The variations that can be achieved with rendering effects only – color, textures, and lighting, and smoothing – are many, even on the same base form. The choice of color and lighting effects may be governed by the desired mood or atmosphere of the model or image being generated (See Chapter 5: Atmosphere for more discussion and examples,) or the colors may be governed by desire for some level of realism. Landform, or the groundplane, can be considered in two large categories: natural surfaces and built surfaces. Landform in nature tends to be either an exposed mineral substrate (rock, sand, gravel, clay, dirt), or to be textured by a vegetative cover (grass, lichen, moss, flowers, shrubs, trees, forest, forest, leaf litter, e.g.), and so colored in the earth tones (grays, tans, browns, or greens and olives). Built surfaces, including paving of all kinds, tend to be more flat, level, and regular, and in a different range of colors (white concrete, black asphalt, red brick, terra-cotta tiles, etc.).

2.5.1 Simple Color

The simplest texture that can be applied is just a solid color, and for some purposes this may be sufficient. For more realistic portrayals, earth-tone colors such as browns, tans, and greens are, of course, the best choice. In most cases a very bright color is inappropriate, but pastel shades and muted values are best. In more fantastic or other less-natural environments, any color at all may appear on the ground form.

Figure 2.35
This series of illustrations represents the types of materials that can be applied to a topographic surface.
a. Simple color.
b. Simple diffuse map.
c. Procedural grass texture. The procedural grass texture was produced with the "Shag:Fur" plug-in by Digimation for use with 3D Studio Max.

2.5.2 Multichannel Textures, Including Photographic Based Textures

For realism, and other effects, more complex textures than simple color are required. Bump maps of various sorts are especially useful in terrain modeling, as the surface often has a grainy, or bumpy quality. Mineral, or geologic surfaces, can be best approximated by a combination of color and surface texture which consists mostly of particles (sand, granite) or facets (of smoother stones, e.g.) In these conditions, irregular tiling is important; no apparent repeating geometric pattern should be visible, for most realistic effects. Many of these surfaces also have a slightly reflective, or sparkling quality, due to mineral components (mica, silicates). Sometimes these highlights are dampened or obliterated by a fine layer of dust giving everything a matte finish. Other rocklike nonvegetative coverings in the landscape include snow and ice, which are most easily modeled simply as color and texture over terrain.

Vegetative coverings, created by plants of all sizes, are more complex – and more common – surfaces, characterized by depth and increased form in the texture. Leaves of grass, or of other small plants, give a specific defining texture to an overall covering. This is best approximated, when needed, by procedural approaches or by embedded image-maps in the texture. See Chapter 3 for a more detailed discussion and more examples of plant textures. Again, in these natural coverings, tilings must be irregular for maximum realism, no recurring geometric tiling pattern should be visible. Simple plant forms, such as algae and moss, can be approximated with a combination of color and bump maps, and masks outlining the patches characteristic of their growth.

Built surfaces, including bricks and tiles, are perhaps the easiest ground plane textures to apply in a realistic way. These can afford to be – in fact should usually be – regular in their tiling, with repeating geometric patterns visible. This pattern often helps to give a sense of depth as the pattern recedes into the background. Bricks and tiles can be applied in a variety of repeating patterns, from the simplest staggered courses of ordinary paving to the most elaborate of arabesque tile designs. For realism, sometimes the crisp geometry and sharp edges of these forms should be softened or broken up in a random way, to increase the appearance of age or natural blemishes and variations. This is hard to accomplish with a simple repeating texture map, except by overlaying layers of

Figure 2.36
Row 1:
a. Example of brick texture.
b. Example of a ceramic tile texture.
c. Example of a grass texture.

Row 2:
Image maps used to define the "diffuse color" channel:
a. Brick image.
b. Tile image.
c. Grass image.

Row 3:
Image maps used to define the "bump map" channel:
a. Brick bump map.
b. Tile bump map.
c. Grass bump map.

other image maps to add noise, and is better managed by a procedural texture generator which can produce minor variations automatically. Irregularly tiled surfaces such as asphalt and concrete are best textured just like other rock surfaces, with a combination of color, speckle, and bump maps.

2.5.3 Draped 2D Image Maps

If an ortho-rectified image is not available, some computer processing is required, usually called *rectification*, or *rubber-sheeting*, since the desired effect is to distort the image as if it were a rubber sheet, to fit to known positions, or coordinates. Some GIS and other image processing or remote sensing software offer this operation. In addition, the image needs to be registered, by determining the coordinates of the corners of the image.

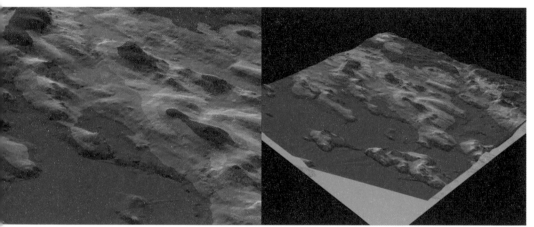

Figure 2.37
a. Detail or draped map.
b. A colored elevation map draped over terrain.

When the image map has been rectified and registered, it can be "draped" over the terrain. Different software systems provide different mechanisms and controls, but the resulting effect is as if each individual pixel, polygon, surface patch, or triangle in the terrain model is textured with the appropriate color and texture.

Sometimes, a complete photographic (or other) image can be mapped, or draped, over the terrain surface. Examples include using a scanned topographic map, or architectural plan, as the image surface. This tends to give a less realistic, but often useful, effect. In such cases, it is most useful if the rectangular image has a proportion identical to the rectangular bounding box of the terrain surface model, since no distortion from scaling in the u/x or v/y axes will be introduced. In the case of grid raster surfaces, ideally one pixel of the mapped image will correspond to one grid cell of the surface mesh. (Some systems may even require this condition). In geo-referenced systems, a GEO-TIFF image may carry the necessary geographic referencing information to be correctly placed on the terrain, and so a set of images, overlapping or fitting together into a mosaic, can be used.

Background landform, such as mountains in the distance, can be modeled by pasting an image map on a flat plane, or surrounding six-side planes, or a cylinder or even half-globe, at the extreme periphery of the model. As with all "image only" backgrounds, such a landform cannot be walked over or through, but simplifies the model for distant features. See Chapter 5: Atmosphere, for more on backgrounds.

Figure 2.38
A synthesized view using GIS data as input, of an aerial view of Minute Man National Park, in Concord, Massachusetts. Courtesy of Carl Steinitz, Harvard Design School. Rendered in ERDAS.

2.5.4 Geospecific Textures

When geo-referenced, scale-corrected imagery is available, you can use it as a surface texture over a digital elevation model to produce a landscape rendering with apparent features in the correct location on the terrain. This kind of image is sometimes called *geospecific texture*. Geospecific images are usually from either aerial photography (at scales from 1:500 down to 1:25000), or from satellite imagery (at resolutions from 30m/pixel down to 10 or even 1m/pixel). The geo-referencing information will either be included in the file format (as with a Geo-TIFF file), or in an associated header file. The USGS makes available *digital ortho-photos* and *digital ortho-quads* (*DOQs*) at the standard scale of 1:25000, to match the printed topographic quad sheets. Finer resolution (larger scale) images are increasingly available from governmental and private sources. Often 5m and 1m resolution ortho-photos are available.

In order for a photograph to be accurately draped over a digital terrain model, the coordinates of the corners of the photograph must be known, and the photograph must have been previously corrected for any distortions such as introduced by lens, camera tilt, etc. This process is called *ortho-rectification*, and the result is an *ortho-rectified* image.

Figure 2.39
*a. Detail of Mt. St. Helens represented with a draped grid surface.
b. Mt. St. Helens surface model with a draped ortho-rectified image.*
Courtesy of 3DNature.

Figure 2.40
*a. Detail of an ortho-rectified image.
b. Images of geo-specific texture.*
Courtesy of Remote Sensing Laboratories, Dept. of Geography, University of Zurich. Satellite image © ESA/Eurimage, CNES/SPOT.

Figure 2.41
*a. Detail of view.
b. View of Beckenried, Switzerland, using SPOT satellite image draped on terrain.*
Courtesy of Remote Sensing Laboratories, Dept. of Geography, University of Zurich Satellite image © ESA/Eurimage, CNES/SPOT.

2.5.5 Geotypical Textures

Geospecific texture mapping as described above only results in a 2D image on a smooth 3D terrain surface – no 3D vertical elements are introduced. This looks moderately convincing from birds-eye perspective views, looking down on the terrain, but the more oblique the view, the less acceptable this approach. When side-views, as of trees or buildings are required, another technique must be used. Some landscape visualization software offers the capability of using a rectified image or landcover map as a key to guide the placement of 2D images (texture maps) and 3D objects into the rendered scene, using values from the landcover map to select appropriate textures and objects. These texture images are sometimes called *Geotypical* textures, since they are not the exact trees or buildings, but representative ones, used in the right place. (You can, of course, use actual photographs of actual trees, and actual 3D models of actual buildings, for accurate depiction of existing landscapes.) A registered and rectified landcover map is required, as well as optional data sources such as additional point files, or polygon files, which specify the locations of individual 3D objects or 2D texture/images to be inserted. Sometimes a random placing method may be specified for objects within polygons, at a specified density, for the rapid generation of forests, or even housing subdivisions.

Figure 2.42
A landscape synthesized using "ecosystem" rules. Courtesy of Karin Egger, Vienna Technical University. Modeled and rendered in World Construction Set.

This technique can be used to model landscapes with natural ecological systems, by combining information from the DEM and the landcover map to procedurally generate appropriate textures or objects according to surface conditions, such as elevation, slope, aspect, concavity, etc. Thus, in a typical New England forest setting you could specify that vegetation on north-facing moderate slopes should be evergreens, and south-facing slopes should be mixed hardwoods; flat areas could take further information from the landcover map, and be rendered as agricultural fields, or grassy meadows, or forests, depending on the code for that area. For this technique, the program needs a library of suitable images, typically provided as JPEGs or TIFFs, which can be placed (appropriately scaled, possibly rotated) into the final image.

The landcover map can be either a raster grid data set, with integer values indicating various objects or textures to be placed, or points and polygons indicating specific locations, or areas, to be filled in.

DRAPING AN IMAGE MAP

Objectives:
To produce an aerial view of a landform, with colored or textured features "draped" over it.

Inputs:
Digital Elevation Model (TIN or Grid, in standard format).
Image (aerial photo, hand sketch, etc., as JPEG, TIFF, or other standard image format).
Coordinates of area of interest, usually a rectangle, in standard geo-referencing system (i.e., known units and projection system).

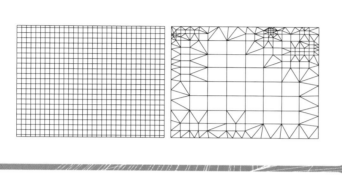

Step 1.
Determine area of interest, and choose software for the drape operation. Some software may require specific image formats, terrain data formats, or have other limitations or requirements. Determine these beforehand.

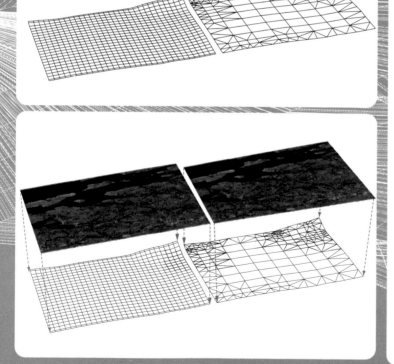

Step 2.
Assemble source material. Terrain and image data must overlap the area of interest.
a. Acquire or generate DEM in desired geo-referencing system, at desired resolution (grid cell size, for a mesh, or minimum triangle size for TIN). Remember that higher resolution will necessitate larger files, and take longer to render. If only contours are available, then some software must be used to create either a grid or a TIN from the contours.
b. Acquire or generate image, at desired resolution. The image can match the resolution of the terrain; if a grid is used, then one pixel will be on one grid cell. Image and terrain resolution need not match, but some interpolation and hence inaccuracy may result if they don't.

Note:

Image must be geo-referenced. If pre-referenced image is used (Digital Ortho-photo, for example) then just verify that image referencing system is same as terrain, or convert as necessary.

If an unreferenced image is used, then you must go through "rubber-sheeting," or registration and rectification process. Using some other source of known geo-referencing (the DEM, if feasible, or some other vector source) identify known points on the reference map with the same feature on the image. When 3 or more points are established, the image can be rectified, producing a new image in the process. This may often warp or distort the outline rectangular boundary, especially if there is a lot of terrain elevation difference.

Step 3.

Verify geo-referencing. Visual inspection should show similar features in similar places on both the terrain and the image (if they are visible, hydrological features such as rivers or lakes provide good references, as they should be apparent in both image and landform). If there are obvious incongruencies, verify the registration and coordinate systems, including projection system and units, in steps 1 and 2.

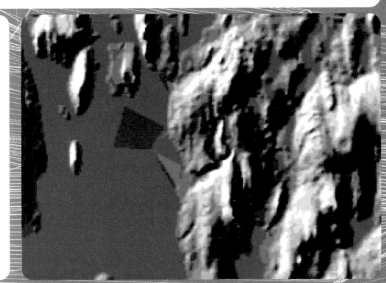

Step 4.

Invoke the DRAPE command in your visualization or rendering software. Usually this is as simple as specifying the source file for the terrain and for the image, and picking some eye position. (Sometimes a default eye location may be provided, typically above and to the northeast of the center of the terrain.) A raster image should be produced.

In some systems, draping is just a generic "assign texture to surface" operation. In this case, the image is specified as the diffuse color map for the surface, and adjustments such as tiling and

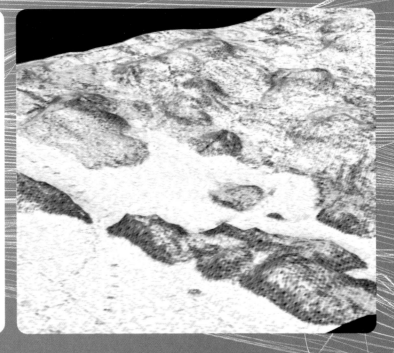

rotation are made as for any texture.

Usually, the proportions of the image should be the same as the bounding rectangle of the terrain; otherwise, some distortion will appear as the image is stretched or squeezed to fit. Additional texture maps, such as shininess, or opacity, or others, may also be added for special effects.

Step 5.

Adjust eye position (azimuth and altitude) for best visual effect, highlighting desired features, and providing sufficient detail in area of interest.

Step 6.

Adjust terrain vertical exaggeration, if desired. Usually, terrain should not be exaggerated if '"realistic" visualization is required, but if an explanatory, schematic, or other "interpretive" rendering is being produced, increased vertical exaggeration may help emphasize landform relationships, especially in very flat or gentle terrain. You may also realize a need to adjust terrain resolution in this process; if the grid is too coarse, exaggeration may produce undesirable artifacts.

Step 7.

Adjust lighting parameters, if possible (locate direct lights or spotlights, for example, to simulate solar lighting conditions.) Simple draped images will not provide realistic microscale shadows from elements such as buildings, trees or forests, but macroscale shadows and illumination on the terrain – showing light and dark sides of a valley for example, or casting shadows from terrain onto itself in steep or hilly areas – is possible.

Step 8.

Adjust color and texture parameters, if possible. Often colors from the original image will be distorted in the projection and illumination process. You can go back to the original image and make color/hue/value adjustments to improve the final result. If the original image is '"false color" such as a landuse map, then you may be free to adjust the colors in any way to create a desired final effect. Also set the background color for the final image (sky-blue, or neutral gray, black or white, etc., depending on the final use.)

Step 9.

Adjust the aspect ratio of the final rendering, accounting for final desired use, and the contents of the image. Choose landscape or portrait format, dimensions, and total number of pixels desired.

Step 10.

Save eye position and other parameters for future reference; save image in desired format (usually JPEG or TIFF) at desired resolution.

2.6 Terrain Visualization

2.6.1 Tiling of Texture Maps

A common problem with visualizations of terrain is the artifacts that appear in textures applied to the ground surface. There are two most common ones: the appearance of a repetitive pattern in the surface, resulting from the regular tiling of a texture map, and the problem of textures which may look great in the midground, but when close-up, in the foreground, tend to be exaggerated, out-of-scale and blurry.

Figure 2.43
a. Tiling of small texture map causes visually disturbing repetitive pattern in surface.
b. Larger map with fewer repetitions appears distorted and blurry in foreground.

The tiling problem arises when a too-small texture has been mapped onto larger polygons, and so has been repeated, or tiled.

The blurring problem arises mostly because the terrain polygons (triangles, or mesh faces) are largest in the foreground, and the texture has been sampled at a mid-ground resolution. There are really only two good solutions to this problem at present: recursive subdivision of the terrain polygons, or procedural terrain texture.

By further subdividing the terrain in the foreground, textures that look good in the midground can be made to look acceptable in the foreground. Adjusting the scaling factors and the alignment of the *u/v* coordinates is necessary to overcome these problems.

Of course, both problems are more easily overcome in a single static image. In an animation, you cannot so easily control what is in the foreground at each frame. In this case, some procedural texturing approach is really the only effective solution.

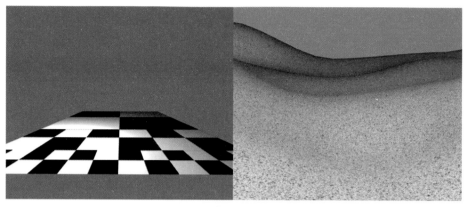

Figure 2.44
a. Diagram showing recursive subdivision yielding smaller rectangles in foreground.
b. Surface texture generated procedurally (note the absence of tiling artifacts).

Tiling of the terrain objects themselves may be required. As terrain models can become very large, it is often useful to subdivide the project into several smaller tiles, whether surfaces, or solids, that fit together for rendering purposes. In this case, it's important to take extra steps to guarantee that the terrain objects will edge-match correctly. Often, small inconsistencies can arise at the edges of these terrain objects, leading to distracting gaps, voids, or overlaps when they are butted up together.

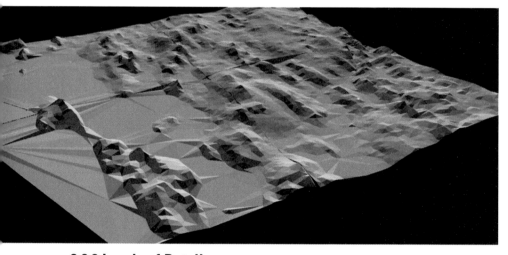

Figure 2.45
TIN representation made of four separately created TINS, joined together. Note the gaps along the edges where the four tiles meet. Modeled and rendered in ArcInfo and ArcView.

2.6.2 Levels of Detail

In many modeling challenges, the extent of the scene calls for different conditions in foreground (close-ups), midground, and background (distance). It can be computationally expensive and inefficient to model all terrain at a similar level of resolution when the area is large. In visualizations where foreground and background area are known in advance, it is possible to use coarser information in the background, and finer in the foreground. For example, a very coarse grid mesh or TIN may be used to establish the base landscape for a large area, a finer TIN for midground areas, and carefully formed NURB surfaces in the very foreground, for maximum control of realism while keeping the overall polygon count (and thus rendering time) down to a manageable size. Often this is the case when specific site or project area is embedded in its larger context, and concentric rings of foreground, midground and background can be established in advance. When the furthest background is mountainous, or at least above eye level, then an additional panoramic photograph can be used to extend the terrain into the distance.

Managing the *Levels of Detail* , or *LOD*, required for objects including ter-

Figure 2.46
TIN of the same terrain, created at three different resolutions:
a: 600 faces,
b:10,000 faces, and
c: 80,000 faces.
Modeled and rendered in ArcInfo and ArcView.

rain at varying distances is one of the greatest challenges for landscape modelers. In all but the simplest, static views, trade-offs and optimizations must almost always be made to achieve desired results with finite resources (mostly computer memory and processing time). Strategically reducing polygon count is the first step, and using carefully chosen textures and image maps is the next. In rendering, especially for animations and most especially for anything resembling real-time, additional steps include precomputing visibilities and surface normals, for example. These steps are usually embedded within the rendering software, and may be beyond user control except for possibly setting some choices about preferred approaches or desired quality of results.

Understanding LOD requirements has much to do with perception, and the desired levels of abstaction in the representation being made. If the background really is just background, filling up the void, or only providing conventional context, you might consider omitting it entirely! If the background contains important information, you might examine that information carefully: is it about color, texture, or placement of landmarks? Identifying the important requirements for the background, and for all the elements of a model, may help to determine best strategies for LOD trade-offs. If you really determine that you care about and need detail everywhere, then you must be prepared for the consequences: usually huge memory requirements and long rendering times, making real-time navigation impractical. Some dynamic LOD management techniques have been developed for animation purposes, which usually involve careful segmentation of data between active memory (RAM) and disk, with only visible elements being loaded in RAM, which helps to speed rendering times; and other elements offloaded to disk storage until they are needed, at which time they are reloaded into memory. Such techniques are fairly exotic, and these and other alternative techniques will surely be further developed over time.

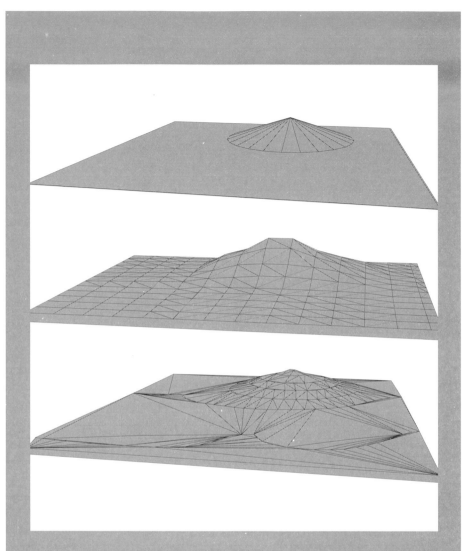

Figure 2.47
Representation of landform at three different levels of detail in VRML.
a. As a flat plane and a cone (simplest).
b. As a grid mesh.
c. As a TIN model (most complex).

TECHNICAL NOTE:

The VRML2 language standard, and the newer "Active Worlds" and X3D specifications, provide an additional mechanism for LOD handling: Every object in a scene may be explicitly given multiple representations for rendering purposes, to be used at varying distances from the viewer. So, for example, a landform might be rendered as a single solid colored flat plane or cone in the far distance, a coarse grid with a texture map in the midground, and as a more detailed TIN model in the foreground. Careful design of these multiple representations can achieve real efficiencies in rendering animations.

2.63 Lights and Shadows on Landform

An important consideration in creating visualizations of terrain models is the establishment of lighting conditions. Since natural terrain often tends to be subtle in its variations, oblique lighting conditions, such as early morning or late afternoon sun's rays, are especially helpful in making vivid landforms. Choosing an illumination model, including both ambient and direct lights, is critical. (See Chapter 5, Atmosphere, for more on lighting techniques.) Also, making sure that shadows are cast, either by the landform itself, or perhaps by objects such as trees, etc., onto the landform, is extremely helpful in making landform visible. Since shadows on the ground are usually viewed obliquely, they need not be perfectly accurate; simple smudges and blurs of dark and light, correctly located with respect to shadow casting objects will suffice. Creating a *shadow map* as an image – in which black or gray shadows are painted on a ground surface – and applying this image to the texture of the landform is one way of achieving this.

More accurate, of course, is to use shadow casting features in the rendering system, whether ray-tracing or others, to create real shadows on the terrain.

In some cases, you will be required to match realistic lighting conditions with accurate sun angle and position, or artificial lighting; in other cases you may be free to place and modify the lights until a desired effect is achieved. Similarly, the color of the lights may have an impact, especially when interacting with the colors and textures of the landform.

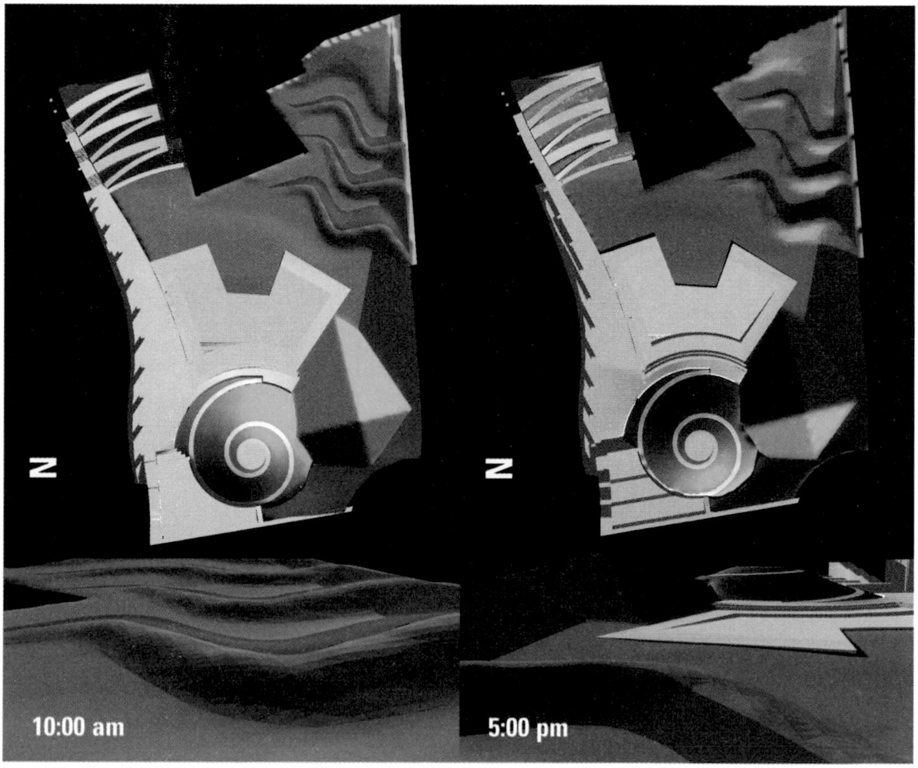

Figure 2.48
The geometric base model of the University Commons project rendered at two different times of day. Notice how the shadows allow for the landforms to read in both plan or perspective view. The sun system allows for the simulation of natural lighting conditions determined by the latitude, longitude, and time of day. The lighting for the model was generated by the 3DStudioMax "Sun System."

10:00 am

5:00 pm

2.7 Calculations on Terrain: Analytic Models

In addition to rendering for visualization, or as an adjunct to the process, analysis of landform is enabled by many of the same data models presented so far. Typically embedded in Geographic Information Systems (GIS) software, some of these operations may be found in CAD or other engineering, modeling, or analysis software.

2.7.1 Cut and Fill Volume Calculations

One common calculation required from digital terrain models, is some indication of volume of earth. Especially when two models are given, one from an existing condition and one for a proposed new terrain model, the calculation of *cut* (earth removed from the original) and *fill* (earth added to the original) is critical. In many cases, one goal is to achieve a balance, or net change of zero, so that soil cut from one place is filled in another on the same site. In addition to simple *cut-and-fill*, a more sophisticated analysis might indicate *mass-haul* requirements, showing what volume of soil is required to be moved over what distance (either within the site or to/from off-site.)

The grid model offers a very simple way of calculation cut and fill: simply subtract all the values for each cell in the existing model from the proposed model. A positive value indicates depth of fill; a negative value depth of cut. Multiply each cell's cut or fill by the area of a grid cell (*x*-resolution multiplied by *y*-resolution) to generate volume (making sure that units, such as feet or meters, match). Other representations can be used also; if boolean operations are available, creating the boolean difference between the two solid models can be used to compute the volume of the change.

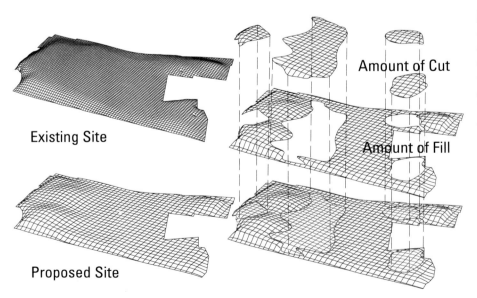

Existing Site

Amount of Cut

Amount of Fill

Proposed Site

Figure 2.49
Grid mesh surface representations illustrating the existing and proposed site conditions, and the resulting volumes from the cut-and-fill operation.

2.7.2 GIS-Based Elevation, Slope, and Aspect Analysis

From a digital elevation model, or *height field*, two important and useful additional surfaces of information can be derived. The first is a *slope* analysis, which computes the steepness of the surface, in percent or in degrees; the second is an *aspect*, or *orientation* map, which computes which direction (north, east, southwest, etc.) the surface is facing. These two characteristics are especially valuable in design for functional purposes. (For example, a northwest facing steep slope is a bad place for a driveway in northern climates, as it may tend to be covered in ice in the winter. Fruit orchards are most desirably located on gently sloping southwest slopes, which encourage cold air drainage. Landscape architects use many slope criteria for different uses: a 2.5% slope is considered maximum for most playfields; 8% for access ramps to be used by wheelchairs, and so on.)

Landscape ecological processes may also be influenced by elevation, slope, and aspect. (In temperate climates, oaks and other hardwoods are most likely found on south facing slopes; hemlocks on north facing, or wet slopes.) Using the slope and aspect maps for information about the likely vegetative covering, or other land use, can be a valuable part of terrain modeling.

Figure 2.50
Slope map and aspect map created from a terrain model.
a. Slope in ten classes; darker reds are steeper slopes.
b. Aspect in 9 classes (8 compass directions, from N to NW, and None); orange colors face south, blues face north. Modeled and rendered in ArcInfo and Arcview.

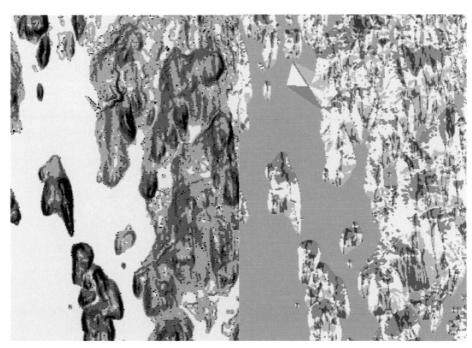

These analytical and overlay techniques can be combined with boolean operations and other solid modeling. Generating a snow-covered mountaintop, for example, might be accomplished by starting with one surface model for the mountain form, generating another which is slightly raised from the first and colored snow-white, and then adding the one surface to the other. Variations in snow cover computed on the basis of the slope and aspect analysis – greater depth at higher elevations and on north slopes, less on south facing or steep slopes, for example – can add a sense of realism to the effect.

TECHNICAL NOTES:

The calculations of slope and aspect are typically made from a raster grid model, and although they yield a value at each grid cell, they must take into consideration the neighborhood of values around each cell. Slope, for example, is calculated by taking pairs of neighbors on either side of the cell in question, calculating the difference in elevation (*rise*) and the difference in horizontal difference (*run*); the slope is then the value of rise divided by run. For each cell, 4 different pairs of cells are used, and so 4 different slope values may be computed. Then it is a matter of choosing an appropriate mathematical function; the two most common are: the average of all the values, or the maximum. The maximum is the more intuitively correct approach.

Aspect is computed by a more complex trigonometric formula, which essentially seeks to find the perpendicular (or *surface normal*) vector at each grid cell, then take the (x,y) component and represent that as an azimuth value ranging from 0° (due north) through 359.99 (where 180° is due south, 270° is due west, and so on). Perfectly flat horizontal surfaces have no aspect, which is usually represented by a special value such as -1. (Or zero may be used for no aspect, and north represented by 360°.)

Note that for both slope and aspect, neighboring cell values are required, and so both calculations may be either undefined, or potentially erroneous, at the very edges of a grid or raster.

2.8 Dynamics – Procedural Models and Representations

For terrain modeling and visualization purposes, dynamics can be thought of in three important ways: generative (and transformative) processes that *create* terrain representations; movement *through* the landscape, over terrain; and movement *of* the terrain, as in earthquakes and erosion processes. In all cases, there are mathematical, or algorithmic, models behind the dynamics, often derived from some underlying physical or natural system. In the special case of *movement through*, characterized by animations, walk-throughs and flyovers, considerations of human experience and perception is also important.

2.8.1 Generation

In the case of terrain models of real, existing, or proposed terrain, specific measurements and recordings of geometry, represented as contours, grids, or TINs, is usually required. But for more mathematically defined landforms, or for imaginary landscapes, it may be possible to achieve significant savings in memory and disk space by using procedural methods to generate, rather than record, the landform geometry.

The simplest examples of procedurally generated landforms are regular geometric solids and other mathematically defined shapes, including curved surfaces, where a mathematical formula can describe the x,y,z relationships quite concisely. A sphere, for example, is defined by $x^2 + y^2 + z^2 = r^2$, or $z = sqrt (r^2 - x^2 - y^2)$. A hemispherical mound is then defined by the above formula, for all $z > 0$. Naturally, in order to render, these mathematical formulae have to be transformed into polygons or surfaces, but often this can be done inside of the rendering software. In this way, arbitrarily fine polygon size, or resolution, can be specified for rendering without having to generate or maintain a huge file of geometry. In many modeling /rendering packages, for example, geometric solid primitives based on the circle (cones, cylinders, spheres, e.g.) can be rendered and displayed with any specified number of facets around the circle, so the same cylindrical description can generate a three-sided or six-sided prism, as well as perfectly smooth-appearing cylindrical form.

These mathematical models which contain variables are sometimes referred to as *parametric models*, since the variable values serve as parameters which influence the final form. The total number of parameters determines the complexity of the resultant form. A sphere has only one parameter (r, or radius), while a cone may have three (height, bottom radius, top radius), and more complex forms may require even more parameters. Generating multiple forms from these parameters yields *parametric variations*, which may be the basis of a composition, or, when parameter values are varied over time, may form animations of changing form. A volcano, for example, may be defined as two cones, one inverted and subtracted from the other at the top, for the mouth, and a simplified cartoon of volcanic formation can be described by varying the parameters of these cones over time

Figure 2.51

A "volcanic" form created by boolean subtraction of one inverted cone from another, then roughened and twisted using modeling tools. Red-colored "lava" textured interior added for visual effect. Modeled and rendered in 3DStudioMax. (See "volcano.mov" on the CD-ROM)

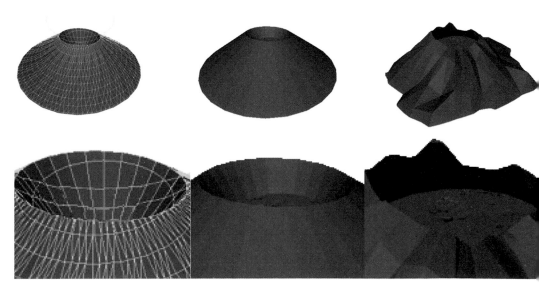

2.8.1.1 Fractal Terrain

Natural landforms are not geometrically regular, however, and some additional techniques must be used to introduce the irregularities which mark natural forms. Some interjection of randomness, or *noise*, is the first step, creating forms which are not perfectly smooth, but which nonetheless follow some basic formal structure.

In his famous analysis of the underlying similarities found in natural forms, varying across scales and sizes from coastlines to cloud forms to leaf-edges, the mathematician Benoit Mandelbrot found a way of describing the roughness of these forms, which he called the *fractal dimension*. The development of the study of fractals, and fractal geometry, has led to a range of techniques for mathematically describing, in relatively simple ways, complex and irregular forms, characteristic of those found in nature. One characteristic of the fractal geometries described by Mandelbrot is their *self-similarity* at varying scales. That is, the roughness found along a coast-line when seen from the air, is similar to that found in examining a stretch of coastline at your feet, or even a single cluster of

Figure 2.52
Synthetic terrain produced by "fractal terrain generation" software. Coloration is determined by elevation.

rocks or grains of sand. This self-similarity of structure can be achieved procedurally, by using a *recursive* algorithm, one which performs essentially the same operations over and over again repeatedly, on ever smaller elements – those produced by a previous operation.

A simple form of this is the *recursive subdivision*, in which a single form is subdivided into smaller, identical forms, and these further subdivided, and so on. If slight variations are introduced at each subdivision, a kind of irregular detail within a larger structured whole results. For example, a landform may be described a starting with a triangular pyramid, then recursively subdividing each triangular face into smaller triangles, until some specified smallest size is reached (or else the procedure would go on forever, in an endless loop!) If at each step of the subdivision, triangle vertices are slightly randomly displaced, the result is an irregular surface conforming to the basic outline of the original pyramid.

Variations on these techniques for creating fractal terrain have been used extensively in the creation of synthetic landforms. For example, Lucas Films' seminal *Pt. Reyes* illustration (right) features fractal mountains in both the foreground and background.

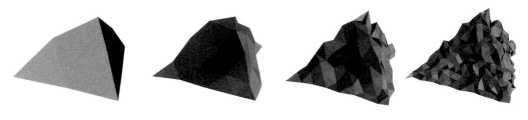

2.8.1.2 Terraforming

While the techniques of fractal terrain have elegance and efficiencies, they can not be used to produce precisely controlled surfaces. But the principle – of encoding rules for the generation of terrain, rather than the desired geometry – can be extended to achieve more controlled results. The basic idea behind such techniques is to specify a set of operations, such as cutting or filling terrain, with parametrically defined shape characteristics (such as angles of slope, depth of fill, etc.) usually to be performed along some path. This set of operations is then swept along the path, either over an existing base terrain, or on a blank surface, and the result is a terrain geometry which has the desired shape.

Simple swept or extruded forms, such as can be produced in most modeling software, are the simplest examples. An earthen mound, or *berm*, for example, can be produced by sweeping a cross-sectional line along a horizontal path, and a road with side shoulders can be produced in just the same way, using a more complex cross section. Some sweep operations allow the parameters of the defining curve to be varied over the length of the sweep, so the berm can be tapered from end to end, and so on.

Boolean operations, or simple intersections, can be successfully used to blend these forms onto existing terrain, when only "fill" operations are required. When "cut" is required, however, more complex operations are required, because the sweeping operation must vary its action according to the underlying terrain. Such *terraforming* operations are less common in modeling software, and are found mostly in special-purpose or custom-built software. The examples below show the results of a "digital bulldozer", in which a blade is swept along a 3D path, leaving a sculpted terrain behind. In this virtual terrain sculpting environment, a digital blade may either cut or fill, with no regard for real-world constraints of balanced volumes, angles of repose, or others.

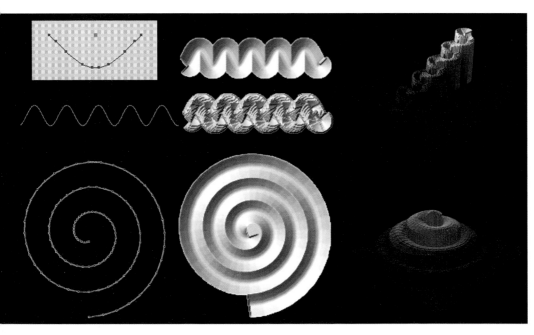

Figure 2.55
Procedural landform produced by sweeping a simple cross section ("U"-shape) along a specified path. Above, a sine-wave path; below, a spiral path ascending along Z-axis. Right, the inverse of these forms.
From Terrain Sculpting Software (TSS) Courtesy of Caroline Westort.

2.8.2 Movement *through* Terrain

Animated walk-throughs or flyover animations generated from three-dimensional models provide a time-based method for evaluating or communicating a design proposal's intent or anthropomorphic experience. Many times, digital models are made specifically for the purpose of creating an animated walk-through or flyover. Consideration of the final purpose(s) of the model (and animation) will help to make decisions such as level of detail, scale and resolution, color and texture of the terrain model.

An animation of a raft trip through the Grand Canyon, a car ride across the Great Plains, a leisurely walk down the steps at Naumkeag or through the schematic model of University Commons, will each require attention to different details in the terrain model and in the final animated path.

For most animation purposes, setting an appropriate speed, and path, are the most critical decisions. The frictionless, constant speed of a helicopter flyover is appropriate for regionally scaled visualizations, but tends to give a disassociated, floating feeling. The anthropomorphic alternative of generating a walk-through at eye level requires close attention to topographic change and its impact on speed. Walking speed is about one tenth to one twentieth of driving speed. Terrain features, such as rough surface and steep slopes, tend to further slow down walking speed. Animations that vary the speed according to the terrain are much more convincing than those that do not.

Furthermore, animations over terrain usually should not be smooth in their path. Changes of surface material, thresholds, and especially steps and ramps cause distinct variations in speed and viewpoint for the normal traveler. One of the biggest challenges to animation is to accurately capture the motion of ascending or descending steps, rather than making the path appear to be on an escalator.

Path creation for both the camera and the camera's target is facilitated by generating a spline curve by snapping directly to the surface or surfaces that comprise the topographic model. Some modeling applications provide tools that allow for sketching on surface entities. In both situations, the spline curve can be refined and then moved to the appropriate eye level if it is to be used to control the movement of the camera or target.

In the VRML language specification, and some modeling systems, it is possible to set the viewer's path to follow terrain, so that the eye level of the camera is held at a constant eye height (1.7 m) above the terrain surface. Also, collision detection can be used to prevent the viewer from walking through solid objects such as the terrain.

Figure 2.56
Plan showing camera and target paths for the animated walk-through of the University Commons Project. Paths were generated by drawing a spline curve over the terrain. Splines were then simplified for smooth movement.

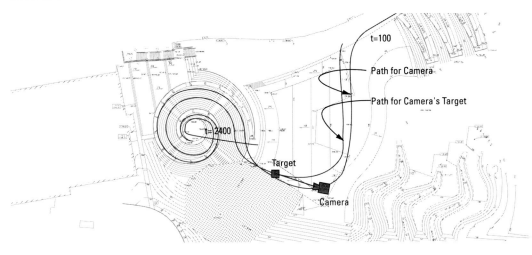

Figure 2.57 *Walkthrough of University Commons Schematic Model*

Over a sequence of 2400 frames, in a simulated walk-through, the camera traverses the turf plain of University Commons, and then proceeds up the path to the top of the cone. (See "uc-walk.mov" on the CD-ROM.)

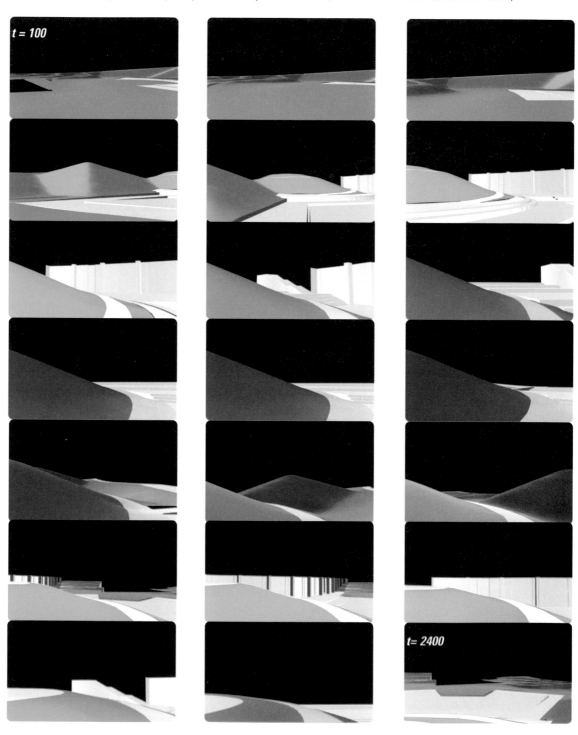

2.8.3 Movement *of* Terrain

Movement through terrain depends on moving camera positions and viewpoints, through a fixed terrain model, but movement *of* terrain calls for a dynamic terrain model itself. Such a condition might be caused by attempting to model natural phenomena such as an earthquake, dune movement, or soil erosion, or might just be a desired effect in some model or animation. The algorithmic and procedural approaches described above are typically the most effective ways to achieve these effects, by creating procedures in which time *(t)* is a parameter. This may be explicit, or implicit as in the intervals implied by the steps between sequential applications of a recursive procedure or a GIS model.

Many 3D modeling and rendering systems have a facility for *morphing* between two forms, a beginning state and a final state. Sometimes, there may be strict conditions on these forms. A common requirement is that both beginning and ending forms have the same number of vertices (since the transformation is then relatively straightforward, involving just a linear interpolation of in-between positions for each vertex point. For this reason morphing is also sometimes called "tweening"). In this way it is possible to create dramatic changes – or apparent motion, in animation – of terrain forms.

Figure 2.58
In this example and the associated animation sequence the pyramid landform erodes over time. Two geometric models were generated from two hypothetical grading conditions. The animation that corresponds to the still frames is on the CD-ROM (see "terrain-morph.mov"). Modeled and rendered in 3DStudioMax 3.1.

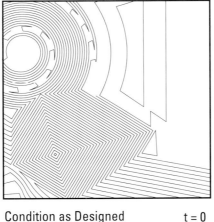

Condition as Designed   t = 0

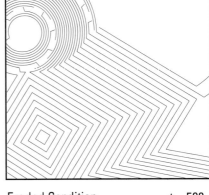

Eroded Condition   t = 500

In addition, some modeling systems have procedural transformations that can be applied to terrain surfaces, especially grids. These may include the introduction of random noise, or displacement, of a specified intensity, or more controlled geometric transformations such as ripples and waves. These can be applied just one time, to create static landforms, or may be animated. Sometimes the parameters of the transformation, such as intensity, or diameter, etc., can be tied to the time parameter, so that they may vary over time, and an animation can be produced by applying the transformation, with time-varying parameters, one frame at a time.

Figure 2.59 *Morphing Terrain – The Eroding Pyramid*

Over a sequence of 500 frames the pyramid landform erodes from a 2.5:1 slope to a 4:1 slope. See "terrain-morph.mov" on the CD-ROM.

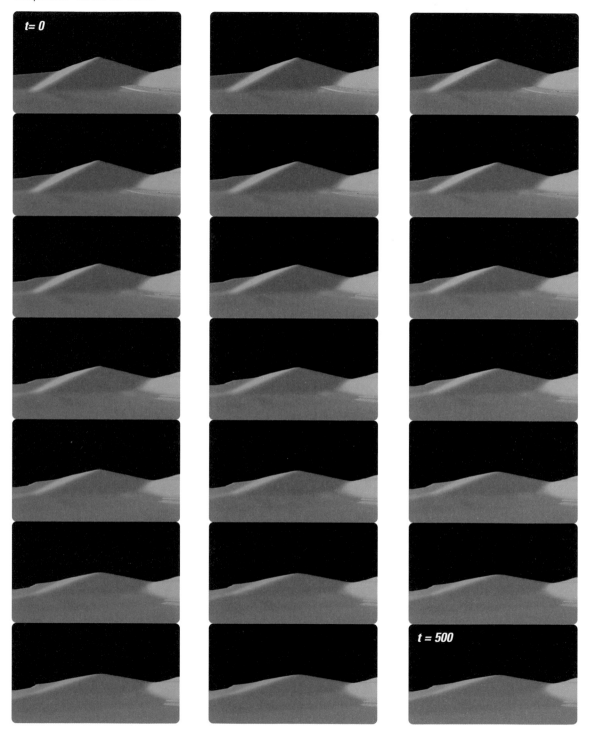

MORPHING TERRAIN

Objectives: To produce an animated "morph" between two terrain objects, simulating motion such as erosion or other geological dynamics.

Inputs: Two mesh representations, of the beginning and end state, with identical number of vertices in each mesh and similar topological directions.

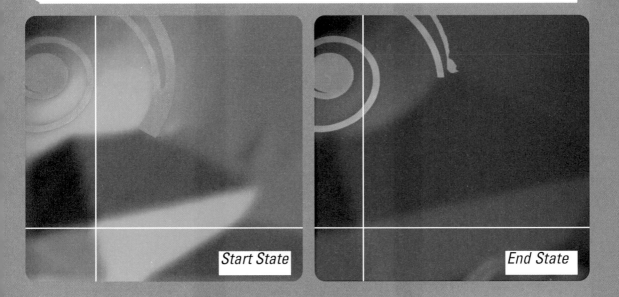

Start State

End State

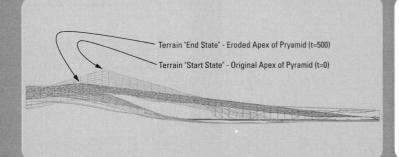

Terrain "End State" - Eroded Apex of Pryamid (t=500)

Terrain "Start State" - Original Apex of Pyramid (t=0)

Process:
1. Generate terrain models that represent the "Start-state" and the "End-state" for the morph.
2 Set the desired duration of the animation. (time=500 frames.)
3. Make sure both terrain states are visible at the start (t=0).

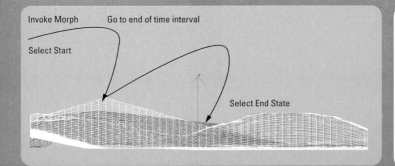

Invoke Morph
Go to end of time interval
Select Start
Select End State

4. Go to the end frame (t=500).
5. Activate the animation mode.
6. Select the "Start-state" terrain object.
7. Invoke the morph (or "tweening" operation).
8. Select the "End-state" terrain object.
9. End animation mode. Save.

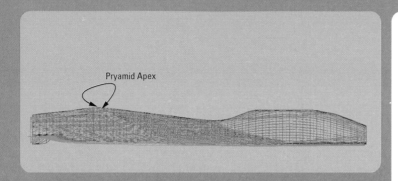

Pryamid Apex

10. Play back the animation. Now, at frame 500 the terrain model has morphed, so that the vertex points of the "Start-state" match those of the "End-state". The 3D modeler has interpolated a new mesh for each time step, moving each mesh point linearly from its start position (t=0) to its end position (t=500).

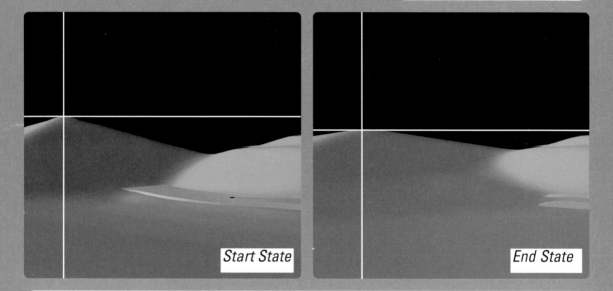

Start State

End State

Troubleshooting:
a) If you are unable to select the "End State" geometry, then your entities may not have the same number of vertices. If your modeler allows, delete excess vertices.
b) If the morph sequence results in an awkward folding and stretching on the way to achieving its "End State" it means that the topological directions of the models vary. If you modeler allows, reverse the topological direction of one of the terrain objects.

Figure 2.60
*a. Rippled land-
form produced by
using parametric
deformation of a
NURB surface,
specifying ampli-
tude and frequen-
cy of wave form.
b. More surface
variation created
by adding some
random "noise."*
Modeled and ren-
dered in
3DStudioMax.

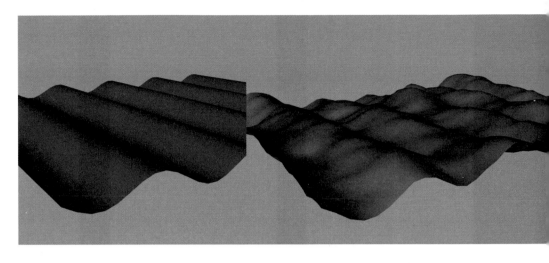

2.8.4 GIS-Based Erosion and Other Dynamic Models

The raster grid system of GIS terrain representation can be used to create time-varying models as well. Writing rules, or procedures, that transform each cell value a step at a time, as a function of similarly located cells in other layers, or neighboring cells in the same layer, can be used as a way to create dynamic models.

For example, a simple grid-based soil erosion model might work like this:

Given a raster terrain model, and a grid layer representing a stream;
Calculate for each cell on the stream its distance from the headwaters;
    (This is the stream reach; assume there will be more water, force,
    and erosion at higher reaches.)
Calculate the slope of the terrain model; assume there will be more erosion
    at steeper slopes.
Now, for each cell on the terrain model that is under the stream, first reduce
    its elevation by an amount proportional to reach + slope.
Then apply a neighborhood averaging formula to cells in the region of
    each stream cell, the radius of the neighborhood increasing
    proportionately to the reach.

Repeated over several steps, this will gradually lower the elevation under the stream, and draw down the neighboring cells as well. Adding some random noise function at each step to prevent the smoothing function from eliminating micro-features might help. This is of course not a real physics-based dynamic model, but serves to illustrate the mechanism. A more geophysically correct model might well be developed from this framework, adding in consideration of soil type and erodability, stream channel mechanics, and other constraints.

See the accompanying CD-ROM for more examples of dynamic landscape models.

The fifteen images on the facing page are a representative sampling of the many forms that representations of terrain data can take. The choice among internal data formats (contours, grids, TINS, etc.) is usually dictated by available data sources and software tools. The many choices about graphical representation — color vs. black-and-white, plan or aerial oblique, using photographic images or not, and others — are made as part of an overall plan for representational purpose and format. Combining the powers and techniques of CAD, GIS, remote sensing, and image processing software is especially valuable in this regard, and evolving tools for making their integration easier will doubtless become essential tools for landscape modeling and visualization.

Figure 2.61 Terrain representations. Modeled and rendered using ArcInfo, ArcView, 3DStudioMax, and Photoshop software.

a. 3D perspective view of TIN model.

b. 3D perspective view of faceted grid model.

c. 3D perspective view of smooth NURB surface model.

d. Aerial view of black-and-white digital ortho-quad photograph draped over TIN model.

e. Aerial view of colored GIS land-use map draped over TIN model.

f. Aerial view of scanned USGS topo map draped over TIN model.

g. Plan view of contours represented as polylines.

h. Plan view of grid mesh derived from contour lines; grid mesh size = 100 meters.

i. Plan view of TIN model derived from contours.

j. Plan view of scanned USGS topo map with contours highlighted in brown.

k. Plan view of grid model, hill-shaded (with light from north-west) to accentuate relief, in grayscale.

l. Plan view of analytical slope map (darker red = steeper slope) derived from grid model, superimposed over hillshaded terrain.

m. Plan view of GIS derived land-use / landcover map. Colors are synthetic, applied to pixels based on classification of satellite imagery, aerial photography, and GIS data layers.

n. Grayscale digital ortho-photo-graph from USGS, ortho-rectified to the same scale as USGS topo map and GIS data layers.

o. Hybrid combination (created with image processing) of col-ored GIS landuse/landcover map with grayscale digital ortho-pho-tograph, conveys color classifica-tion information from GIS, while retaining apparent detail of the grayscale photograph.

2.9 Summary

Digital models of landscape almost always start with – and sometimes end with – a digital terrain model. Whether the landform is conceived of as regional context, site-scale field, or sculptural object, will help to determine an appropriate modeling and rendering approach. In many cases, data sources for terrain can be found from public sources or design professionals; some transformation from one format to another is almost always required. Digital terrain models can become cumbersomely large files, so some simplifications, compromises and abstractions are often necessary. Making the physical form, whether 2D surface or 3D solid, is just half of the necessary effort; the other half is choosing and applying a texture and lighting to create the desired image or effect. For the purposes of animations, either *over*, or *of*, terrain, the characteristics of the terrain should help inform the animation path and other parameters. Procedural methods for generating, transforming, or animating terrain can be especially useful in cases where specific real landforms are not required.

Chapter Matrix Picture Credits [Page 38]

1. Harima Science Garden City, Hyogo Prefecture, Japan, Peter Walker and Partners. [Courtesy of Peter Walker and Partners.]

2. Hillock Mounds, Byxbee Park, Palo Alto, California,1988-1992, Hargreaves Associates. [Courtesy of Hargreaves Associates.]

3. Model: Memorial to the Belgians who died on 18 June 1815, Yves Brunier.

4. Screen Capture of University Commons, University of Cincinnatti, Hargreaves Associates, 1999. [Hope H. Hasbrouck]

5. Plaza De La Constitucion En Girona, Girona, Spain. 1983/1993. [Elias Torres & Martinez La Pena.]

6. Les Pyramids et Les Arbres, Pages Paysage.

7. Harima Science Garden City, Hyogo Prefecture, Japan, Peter Walker and Partners. [Courtesy of Peter Walker and Partners.]

8. Shell Petroleum. Rueil-Malmaison, France Kathryn Gustafson [Courtesy Kathryn Gustafson.]

9. Aerial View Minute Man National Park,1984. Generated for Graduate School of Design, Harvard Unveristy by ERDAS, Inc. [Courtesy of Carl Steintz.]

10. Fractal Terrain. [Stephen M. Ervin]

11. Student Work – Graduate School of Design, Harvard University. [Courtesy of Kevin Fisher.]

References

Beardsley, John. *Earthworks and Beyond: Contemporary Art in the Landscape.* New York, NY: Abbeville Press, 1984.

Brunier, Yves. *Yves Brunier: Landscape Architect Paysagiste.* Basel, Switzerland: Birkhauser-Verlag fur Architektur, 1996.

Levy, Leah and Peter Walker. *Peter Walker: Minimalist Gardens.* Washington, DC:SpaceMaker Press, 1997.

Laurini, Robert and Derek Thompson. *Fundamental of Spatial Information Systems.* London, England: Academic Press, 1992.

Maguire, David, Michael Goodchild and David Rhind (Eds.). *Geographical Information Systems: Principles and Applications.* New York, NY: Wiley, 1991.

Mandelbrot, B.B. *The Fractal Geometry of Nature.* New York, NY: W. H. Freeman and Co., 1982.

Figure 2.62
Four views showing time-based simulation of idealized stream channel erosion, using GIS software and the algorithm described in the text on page 113. This sequence was modeled and rendered using ArcView and ArcInfo.

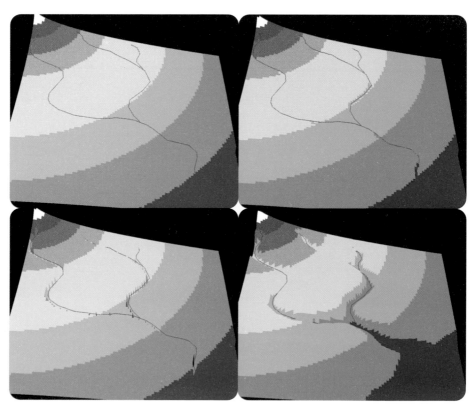

canopy

understory

groundcover

paraline

silhouette/surface

parametric sol

specimen

composition

forest

branching-2D
branching-3D

exotic

dynamic

Vegetation 3

3.1 Introduction

Trees, and assorted other vegetation including shrubs and groundcovers, are perhaps the most visible elements of the usual landscape. They surround us at eye level with their trunks; they embrace us overhead with their canopies, their textures are underfoot. Leaves frame our views, grasses carpet the foreground. Foliage provides texture and color in the landscape – infinite varieties of green and brown, then, in temperate climates vibrant yellows, oranges, and reds. Trees with their verticality and shadows accentuate the terrain they stand upon; groundcovers, like grass, provide the texture and grain of the landform. For landscape painters, trees are sculptural things, majestic, comforting, or twisted, almost mystical, in the foreground, blanketing, shaping, framing in the background. For landscape architects, trees and vegetation are both armature and covering, forming spaces, rooms, allees, focal points, and framed views, at the same time providing color, texture, and mass to compositions.

This chapter describes the basic forms that vegetation can take in the landscape: as discrete *objects* (plants), and as continuous *fields* (or forests); illustrates the most important forms of digital representation of vegetation: 2D symbols, 3D *surface models* including planes with texture-mapped images, and 3D *solid models*, and gives examples of construction of each; explores the space-forming and design uses of vegetation; and concludes with some information on procedural, or algorithmic vegetation models, and describes aspects of *dynamic*, or animated vegetation models. Further examples of the latter are given on the accom-

119

INTERNAL REPRESENTATION

canopy & understory

	2D representation		3D representation	
EXTERNAL REPRESENTATION	paraline drawings, symbols	procedural	surface/silhouette	parametric solid
wireframe		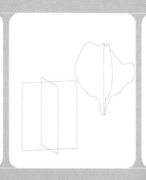		
simple color			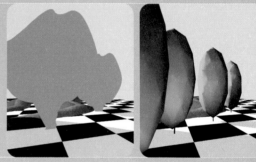	
texture maps				
diffuse map				
multichannel /procedural				

120

groundcover
2D representation
photobased

3D representation
tiling

hybrid | 3D procedural | | | procedural

121

panying CD-ROM.

For modelers, trees and vegetation present a variety of challenges. Fractally detailed, asymetrically branching and twisted, with corrugated bark and multi-veined leaves, there are far too many surfaces and details to imagine modeling even one with accuracy or completely. And plants are also often numerous, with hundreds or thousands of trees in a scene, or millions of blades of grass. They are porous, light permeating unevenly to their interiors, casting ragged shadows over undulating earth below. And they blow in the wind, change colors with the seasons, and grow, transform, even die, over time. How far from the truth a simple "lollipop" tree seems to be!

Figure 3.1
a. The precise geometry of the topiaries seen at the Chelsea Flower Show recalls the form of the lollipop tree, generated from solid geometric primitives. Chelsea Flower show 1999, Hope H. Hasbrouck.
b. The student exercise at the left clearly illustrates the use of solid geometric primitives to represent a structured and maintained planting of trees. Student Exercise 1999, Harvard University Graduate School of Design, Misty March.

And yet, as a first approximation, lollipops capture the essentials – a vertical column, a volumetric canopy – and are easy to create and clone in geometric modeling software: forming the trunk of a single line, a plain cylinder or a tall tapered cone, and the canopy a simple form such as cylinder, sphere, cone, or even tetrahedron. For illustrating and evaluating masses of plants, as in a grove, hedge, or allee, or for those occasional plants that actually are simple geometric solids (or candy-shapes: lollipops and gumdrops), simple forms are sufficient, and the addition of even a little bit of texture, color, transparency, and lighting provides for endless variation

3.2 2D Models of Vegetation

Two-dimensional digital vegetation models are comprised of either vector or pixel/photographic entities. The choice of data type is dependent on the intent of the model or representation. Vector entities are easily combined to form symbols which suggest location and size while the photograph is more suggestive of character, density, and habit. Choices are not limited to one or the other, both data types can often be integrated into the same model.

3.2.1 Photographs for Collage and Drawing

Photography is an effective medium for the capture and representation of vegetative complexity. Modern digital technology allows for slides or photographs to be scanned at very high resolution for incorporation into digital media. Digital cameras create digital images directly on disk, RAM-chip or CD-ROM which can be shared across software applications and platforms. In addition to collecting or generating your own images, there are numerous published collections of images and textures on CD-ROM, as well as sources on the web. Compiling photographs in digital landscape models is invaluable, for the photograph captures the intangible complexity, variation, and textures that are integral to the suggestion of landscape space and experience.

Despite the numerous benefits of integrating photographs into digital models, limitations exist. Images can be too realistic, or detailed, and they represent a specific time of day, so lighting and shadow conditions are fixed. An approach can be using the photograph or photographic entities as elements of a collage. The photographs are pasted on the pictorial plane or onto geometric entities in digital space. The photographs can be used in plan, section, and elevation and in projective or constructive views.

Figure 3.2
This image illustrates the combination of images with vector entities to produce an illustrative plan and section. Courtesy of Peter Walker and Partners.

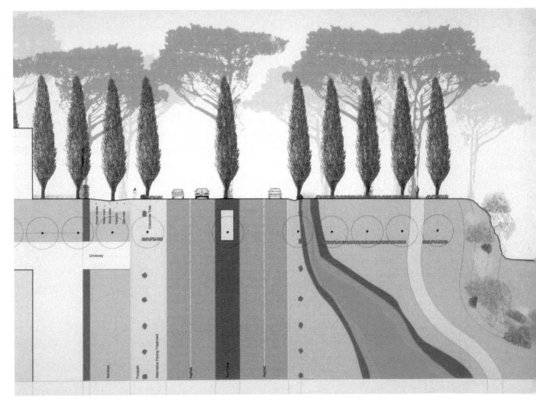

3.2.2 Paraline/Orthographic Drawings

When the two-dimensional image is too suggestive or detailed, design professionals rely on a vocabulary of simple shapes developed for representing trees in plan, section, or elevation. For plan representation the most obvious is a circle (representing the canopy) with a dot in the center (representing the trunk). This representation describes not only the exact location of the center of the trunk but the radius of the spread of the canopy. When several such tree symbols are overlapping, or many are, as in a grove or forest, graphical highlighting may emphasize just the outline of the joined circular forms. Sometimes these are even shown with a stylized shadow, to emphasize the 3D and spatial qualities of the trees represented.

3.2.2.1 Planting Plans

Landscape architects and garden designers typically produce special *working drawings* or *construction documents* to guide the creation of a landscape or garden. Included among these, along with the *dimensional plan* and *grading plan* which defines the landform, is a *planting plan*, showing the locations and species of all plants. Usually this is given as an overlay on the grading plan, so that planting relationships to landform are evident. The location of each new or existing plant is indicated by a symbol, often a cross, indicating the approximate center of the

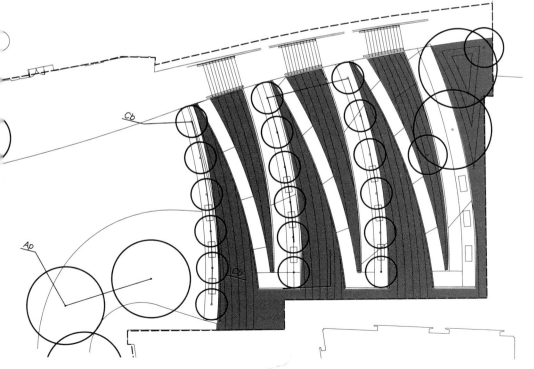

Figure 3.3
Partial planting plan of the University Commons Project at the University of Cincinnati, Hargreaves Associates. Using vector entities the plan describes the location of trees and groundcover. When describing the trees, note that the symbol describes both the trunk location and the extent of the canopy.
Digital data courtesy of Hargreaves Associates.

stem, or bunch of stems, and a circle indicating the approximate size. These graphical symbols are highly simplified, and the sizes may be only general and relative to distinguish different larger and smaller species. When several similar plants are to be located in a clump, or other organized group, a connecting line is drawn between all the members of the group, to clarify that relationship. Finally, each plant or group is identified by name (or by a symbol) which can be looked up in an attached planting schedule, which identifies each plant, genus, species, and variety if indicated, as well as any special notes or other instructions to the planting crew.

You can use a planting plan as a starting point if you have it, by digitizing all the plant locations (or acquiring the planting plan in digital form). These spot locations become the insertion points, or markers, for putting the appropriate 3D plant object into place in the model.

3.2.2.2 Plan Symbols

Elaborating on the simple circle, other symbols attempt to capture more specifically the branching structure and irregular outline of trees in plan, leading to the semirealistic, botanically derived tree stamp, sometimes even drawn with stylistic leaves, or clumps of foliage.

Figure 3.4
These tree symbols have been adapted from the tree stamps used by the landscape architect Dan Kiley.

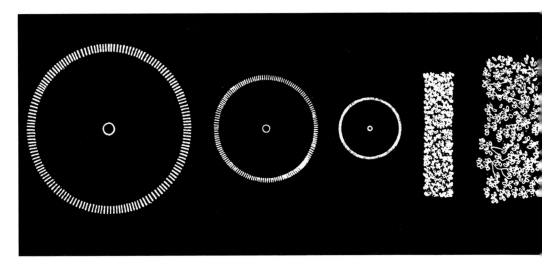

3.2.2.3 Elevation and Section Symbols

In eye-level views (perspectives, sections, elevations, even axonometrics, and aerial oblique views) similar 2D representations can be used to present tree profiles. The characteristics of trees in side view – their proportion of height to width, shape of canopy, form of branching, and others – combine to form species-unique outlines, which can be used to identify and visualize specific tree forms, both in isolation and *en masse*. Some standard reference texts provide these profiles, sometimes derived from photographs of perfect specimens in winter conditions, for many kinds of trees, including deciduous, coniferous, and palms.

These sparse, but evocative illustrations are common in architectural and landscape architectural renderings, capturing realistic tree forms in simple enough style to readily draw by hand, in black and white, and providing enough texture and associative information to help the viewer imagine the full-grown, shady-green, swaying-in-the-breeze version, without having to try to draw all of that. This role of simple but suggestive graphics is important for designers, especially in early design stages, and as a representational technique is often preferable to photographs or "photo-realistic" efforts.

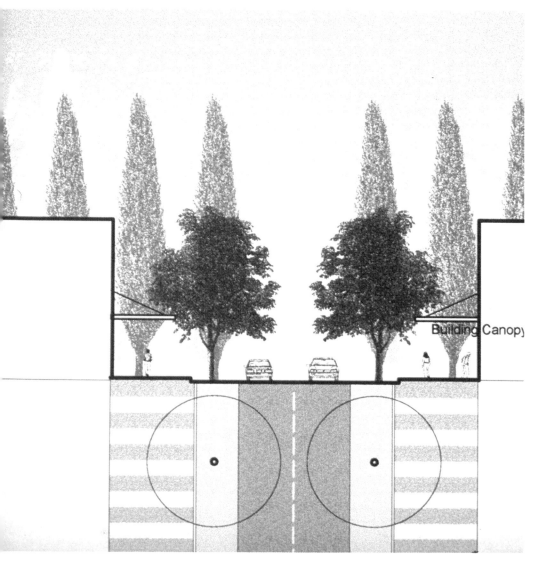

Figure 3.5
This image illustrates the combination of images with vector entities to produce an illustrative plan and section. Note the effectiveness of layering and transparency for conveying depth and spatial relationships within the project. Courtesy of Peter Walker and Partners.

3.3 3D Vegetation Models

2D images of plant forms are useful for a variety of purposes, but to create a virtual landscape, which can be viewed from a variety of angles, or walked through, 3D is required. A full 3D model of any but the very simplest plant is a daunting prospect. The sheer number of polygons and solids required for even a small tree can be well in the millions. So the most common method for rendering plants is to use a very simple geometric figure, such as a flat plane, or *billboard*, and texture-mapped images.

Figure 3.6
Rendered plan and Perspective of the Miller Garden, by the Landscape Architect, Dan Kiley.
Gary R. Hilderbrand, principal investigator; with Scot Carmen, Mami Hara, Pierre Belanger. Harvard University, Graduate School of Design, 1998. Courtesy of Gary R. Hilderbrand.

3.3.1 Surfaces

In general, 3D models may be classified as either *solids* or *surfaces*. For most purposes, models of plants are most readily made as surfaces, as these are easier to form and to manipulate in irregular ways. The simplest surfaces are just rectangular flat planes, or polygonal cut-outs; more complex ones are meshes or other combinations.

3.3.1.1 Billboards

Side-view photographs of trees, shrubs, and flowerbeds can be easily be image-processed and used as a texture map on a transparent vertical plane in a 3D scene. This technique is often called "*decals*" or "*billboards,*" and provides a direct way to introduce 2D images into the 3D scene. Photographs for this purpose need to be of high quality (resolution and clarity), and are most useful when made of single plant specimens against a solid color background (such as the sky) so that they can be isolated and then recombined in the final model. The solid color can be set to transparent in your rendering software, and so you can see through the trees in the final model, to give a more realistic, layered look.

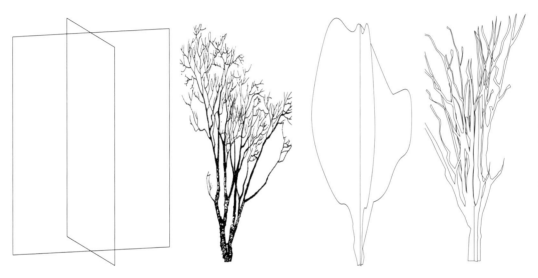

Figure 3.7
a. Two intersecting vertical planes (billboards).
b. An image map.
c. Silhouette cut-out billboards including envelope.
d. Silhouette cut-out of branching structure.

In order to set the background color to transparent, you will often need to create a transparency *mask* – a bitmap image that corresponds to the full-color textured image, but which has only black-and-white, or gray-scale values. Many rendering systems allow you to use such a mask to specify transparency – either on/off, in a monochrome black-and-white mask (which may be embedded within the image in the *alpha channel)* or in 255 levels, using a gray-scale mask, in which all black, or 0, is completely transparent; gray, or 128 is 50% transparent; and white, or 255, is opaque. (These values may be user-selectable, as to whether black, white, or some other solid color is transparent.)

To make a mask, you will need to use some image-processing operations, to select those pixels that are outside the image. If you are using a photograph taken with a distinct, solid color background, such as the blue sky, you will be able to use this color value to select all sky pixels; otherwise, you might have to (tediously) select out all the background pixels one by one. It's important to recognize the role of *anti-aliasing* in this process. Many color images have pixels with intermediate or *ramped* values (between blue and green, for example, at the edge of foliage and sky) and a color-picking tool might have a tolerance, or threshold, set to include pixels with values close to the specified value. In some cases, if you have anti-aliasing on, and make a mask from a selection, you will include edge pixels which can give a disturbing halo effect when the image is used in a rendering.

When you create a rectangle to be used for the image map, (sometimes called a *decal*), you will want to make the proportions similar or identical to the image. If identical, you will have an easier time mapping the pixels of the image to the rectangle. If the proportions are different, then some distortion may be introduced when you apply the image. The rendering software may allow fine control of the scaling of the image, which can help in reducing these distortions and artifacts.

You also need to be aware of the file format used for images as well. Using a compressed file format that is *lossy*, such as JPEG, you may find some artifacts are introduced when the image is used as a texture. TIFF files do not lose any pixels, even when compressed, and so are better used as image maps.

These same kinds of photographic images – whether in full leaf, or barren winter conditions, etc. – can be used as image maps, or texture maps in 3D geometric modeling software to bring instant photographic qualities to simple geometric forms. A leafy texture mapped onto a simple rectangular hedge, or a tree photograph onto a flat plane, like a billboard in the landscape, is an effective way to combine solid modeling with image processing.

3.3.1.2 Silhouette

Another potential problem with the billboard approach is that the billboard may cast a rectangular and most untreelike shadow. In modeling environments where shadow casting is supported, the image or texture map itself probably will not cast a shadow, but the object to which it is mapped will. In this case, it's necessary to further refine the billboard to become a *cut-out*, of an appropriate shape for – if not exactly the same as – the object mapped on it. In many cases, a simplified form, such as lollipop, will be satisfactory for the cut-out, if the shadow it casts will be further obscured by being on rolling or textured terrain, e.g., or mixed up with others. However, if the shadow cast by the tree cut-out will be plainly visible, or in the foreground, then it may be appropriate to strive for further realism by allowing some rays of light to pass through, as in nature, creating dappled sunlight in the shadow. See below for more on shadows.

These cut-outs can be made in several simplified forms – lollipops, triangular, and elliptical – and used in combination with different photographic textures to achieve a wide range of results.

BILLLBOARD

Objectives: *To illustrate the procedure for constructing 3D representations of vegetation using simple surfaces as "billboards."*
Inputs: *Closed polygonal surface – complex or simple.*
High resolution image of plant material to be modeled/rendered. (*.tif, *.tga, *.jpg). For accurate branching and habit consult a reference such as Hightshoe's "Native Trees Shrubs and Vines for Urban and Rural America."
Note: *When generating or scanning the image of the plant material to be represented, take note of whether or not the image or plant is symmetrical. Trees with a central leader, are more successfully represented in this manner when compared to the multistemmed forms of understory trees.*

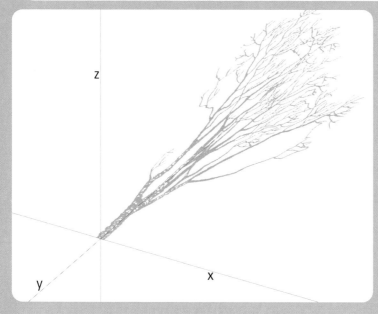

Process:
1. Tracing the tree image for accurate proportion or "true" habit configuration.

In the CAD or modeling application – place the image of the tree as an "underlay" so that you can trace its outline for accurate proportion of height to width. This can also assist in the setting the right proportions for mapping coordinates when anticipating that the tree image will be used as rendering material.

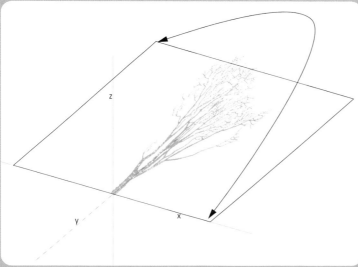

2. Using the rectangle or simple polygon command – construct a closed surface in the proportion of the "tree" on the XY construction plane.
3. Check the dimensions of the tree form, and scale as necessary.
4. Rotate the polygon, so that it is

perpendicular to the XY construction plane. You now have a simple billboard form. Depending on the complexity of your model and whether the tree is symmetrical or not you can copy the billboard around its midpoint to provide the illusion of three dimensions.

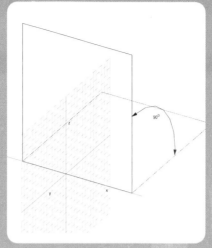

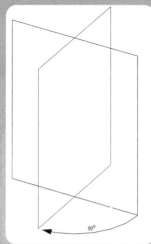

5. The billboard or billboards can then be moved to appropriate location in the model, and assigned a rendering material. It is suggested that you create a symbol, group, or block, after the material is assigned and then replicate throughout the model as designed.

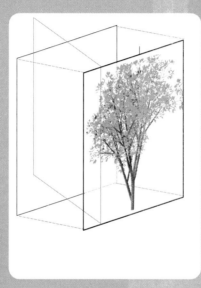

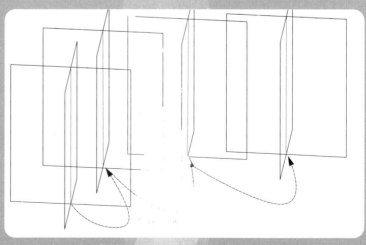

SILHOUETTE

Objectives: To illustrate the procedure for constructing 3D representations of vegetation using simple surfaces, silhouettes, or "billboard cutouts."
Inputs: Closed polygonal surface – complex.
High resolution image of plant material to be modeled/rendered (*.tif, *.tga, *.jpg). For accurate branching and habit consult a reference such as Hightshoe's "Native Trees Shrubs and Vines for Urban and Rural America."
Note:
When generating or scanning the image of the plant material to be represented, take note of whether or not the image or plant is symmetrical. Trees with a central leader, are more successfully represented in this manner when compared to the multistemmed forms of understory trees.

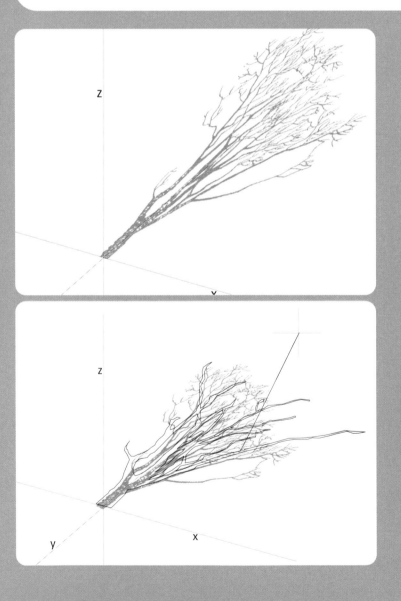

1. Trace the tree image for accurate proportion or habit. In the CAD or modeling application place the image of the tree as an "underlay" so that you can trace its outline for accurate proportion of height to width. This can also assist in the setting the right proportions for mapping coordinates when anticipating that the tree image will be used a rendering material.
2. Using the polyline or running line command, trace with detail either the branching structure or branch structure with canopy of the tree, on the XY construction plane. Make sure that the polyline is closed.
3. Check the dimensions of the tree form, and scale as necessary.

4. Rotate the polygonal form, so that it is perpendicular to the XY construction plane. You now have a "cut-out billboard" form. Depending on the complexity of your model and whether the tree is symmetrical or not, you can copy the billboard around its midpoint/center to provide the illusion of three dimensions.

5. The billboard or billboards can then be moved to appropriate location in the model, and assigned a rendering material. It is suggested that you create a symbol, group, or block, after the material is assigned and then replicate throughout the model as designed.

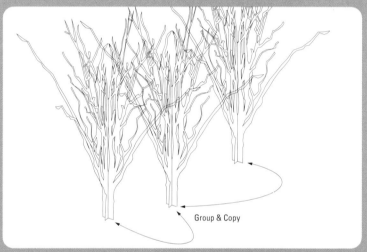

Group & Copy

3.3.1.3 Layered Canopy

In between simple flat planes and more complex 3D representations, is a class of interesting models that are useful shorthand for plant materials. These are made by combinations of bent and curved surfaces, much like pieces of construction paper, sometimes impaled on a pole or stem. Useful at high levels of abstraction, like lollipop trees, these have the added advantage of being a bit more volumetric and slightly more realistic in that they have depth and layers of canopy, and can cast more interesting shadows, especially for conifers.

Figure 3.8
The strategy used to model trees in this student thesis can be adapted to create digital representation of trees by combining typical entities found in geometric modeling, most notably swept forms for trunks and branches with simple surfaces for the depiction of tree canopies. This photograph is from the landscape architect Garrett Eckbo's Master's thesis "Contempoville: Los Angeles World's Fair 1945." Mr. Eckbo completed his thesis in 1938 at the Harvard University Graduate School of Design.
Courtesy of Special Collections, Frances Loeb Library, Graduate School of Design, Harvard University.

LAYERED CANOPY

Objectives: *To illustrate the procedure for constructing 3D representations of vegetation using simple surfaces and swept shapes.*
Inputs: *Closed polygonal surface – complex or simple, polylines.*
High resolution image of plant material to be modeled/rendered (*.tif, *.tga, *.jpg). For accurate branching and habit consult a reference such as Hightshoe's "Native Trees Shrubs and Vines for Urban and Rural America."
Note: *When generating or scanning the image of the plant material to be represented, take note of whether or not the image or plant is symmetrical. Trees with a central leader, are more successfully represented in this manner when compared to the multistemmed forms of understory trees.*

1. Place an underlay of the tree species that you wish to model into the XY construction plane of your model. Invoke either the polyline or line commands and trace the extent of the branching structure and trunk form in the XY construction plane using two separate layers.

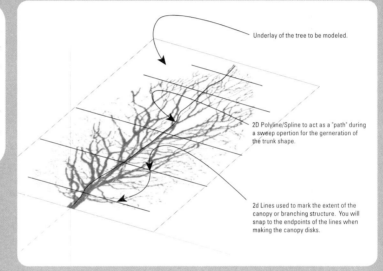

Underlay of the tree to be modeled.

2D Polyline/Spline to act as a "path" during a sweep opertion for the gerneration of the trunk shape.

2d Lines used to mark the extent of the canopy or branching structure. You will snap to the endpoints of the lines when making the canopy disks.

2. Rotate the entities 90 degrees around the YZ construction plane so that they are now perpendicular to the XY construction plane.

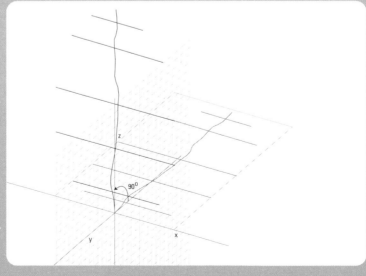

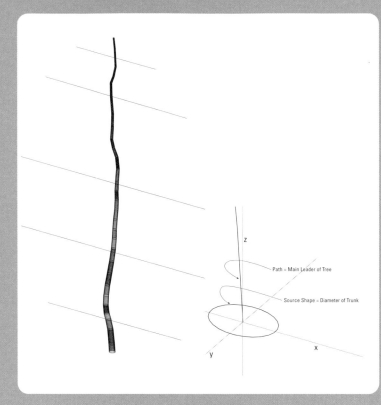

Path = Main Leader of Tree

Source Shape = Diameter of Trunk

3. With either a closed polyline, circle, or ellipse, model the diameter of the trunk or branching structure.

4. Using the sweep command sweep the trunk profile along the traced path of the trunk or central leader. The resulting solid entity will be the trunk entity.

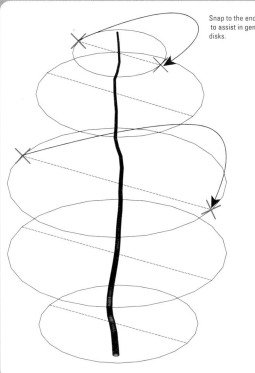

Snap to the endpoints of the 2d lines to assist in generating the Canopy disks.

5. The line entities that represent the extent of the tree branching structure will be used as a guide in constructing the canopy disks. Make sure the XY construction plane is current and activate the endpoint snap.

6. Using an ellipse, circle, or rectangle, generate a series of surfaces to represent the canopy. The "endpoint snap" will enable you to use the canopy extent entities as guides for constructing the geometry.

7. Anticipating material assignments in a rendering application, make sure that the canopy entities are on a different layer than the trunk entities.

8. This image compares a wire-frame representation with a hidden line view.

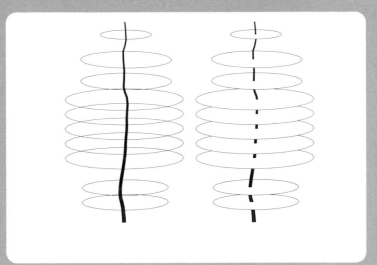

9. The entities can be grouped and replicated in the modeling or rendering application similar to a block and instances procedure in CAD applications.

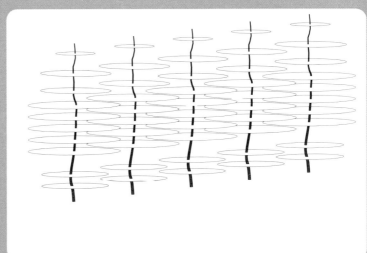

10. These two images illustrate both the strength and the weakness of the layered canopy tree model. The eye level accentuates the thinness and planarity of the canopy entities, while the aerial view adequately represents the canopy coverage.

3.3.2 Solid Representations

To overcome the limitations of photographic textures on flat planes, true 3D models of plants may be used. In some cases, simple geometric forms such as cones and cylinders can be effective. Usually, though, these are limited to formal gardens with very specific characteristics. Plants in general need to be represented with more complexity and more variation in shape, and creating plantlike forms requires some very specific techniques.

3.3.2.1 Simple Parametric Solids – Cones, Cylinders

The clipped hedges and pruned evergreen shrubs of some European gardens and many suburban ranch houses can be effectively modeled with geometric solids. These can even be simple, solid colors, and achieve a certain cartoonlike clarity of representation. For slightly more subtlety, try applying a few more complex textures, including transparency, eroded surfaces or bump maps. These combinations are endless.

Figure 3.9
The geometric forms seen at Hampton Court Palace in Richmond, England, can best be represented with the parametric solid forms of cones and cylinders.
Hope H. Hasbrouck, 1999.

3.3.2.2 Cylinder-based Hand-built Models

Modeling branching forms can be constructed by hand, at least for a simplified structure. In this case, you can use a 3D modeling system to create tapered cylindrical forms, following a path in 3-space, which may be either straight or curved. Using some geometric snap operation to connect subsequent branches, you can draw a branching 3D form. Usually, attempting to draw in every small twig at the end is a losing proposition, so these forms are best when left slightly diagrammatic. They can be quite effective, especially for representing more angular, or sculptural tree forms.

PARAMETRIC SOLIDS – SIMPLE

Objectives: To illustrate the procedure for constructing 3D representations of vegetation using simple parametric solids.
Inputs: Simple parametric solids or geometric primitives.
High resolution image of plant material to be modeled/rendered (*.tif, *.tga, *.jpg). For accurate branching and habit consult a reference such as Hightshoe's "Native Trees Shrubs and Vines for Urban and Rural America."
Note: When generating or scanning the image of the plant material to be represented, take note of whether or not the image or plant is symmetrical. Trees with a central leader, are more successfully represented in this manner when compared to the multistemmed forms of understory trees.
Overview: These simple lollipop forms can be generated in a multitude of ways. The most common would be the definition of simple geometric primitives or solids derived from extruded, swept , or revolved shapes.

Process:

1. The Trunk:
With careful attention to the trunk height and form select the appropriate geometric primitive for the trunk (cylinder or cone), and either generate directly or through coordinate input. Using a strategy similar to the "Layered Canopy", sweep a shape along a path to represent the central leader or trunk of the tree.

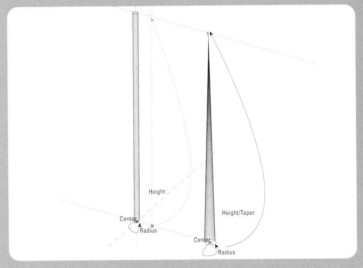

The procedure to make a swept form for the trunk follows the procedure outlined in the "Layered Canopy" tutorial.
a. Trace the central leader in the XY construction plane. This is now the path.
b. Rotate the path around the YZ construction plane so that it is perpendicular to the XY construction plane.

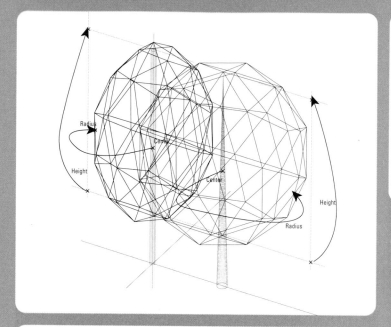

2. The canopy:
With knowledge of the canopy's width and height determine whether it would be best represented with a sphere or a 3-dimensional ellipse. The solid canopy form might be best constructed through coordinate input rather than snapping to the trunk geometry.

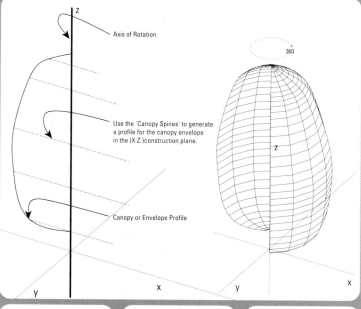

Axis of Rotation

Use the 'Canopy Spines' to generate a profile for the canopy envelope in the (X Z) construction plane.

Canopy or Envelope Profile

360

If you wish to define canopy with revolved or lofted entities, it is suggested but not necessary to use the underlay as a method for generating true-to-habit tree volumes. Using the procedure outlined in the "Layered Canopy" tutorial, the profile of the tree envelope can be generated from either tracing the tree profile or snapping to geometry that suggests the limits of the tree envelope.

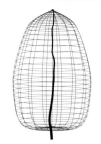

In anticipation of applying rendering materials to the solid canopy forms, you can make a double layer canopy. The double layer canopy will allow you to assign two materials: one to suggest branching structure, the other the canopy texture.

When applying complex textures to the tree canopy, use the cylindrical mapping with a cap. Depending upon whether you use a double layer, the mapping parameters can be tiled in the "u-axis" to adjust density of the canopy material.

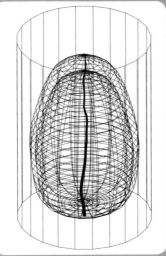

a. This is an example of the type of bitmap used to define the diffuse color of the branching structure layer. For the purposes of the rendering it is usually coupled with a transparency map
b. This is an example of a type of bitmap that could be used to suggest the texture of the tree's envelope. At the time of rendering it is coupled with a transparency map, so that the interior branching layer is visible.

Rendered examples of the double layer canopy from eye level and from above. Note that the shadows include visual information about both branching structure and canopy volume.

A related approach which may have some success would be to use a 3D digitizer, to collect points and surface geometry from a real sample – perhaps in parts, branches, twigs, leaves – and use these to compose a 3D model. Modern laser-based digitizers can be used to capture *point clouds* of 3D coordinates, which can then be organized into solid or surface forms. This technique is most valuable for capturing unique forms which may only be found in nature.

3.3.3 Hybrid (3D and 2D) Plant Forms

For many purposes, a hybrid combination of 3D and 2D approaches may the best. Having a 3D solid skeletal framework is a great benefit for animations and virtual reality, since these can withstand close inspection from any angle. Having detailed foliage, bark, and flowers in 3D form is intractable for most systems, requiring far too much memory and rendering time. So the approach of combining texture-mapped foliage with a geometric solid tree trunk, or skeleton, makes sense for many applications.

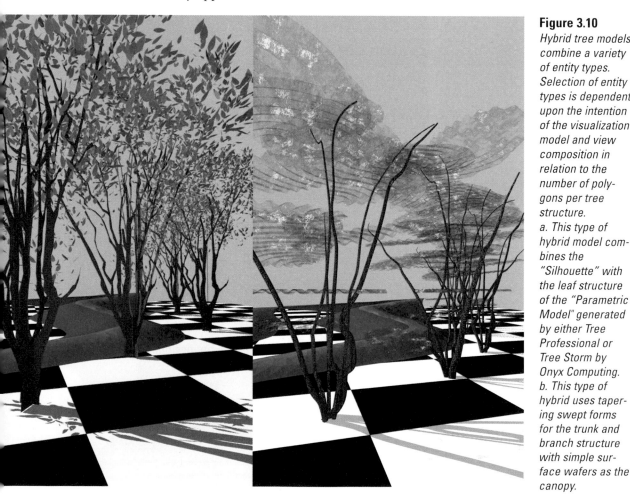

Figure 3.10
Hybrid tree models combine a variety of entity types. Selection of entity types is dependent upon the intention of the visualization model and view composition in relation to the number of polygons per tree structure.
a. This type of hybrid model combines the "Silhouette" with the leaf structure of the "Parametric Model" generated by either Tree Professional or Tree Storm by Onyx Computing.
b. This type of hybrid uses tapering swept forms for the trunk and branch structure with simple surface wafers as the canopy.

HYBRID MODELS

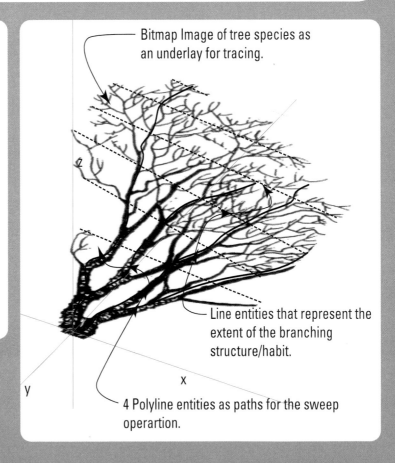

Inputs:
a.) Trunk or branch profile – closed polygonal surface – simple.
b.) Branching structure – open polylines.
c.) Canopy – simple/complex surfaces or disturbed meshes.
d.) High resolution image of plant material to be modeled/rendered (*.tif, *.tga, *.jpg). For accurate branching and habit consult a reference such as Hightshoe's "Native Trees Shrubs and Vines for Urban and Rural America."

Note:
This method seems to work best with multistemmed understory trees without a central leader.

Overview:
The hybrid combines a more complex branching and trunk structure with the simple canopy surfaces of the "Layered Canopy" tree. The complex branching and trunks are swept shapes. The swept shapes use paths derived from tracing the branch structure of an image, and a simple closed form for the trunk or branch profile. In the end the complex branching is then combined with the layered canopy shapes, envelopes, or leaf entities, to form the hybrid model. Many types of hybrids tree models are possible through skillful combination of the entity types described throughout this chapter.

Process:

1. In the CAD or modeling application – place the image of the tree you wish to represent as an "underlay" for tracing tree structure and habit.
2. On the XY construction plane, using the polyline command trace individual branches or the trunk as one entity from base to tip. This will result in a series of paths along which you will sweep trunk and branch profiles.
3. On a separate layer, generate a series of line entities that represent the extent of the branching structure or canopy.

Bitmap Image of tree species as an underlay for tracing.

Line entities that represent the extent of the branching structure/habit.

4 Polyline entities as paths for the sweep operartion.

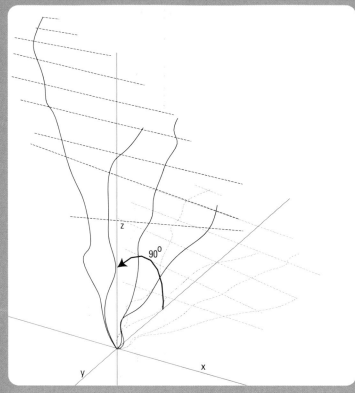

3. In three dimensions rotate the paths and the line entities so that they will be perpendicular to the XY construction plane.

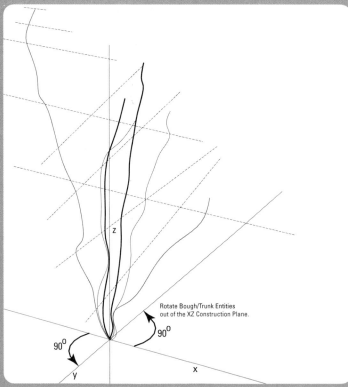

Rotate Bough/Trunk Entities
out of the XZ Construction Plane.

4. Even though the paths are perpendicular to the construction plan they are 2-dimensional. Using the rotate command, rotate the paths individually around the "origin," so that they begin to define or suggest volume.

144

5. With either a closed polyline, circle, or ellipse, model the diameter of the trunk or branching structure.

6. Using the sweep command sweep the trunk profile along the traced path of the trunk or central leader. The resulting solid entity will be the trunk entity.

Variation:
In the sweep operations there are many options for transforming the swept object, providing variations and irregularities. The swept object can be scaled or rotated along the path. These options are set during the command.

7. The line entities that represent the extent of the tree branching structure will be used as a guide in constructing the canopy disks. Make sure the XY construction plane is current and activate the endpoint snap.

8. Using an ellipse, circle, or rectangle, generate a series of surfaces to represent the canopy. The "endpoint snap" will allow you to use the canopy extent entities as guides for constructing the geometry.

9. Anticipating material assignments in a rendering application, make sure that the canopy entities are on a different layer than the trunk entities.

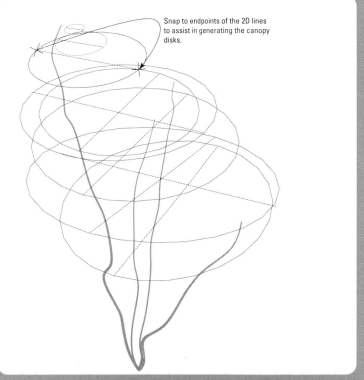

Snap to endpoints of the 2D lines to assist in generating the canopy disks.

Variation: To add texture to the canopy wafers, mesh the polygonal faces and then disturb the points in the mesh.

a. "Disturbed Wafer" canopy with swept trunk entities.
b. "Disturbed Wafer" canopy with Silhouette/Cutout Branching Structure.

a. Canopy envelope with silhouette branching structure.
b. Canopy envelope with swept branching structure.
[The procedurally derived canopy and envelope were generated with "Tree Professional" by Onyx Computing. The method for generating the procedural tree is covered in the next section.]

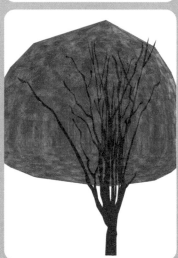

a. Procedurally derived canopy with swept branching structure.
b. Procedurally derived canopy with silhouette branching structure.
[The procedurally derived canopy and envelope were generated with "Tree Professional" by Onyx Computing. The method for generating the procedural tree is covered in the next section.]

3.3.3.1 Parametric 3D Models

Given the complexity of plant forms, and the repetitive nature of the branching structure, it's far more effective to use computer generating techniques to create 3D models of trees and other plants. Using rather simple basic branching and recursion algorithms, as explained below, modern software tools are capable of quite remarkable botanically-correct plant forms within a wide range of parameters of shape, size, and complexity.

These plant models fall into three broad categories of plant types: deciduous trees (broad-leaved, which lose their leaves in the winter in temperate climates), coniferous (the evergreens, which have needles and cones, rather than leaves), and palms (yet another vegetative variant, which have fronds rather than needles or leaves, and are almost entirely tropical in their habitat).

Plant modeling software, much of which derives from work on *L-Systems* by the mathematical botanist Lindenmeyer, typically gives control over a large number of parameters, or numeric variables, which control the specific forms of branching, leaf formation, overall shape, proportion, height, etc. By controlling somewhere between twenty and two hundred such variables, a wide range of forms, corresponding to many of the actual genera and species of the plant kingdom, can be generated.

These can be created as 3D models, with multiple flat triangular, curved, or mesh surfaces, numbering often in the millions of polygons for a medium-sized tree. The size of the file produced for such models can be many tens or hundreds of megabytes. Choosing parameter values carefully, and exercising any optimizing or simplifying options that are offered in the plant modeling software, is essential.

Figure 3.11
Parametric Trees:
a. Blue Spruce
(Abies concolor).
b. Butia Palms.
c. Paper Birch
(Betula paper-
ifera).
Created in Onyx
Tree Pro software.
Courtesy of Pjer
Zanchi.

PROCEDURAL MODELS

Overview:

Using a procedural modeling application such as Onyx Computing's "Tree Professional", botanically correct tree representations can be generated as either 2D bitmaps or three-dimensional geometry in a variety of file formats. The two-dimensional image files can be used as materials at rendering time or can be used in digital collage or montages. The three-dimensional geometry can be imported in modeling applications and can receive material definitions. The "Tree Professional" application allows the modeler to adjust plant structure according to characteristics of Trunk, Bough, Branch and Leaf, and Color. Precise manipulation requires familiarity with species characteristics, these characteristics are saved in a library of Tree Parameters and can be recalled at any time. "Tree Professional" comes with an extensive library of tree parameter files, that describe trees at various stages of maturity and seasonal habit.

Requirements:

"Tree Professional" by Onyx Computing, or equivalent tree-generation software.

Tree Parameter File: Provided with the "Tree Professional" software, or from other source

Objectives:

The objective of this tutorial is to identify features of the interface that aid in the development of botanically correct tree species in two and three dimensions.

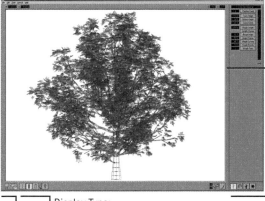

Species Feature Editing Dialog
-- Branch Length, Trunk Height, Diameter, Leaf Type & Color

Specify Species Feature for editing:
--Trunk, Bough, Branch, Leaf

Display Type:
-- Stick Figure, Wireframe, Surface Render, Canopy Volume

Visibility of Species Features
-- Trunk, Bough, Branch, 'Leaf'

3.3.3.2 Special Trees – Palms, Others

Certain kinds of trees call for special modeling approaches. Palm trees, for example, which are widespread throughout warm climates, have a radically different structure and pattern of growth than the coniferous or deciduous plants of the more temperate climates. The simple technique of texture mapping photographs works equally well for any plant (or other object). But the palms, being in fact botanically simpler plants, are especially well suited to algorithmic generation methods for computationally growing the trunk and fronds. The fronds occur in a simple radial pattern, sprouting from the top of the tapered trunk, and have a clear, repetitive, geometric form. They are often arched in a curved form that can be modeled mathematically.

Figure 3.12
Parametric variations on palm tree form.
Modeled in TreePro, rendered in 3DStudiomax.

Although there are many different species and forms of palms, many of these variations are simple parametric variations upon a theme: ratios of trunk length to width, or height of fronds, etc. A parameter-based plant modeling system provides a convenient way to produce a range of related, but different, palm forms.

Cacti are like palms, occurring in a variety of forms, but many simple and parametrically varying ones. Trees with unique characteristics – the mangrove and baobab, for example, whose drooping branches take root in the ground and form a concentric, spreading mass – will require customized modeling approaches, with special algorithms to describe these behaviors and forms, or a combination of texture mapping and other techniques.

Figure 3.13
Solid models of representative cacti.
Modeled and rendered in 3DStudioMax.

3.3.4 Plant Structures: Groves and Allees

Often, in landscape and garden designs, plants are placed in geometric arrangements, creating lines and clumps, used to define space, such as paths and rooms, or just as a visual organizing technique. Most 3D modeling programs provide a range of tools for creating evenly spaced arrangements, in lines, or rectangular, or circular arrays with specified spacing and dimensions. When repetitive elements are used, some techniques to introduce some amount of variation, such as is found in nature, should be employed. Using two or three slightly different, but similar, tree images is a good technique; these should be randomly allocated to the array. Also, mirror flipping of a photographic image, or very slight stretching, horizontally or vertically, can be used to introduce some minor variation in repetitive groups. (But be sure that the resulting lighting model is not incongruous; images with a strong directional lighting and shadows in them should not be flipped horizontally and used together!)

Figure 3.14
*Using image processing to create a row of trees.
a. A row of arborvitae, made by simply copying and repeating a single image.
b. Another row, made by first creating several variants of the image (reversed, shortened, modified) and using them in a random mix.*

151

3.4 Textures on Plant Material

3.4.1 Maps on Solids

Texture maps need not be limited in their application to planes. While effective especially at eye level, these models cannot capture other massing qualities of plants. Trees, for example, often form an overarching, intersecting canopy overhead. Using funnel-shaped solids to capture this characteristic can be effective, combined with texture maps applied for bark (on the trunk) and for branching and foliage overhead. With this method one can even look up and through the branches.

Other vegetation, of course, may enter into the landscape model. Understory plants – small trees and shrubs, as well as groundcovers, woody perennials, flowers and grasses – all are essential parts of the texture and color of the landscape. Some may be modeled just as miniature trees. Others may be more well-suited to texture mapping, depending of course on the representational purpose and role (background vs. foreground, e.g.)

Shrubs can usually be approached as textured masses. Either simple geometric forms (the cones, balls, and rectangles of clipped hedges and topiary evergreens so common in the English tradition) or organic, flowing mounds may be used for structure and color in many landscapes.

In this case, a combination of texture and transparency is required. In smaller masses, light must be seen to be passing through, often especially so at the base (where the stems touch the ground and foliage is sparser) and the perimeter (where foliage is again, sparser and characterized by spurts of growth).

Figure 3.15
Carefully trimmed and shaped hedges and evergreen shrubs in the ornamental garden at the Villa Lante in Italy.

3.4.2 Simple Color

"Plants are green" is a relatively safe assertion, but of course is not completely or always true. Plants come in many different shades of green, from almost yellow to nearly blue, thanks to their chlorophyll content; but they also come in deep purples, vibrant oranges and reds, and muted browns and tans as well. Choosing a good base color is a first step when creating a plant model. A solid simple green is a good choice with simple geometric forms and highly abstract models, but more detailed models need more subtlety and range of texture. When coloring plants in a scene, choosing very small variations in color by varying the amount of red and blue in the RGB values chosen can be helpful in adding variety; the amount to vary will depend greatly on the available color resolution of the display device. (A screen with only 1024 colors has far fewer greens possible than one with millions of colors, or 32-bit color.)

Figure 3.16
Simple solid shapes and simple color are used in this digital model of the Gropius House in Lincoln, Massachusetts. The model is a student project by Eric Kramer '98 at the Harvard University Graduate School of Design. Modeled and rendered in FormZ.

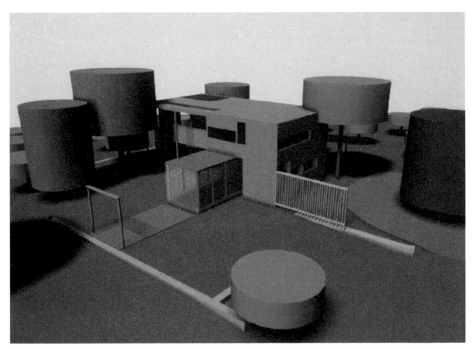

3.4.3 Bump Maps and Other Compound Textures

For some purposes, using the built-in textures or bump maps available in a rendering system may be an adequate representation of vegetation, bark, or foliage. Exploring different settings is a useful way to start, since in many rendering systems small chanegs in settings can make distinct visual differences.

3.4.4 Photograph-based Textures

For many purposes, especially when plants or vegetation details are in the foreground, more realistic photographic-based textures are appropriate. Using basic image processing techniques, you can create a library of textures for bark, leaves, flowers, and foliage that can be used and reused in various combinations.

The images below show a range of examples of using photographic textures for plant forms.

TEXTURED TREE BARK

Objective:
To produce a rendered image of a tree trunk, with branches, etc., textured and colored with a bark-like surface.

Input Items:
3D tree geometry
Digital Image of Bark

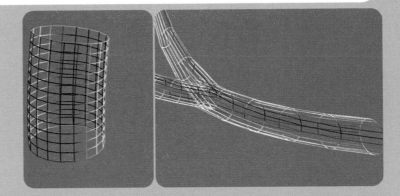

Step 1. Assemble source material.

a. Acquire or generate 3D tree geometry. This may be procedurally generated by some plant-form producing software, or built by hand out of cylinders, possibly with bending, tapering, and twisting modifiers.

b. Acquire digital image of tree bark, either by scanning a slide or print, or by capturing with a digital camera. It is best if this image is captured with a minimum of lighting conditions evident; that is, the image should not have one bright and one shadowed side, as this will influence the final result. Often taking a detail photograph of the trunk of a large diameter tree will give good results, free from curvature or lighting artifacts.

Step 2. Apply texture to geometry. Typically this involves selecting the desired geometry (all of the tree, or selected portions) and specifying a texture map for the selection. In this case, you need to specify a "cylindrical mapping," so the texture is wrapped around the

The texture map, a photograph such as those above, needs to be applied to the trunk or branches with a *cylindrical mapping*. At left, the mapping coordinates are shown in yellow, wrapping around, and aligned with, the central axis of the trunk.

cylindrical trunk and branches. You may have to rotate the texture 90°, depending on how your original photograph was oriented. You may also want to specify a "bump map." A good procedure is to use the original photograph as the bump map as well, though you may wish to experiment with additional options, including using other bump textures.

Step 3. Modify texture map parameters. Changing the scale and rotation of the texture map can have dramatic effects on the image. Choosing finer scale for smaller branches, and coarser scale for larger trunk can be effective. Controlling the depth of bump map can also make a difference. Other maps, such as shininess or reflectance can be added for special effects such as wet branches, glossy bark, etc. You may wish to overlay two or more textures, or add an additional speckled or other texture to the final result.

Step 4. Adjust eye position and rotation of the tree/object for best visual effect, highlighting desired features, and providing sufficient detail in area of interest.

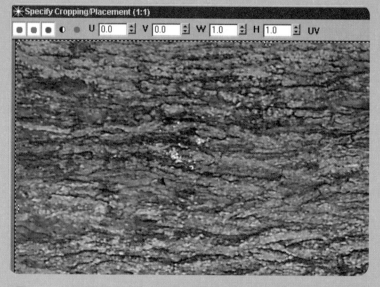

Specify Cropping/Placement (1:1)

U `0.0` V `0.0` W `1.0` H `1.0` UV

3.4.5 Procedural Textures

Vegetative coverings, created by plants of all sizes, are more complex surfaces, characterized by depth and increased texture. Leaves of grass, or of other small plants, give a specific defining texture to an overall covering. This is best approximated, when needed, by procedural approaches or by embedded image maps in the texture. Simple plant forms, such as algae and moss, can be approximated with a combination of color and bump maps, and masks outlining the patches characteristic of their growth.

3.4.6 Grass and Groundcovers

Grass – or more correctly, many different grasses – are plant materials common in all cultivated landscapes. While it is tempting to portray them as undifferentiated green, they are in fact characterized by ranges of coloration and texture. For many purposes, grasses have little form of their own, rather taking on the form of the underlying terrain, and so for modeling they can be dealt with as textures applied to to terrain.

The simple approach of repetitive tiling of a grassy texture map over terrain needs to be modified to eliminate the artifacts formed by the repeating pattern, which can be visually disturbing. Unlike bricks, or paving stones, no repeating structure should be visible on a grassy surface (except perhaps, the linear mowing pattern left on recently mowed athletic or agricultural fields, but even these tend to follow the contours and outlines of the surface).

The best way around these problems is to use procedurally formed textures, which have no inherent repetitive order. Bump maps are one approach, but tend not to generate the spiky character of grasses. For these purposes, some other algorithm is appropriate. A number of rendering and modeling environments now have special parametric procedural effects for generating hair, or fur, which tends to be similar to grasses, and can be used to good effect.

Figure 3.17
a. Tall grass rendered on berms of the University Commons Project. The tall grass is procedurally generated with the Digimation "Shag Fur" plug-in for 3DStudioMax.
b. Detail of grass.
c. Solid model of grass blades in 3DStudioMax.

Bamboo, cattails and tall grasses offer a challenge in between fully branched trees and simple furry grass. Occurring in broad masses and clumps, the procedural generation approach is appropriate, and the results are simply more massive than with smaller grasses. Giant bamboo, of course, has color, form, and texture on every stalk, as well as branches and individual leaves, and so is best modeled as a special tree – all straight trunk, with lesser branches and spiky foliage.

Other surface-covering vegetation, such as moss or lichen, can be approached as various kinds of algorithmic textures. Mottled or splotched effects can be had by combining one or more procedural textures.

Figure 3.18
Harima Science Garden City, Hyogo Prefecture, Japan by landscape architects Peter Walker and Partners.
Courtesy of Peter Walker and Partners.

Figure 3.19
Detailed 3D model of a flowering plant (wild lily) witha photographic textured background.
Modeled and rendered in 3DStudioMax.

3.5 Visualization Concerns

3.5.1 Transparency

Even with holes in the cut-outs for shadow purposes, trees painted on billboards may sometimes look just like that. An additional refinement can be to add some levels of transparency to the image. Many modeling environments provide a facility to enable you to specify a *transparency map,* as well as an image map. Typically, one 8-bit value (from 0 to 255) will be used to specify a level of transparency, with 0 (black) being completely transparent, and 255 (white) completely opaque (or the other way around – be sure to check the manual!) This can allow a kind of fuzziness around edges, and a speckled pattern of transparency, which may be desirable, or not. You will need to experiment with different settings for your individual task. This transparency mask may be either separate image, or embedded in the plant image in the "alpha channel."

Figure 3.20
Images of photographic tree textures, scanned from slides and cropped for a transparent background; also corresponding "alpha-channel" mask for transparency.

3.5.2 Lighting

Complex plant forms and their structure on the landscape are subject to great variation from lighting conditions. Plants can have both diffuse/matte (bark) and specular/reflective surfaces (leaves), and their open interiors may be in deep shade when their crowns are fully lit by sunlight. The shadows cast by large trees are important form-givers to any scene, and 3D plants will often cast shadows on themselves. Complex 3D shapes like trees and shrubs have subtle illumination and self-shadowing characteristics, and these need to be matched in the composite scene.

When using any of the photographic texture-based techniques, such as billboards or cut-outs, it's critical to match the lighting conditions of the pasted-in plants to the lights in the 3D scene; both the direction and the intensity must match. If the photographs have low contrast, from ambient-only lighting, they will look jarring in a scene with strong directional light and stark shadows. Similarly, photographic textures with strong shadows will look out of place in a scene with only ambient light, or photos lit from the left side will look incongruous in a scene where the light is from the right-hand side. Fortunately, most plant images can be mirror-flipped horizontally with no other visual impact, so that left-lit photos can be come right-lit ones, and vice versa.

Figure 3.21

A vegetated back-yard scene in differing light conditions: early morning, late afternoon, and cloudy. Note change in sky color, shadows, outlines, color intensity, and apparent depth with different lighting.

A good library of plant images will therefore contain both indirectly, ambient-lit images taken on a cloudy or overcast day, and also ones with strong lighting, ideally from two conditions, once at noon when the sun is overhead and shadows are smallest and directly underneath, and again in mid-morning, when the sun's rays are from the side; these can also serve for the afternoon, when the shadows will be cast to the other side, by flipping them over.

3.5.3 Shadows

The dark shadows cast by plants, on the ground, on their neighbors, and on themselves, are visually important in anchoring them to the scene and to the terrain. The long shadows of tree trunks are often one of the most effective ways of illuminating the subtle shapes of landform, both in real life and in a landscape model. When using a complete 3D model and rendering software, the shadows can be cast by the rendering system. In this case, some parameters may be available to control the apparent fuzziness of the shadow (sometimes called *soft shadows*), and to set the maximum darkness of fully-shaded areas. There may also be controls required when setting up the lights, surfaces, and objects to specify them as shadow-casting. When a high-quality rendering system (with ray-tracing or equivalent methods for shadow-casting) is not being used, it is still possible to hand-place shadows on the ground. Simple dark smudges, elliptical or irregularly shaped patches placed underneath and slightly to the side of each tree or plant will add greatly to the illusion.

Figure 3.22
Hand-placed shadows, created as fuzzy, black blobs, placed on terrain just below each tree.
a. Shadows alone;
b. with trees placed.
Modeled and rendered in 3DStudioMax

Some shadow-casting systems distinguish between *hard* and *soft* shadows. Hard shadows have a crisp edge between light and dark, and a single solid shade of darkness within the shadow zone (*umbra*); soft shadows have a fuzzy edge, and gradations of darkness within the shadow zone. These soft shadows are often produced by a process of iteratively moving each light source a small amount and recomputing shadows, then effectively summing up their results and overlaying them. This necessarily takes a longer time in rendering, but can add to the verisimilitude of shadows, especially in the foreground, because in the real world there are so many sources of light, reflected off of other objects and so on. Hard shadows are rarely found except under harsh artificial lighting conditions.

For many landscape visualization purposes, where the viewpoint will be taken from eye level, and the ground-plane surfaces are fuzzy and/or undulating, it's not necessary to cast perfect shadows from plants on the ground; they will be seen so obliquely that only a generalized sense of darkness in the approximately

Figure 3.23
*Comparison of
hard and soft
shadows created
by:
a. Ray-tracing;
b. "shadow map."*
Modeled and rendered in
3DStudioMax

correct location will be perceived. This fact makes it quite possible to use the hybrid technique of a photographic texture mapped to a cut-out, where the cut-out casts a simplified shadow that is perfectly acceptable. Obviously, in special conditions such as foreground shadows under lacy foliage, or in areas of dappled sunlight, these simplified shadows need to be elaborated. Even so, simply perforating the billboard in an irregular pattern, or placing a perforated cut-out over the light source, may be a suitable approximation. Since shadows of complex vegetation forms are so time-consuming in rendering, placing and using them judiciously is important; make sure that cast shadows are adding information, realism, or "feel" to the scene, otherwise they are wasted.

Another useful technique for casting dappled shadows from vegetation is to use a "projector" on a directional light, using a black-and-white silhouette bitmap as the image to be projected. This is usually faster than ray-tracing for equally detailed shadows, especially when the source tree is out of the scene.

Figure 3.24
*A projected shadow, using the
black-and-white
bitmap image
shown, assigned
to a light in the
lower left corner
of the scene.*
Modeled and rendered in
3DStudioMax

3.5.4 Levels of Detail

Plants in the landscape present one of the most daunting challenges to modeling and visualization because they encompass such a range of *levels of detail.* That is, a tree has branches, leaves, and flowers at the micro scale, but also exists within a continuous forest at the macro scale. And in between, the tree itself has a unique and recognizable form. When seen in the background, or at a distance, every leaf and flower cannot be seen; but when seen close up, they are the dominant visual features. Modeling every leaf in a forest is still an infeasible task.

Landscape models, then, have to be constructed in such a way that the appropriate level of detail (or *LOD*) is presented. In static views, this is a much more manageable task. If you know where the view is taken, you can predict which trees and other features will be in the background, midground, or foreground, and model them accordingly. Use texture-mapped images on long horizontal billboards coupled with an environment map for the far background; in the midground, use texture-mapped images on billboards, and in the foreground expend your polygon budget on some real 3D models of branches and leaves for texture, verisimilitude, and possibly detailed shadows.

For dynamic views, or when an animation or virtual tour are to be rendered, the problem is more difficult, since objects may be moving from the foreground to the background, or vice versa, over the course of time. In this case, you may be able to get away with selectively modeling some objects in higher detail, that start out in the background, knowing that they will come to the foreground, and so provide a continuous experience. You naturally expend some extra rendering time in putting those objects into the background, but it's a necessary trade-off.

In the VRML 2.0 language specification, there is a simple and powerful idea implemented for managing LOD. In this system, you can specify different representations altogether for a single object, to be applied at different distances. Thus, a tree can have a simple billboard with a low-res image at a great distance,

Figure 3.25
Tree images at three levels of detail: as a simplified 3D lollipop; as a volume with basic branching and transparent canopy; and as a detailed 3D model with full branching and foliage. Modeled and rendered in 3DStudiomax.

Figure 3.26
*Multiple images of
a tree texture map,
at 32, 64, 128, 256
and 1024 pixels.*

a set of intersecting planes with high-resolution texture map at midrange, and a full 3D model with textures, branches, and leaves when viewed up close. The rendering system should handle the switch between levels automatically. Of course, it can be visually disturbing when the switch from one level to the next happens, especially when it is a dramatic change. This is one aspect of animation and visualization that is still evolving in technology. A good solution would be some kind of more finely graded intermediate steps, like a kind of morphing between representations. At the time of this writing (summer of the year 2000) there is no commercial modeling, rendering, or visualization system that handles this kind of transition well; but there are many research developments under way to improve the management of multi-resolution scenes, and no doubt new techniques for describing and controlling LOD will appear on the scene.

Figure 3.27
*Scene with differ-
ent levels of detail
in tree representa-
tion: a 3D solid
model of pine tree
in foreground
(left); photographic
texture-mapped
billboards in mid-
ground (center);
and bump-mapped
textured terrain in
distant back-
ground.*
Modeled and ren-
dered in
3DStudiomax.

3.5.4.1 Forest Models

In the foreground, forests are made up of a number of trees, typically, with some varying layers of lower, understory plants. Different forests in different regions and climates are quite different in structure and composition, but typically there are one or more large species which dominate the canopy and control most of the sunlight, then there are smaller, often big-leaved species which fill in below, right down to the ground level. Modeling this mix is a process of interplanting the various species and textures to achieve a desired blend.

Some abstraction and simplification schemes can be quite useful, such as emphasizing trunks and stems, generalizing the canopy and using overlapping layers of texture maps to achieve a layered look.

In the background, two alternative methods are useful for forests. The first, which works best with rolling terrain, is based on applying a texture layer to a terrain model. This can be a fur or hair procedural texture, or a semitransparent mass. For forests seen against the skyline, it's important to get the ragged look of treetops, as this is the most important visual characteristic. If you are modeling a real forested landscape, using aerial photography or satellite imagery as the basis is necessary. These images can be used as a geospecific texture draped over the terrain; then 3D vegetation massing, and other features such as buildings and roads ("geotypical" objects), can be added to the model; either automatically, by software, or manually.

Figure 3.28
Forest model with considerable detail and botanical realism.
Created by the Forest Simulation Lab at Texas A&M University with special research modeling and rendering software. Courtesy of Midori Kitagawa de Leon, Greg Schmidt and others.

Figure 3.29
Forested lake shore scene.
Modeled and rendered in Blueberry3D software.
Courtesy of A. Ögren.

Figure 3.30
Forested hillside showing emergent tree species (birch or poplar) and understory vegetation over rocky terrain.
Modeled and rendered in Blueberry3D software.
Courtesy of A. Ögren.

3.6 Plant Dynamics

3.6.1 Generation

To overcome the obstacles to creating realistic, complex plant models by hand, a number of approaches have been developed for automatic, algorithmic plant generation. These techniques take advantage of the underlying mathematical structure found in most plants, and of codified botanical rules of growth, to generate plant forms automatically, from a number of mathematical parameters, or numbers which describe species characteristics, age, and so on.

3.6.1.1 Recursive Plant Forms

Drawing these 2D tree symbols by hand, whether with pencil or computer mouse or stylus, one quickly realizes the repetitive and highly-structured nature of these forms. Basically, they are "branching:" each straight line, trunk, stem, or twig, leads to one or more branches, each of which is a straight line which leads to one or more branches, getting smaller and shorter at each repetition, until eventually they stop branching, and perhaps terminate in a leaf or a bud. This description, of a repeated action, each repetition somehow connected to its predecessor, making some change like getting smaller, until finally stopping, is called a *recursive* algorithm. Each successive branch from a previous branch is a recursion, and can basically use the same procedure each time, perhaps some minor variation in parameters such as length or thickness. Recursive algorithms can lead to repetitive structures, but are distinguished from simple repetition by using the result of a previous recursion as the starting point for the next. Also, recursive algorithms don't need to specify in advance the number of times that a repetition, or recursion, will be performed; rather some "stopping rule," such as a minimum size, or length being reached, is used to terminate the procedure.

Simple branching plant forms, like tree silhouettes and plan symbols, can be created by a simple recursive algorithm. The algorithm looks something like this:

> To draw a **branch** at a point, given a length, a direction, and a branching angle:
>> First draw a straight line from the point, in the direction, for the length specified.
>> Then draw a **branch**, from the end of the line, half the length, in the direction **plus** the branching angle (this branches to the right).
>> Also draw a **branch**, from the end of the line, half the length, in the direction **minus** the branching angle (this branches to the left).
>> (Whenever length gets below some minimum size, stop, don't draw anymore.)

This form, and the algorithm, derive from the fact that a small twig on a stem has a similar structure to a stem on a branch, which is similar to a branch on a trunk, and so on. This *self-similarity* at varying scales is the characteristic property of *fractals*, and so these recursive forms may sometimes be called *fractal geometries*.

The algorithm as given above has six essential parameters which govern the appearance of the final form:
- starting length
- starting direction
- branching angle
- the ratio of each successive branch length, in this case 50% (half)
- the implicit two-way branching, one to each side
- the minimum branch size, causing the branching to stop

By varying each of these parameters, by introducing some randomness such as in the branching angle or in the probability of branching to one side or another, and by adding some, such as changing colors or thicknesses at various steps, dependent on the length, and enormous variety of plantlike forms can be generated. In addition, by repeating these treelike forms around in a circle, tree-stamps can also be generated. The following gallery shows images of tree-forms and tree-stamps, all created by the same computer code – a JAVA procedure which can be found on the accompanying CD-ROM.

Figure 3.31
The generation of branched form by succesive Y-shaped branches recursively applied.

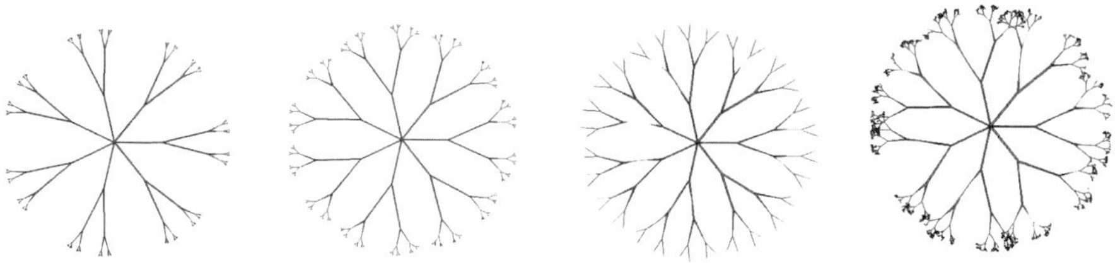

Figure 3.32
*Various parametric
alternative forms
using the same
recursive branch-
ing formula; from
the "java_tree"
program on the
attached CD-ROM.*

3.6.1.2 Other Plant-Generation Codes

This same algorithm is easily extended into three dimensions, where tapered cylinders instead of lines are generated (for trunk and branches), producing 3D treelike structures. The 2D angles of branching are replaced by 3D angles, and more branches around the trunk are generated, filling space instead of limited to a plane; otherwise, the algorithm is nearly identical.

Figure 3.33
Four frames from an animation showing a 3D branching growth process. Note also that this displays phototropism; it is growing towards, and has more leaves on the side of, the light source. Modeled and rendered in special research software. Courtesy of Cyril Soler.
(see the "plant-growth.mov" animation on the attached CD-ROM)

These recursive forms are created by mathematical, rather than botanical, approaches. To more closely approach botanical realism, more complicated and variable approaches are required. The L-systems, or generative grammars, explored by Lindenmayer and Prusinkiewicz and others, attempt to introduce more botanically correct growth characteristics into these forms. Basically, these systems are similar to the recursive systems described above, but add more levels of variety, so that trunks, branches, stems, and twigs, while similar, are not identical, and have forms that change with various growth stages. (Technically, these systems use a *replacement grammar*, in which, for example, a trunk gets replaced by a trunk plus a branch; a branch may be replaced by a branch and several stems; a stem may be replaced by a stem plus a bud; a bud replaced by a leaf or flower, and so on.) The interfaces to such programs are similar: you set various parameters and make selections, then the program generates the form in 3D. These may then be exported as polygons or meshes into other modeling and rendering systems.

Some modeling systems may provide for procedural definitions of plantlike materials. Climbing ivy, for example, has a repetitive structure which, by introducing minor random variations, can be made to look quite organic.

3.6.1.3 Growth, Change, and Seasons

Plants in the landscape grow, change and die. Too often, well-meaning designers place plants into environments which look great when they're young, but become much too large for the space; or, alternatively, would look great when mature, but grow so slowly that they look too small and out of place for years after planting. Computer models can help, by visualizing different ages and forms of plant material. Image processing, or parametric generation can be used to generate foliage colors and densities for different seasons.

The simplest approach is to use photographic images of plants in their various stages of growth (as well as with and without leaves, if they are deciduous, for example). This need just increases the value of a large library of well-identified plant images for use.

If 3D models are desired, then the purely photographic approach needs to be augmented by algorithmic solid modeling, using procedures that can generate plants at various growth stages. It's important to note that growth in plants is not just enlarging in scale! Immature forms of temperate deciduous trees typically have a long slender structure, often with overlarge leaves apparently out of scale, and with less developed branching, dominated by a central stem; over time they become more rounded, branched, and filled out.

(Other plants types and species may have different growth habits; many palms, for example, basically develop their foliage fronds very early, and then just grow taller and taller over time.)

Specialized plant-growth simulation and modeling software has been developed that uses botanical rules and observations to generate realistic plants over time. These may create 2D images, like photographs, or 3D models than can be exported into modeling and rendering systems.

The work of Premislaw Prusinkiewicz and his colleagues, at the University of Calgary, has been foremost in demonstrating the use of computer graphics and procedural modeling for plant growth. The French research organization CIRAD has similarly developed models for plant growth and morphogenesis.

Figure 3.34
*Parametrically generated Sugar Maple tree (Acer saccharum) shown with
a. fall foliage;
b. in winter with no foliage.*
Modeled and Rendered in Onyx TreePro. Courtesy of Pjer Zanchi, Onyx Software.

Figure 3.35

a. Illustration showing stages of growth in a pine tree over multiple years.
From plant growth simulation software by AMAP; Courtesy of Stephane Gourgot.
b,c. Summer and fall foliage conditions of the same tree image. Colors adjusted in Photoshop.

Figure 3.36

Illustration of the effect of plant growth over several years, as mature trees screen unattractive views of wires and poles, also providing shade and greenery on residential street. Trees created in AMAP plant simulation software, then inserted by image processing into existing photograph.
Courtesy of Andreas Muhar.

FIgure 3.37 Walkthrough of University Commons with Vegetation

Over a sequence of 950 frames the viewer traverses through the University Commons project with seaonal lighting conditions and vegetative cover. (See the animation "veg-walk.mov" on the CD-ROM.)

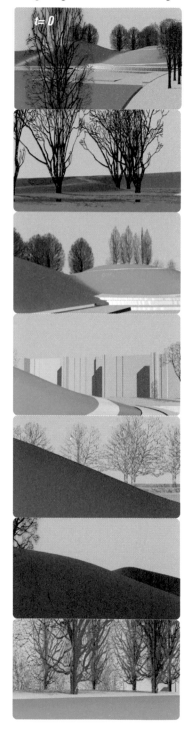

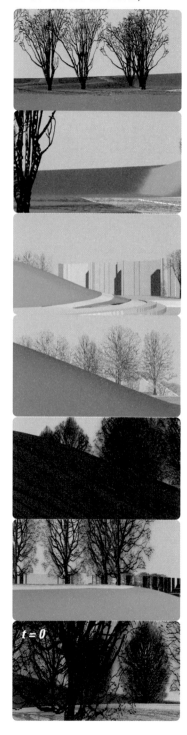

3.6.2 Movement *through* Vegetation

Plants provide vertical structure to the landscape, and in animation, when moved through, contribute visual effects, now obscuring, then revealing other parts of the landscape, covering overhead, providing shade, shadow, and filtered light. The biggest challenge to modelers creating animated virtual tours, walk-throughs and flyovers through landscapes with vegetation, is to use these characteristics of plants to enhance the visual and virtual experience.

3.6.2.1 Vegetation Walk-throughs

In 3D models, especially those which the viewer can move through, whether interactively or along a pre-choreographed path, two complications arise from the simple billboard technique. The first problem is that billboards have only one or two good sides; when viewed end-on, they vanish to an infinitely thin line (cross section of a plane), and as viewing angle changes from head-on to more oblique, the flat plane shrinks in apparent size. These two combine to create the unnerving visual effect of trees shrinking and expanding as the viewer moves around, even disappearing and then winking back into partial view.

For purposes of animations or walk-throughs, or virtual reality simulations, when the viewer's eye level and vantage point may change continually and unpredictably, this flaw needs to be overcome with some technique that presents trees with all good sides, which are visible and correct no mater what the viewing angle. Making a full-blown 3D model is of course one option, but the billboard technique can be extended in two simple ways to retain much of the efficiency and visual appeal of the technique, while allowing for multiple viewpoints. The first technique is to provide two, three, or more intersecting billboards, crossing at the center point, each with the photographic tree image mapped onto it, and transparent otherwise. Then, no matter from what position the image is viewed, there is always at least one photographic image facing the viewer. For most tree images, the shrunken oblique images facing the viewer simply merge into the full-width one with little visual disturbance.

Another approach, in an animated rendering with sufficient computational control to allow it, is to adjust the rotation of each billboard so that at each frame, each texture-mapped plane is rotated to be always perpendicular to the axis of the camera view. Some animation and modeling environments allow for objects to "always face the camera," a useful specific version of the more general constraint "maintain some constant relationship to one or more other objects."

Either of these two methods fails, of course, in the extreme case when the viewer flies up from a side view to have on overhead "bird's-eye" view: either the planes in the first version will vanish again, when viewed from above, after first forming a cross, or a six-rayed star-pattern; or in the second approach, the trees will all appear to lay down on their side when viewed from above!

3.6.3 Movement *of* Vegetation

Other than the phenomenon of their growth, change, and death over time, many plants are also in motion over short time spans, usually under the influence of the wind, rain, and sun. The rippling of blades of grass or rustling of leaves is an essential part of the natural landscape. Less perceptibly, many plants exhibit *phototropism*, the process by which they slowly turn to face the sun as its position changes over the course of the day. Naturally, static images can't show these, except indirectly by, for example, strongly leaning treetrunks and branches, such as are found in windswept landscapes like some mountains or coastlines. Animations are required to truly portray these dynamics.

3.6.3.1 Physics-based Kinetic Systems

While it is possible to generate some motion in 2D and 3D models purely "by eye," using the tricks of sprite animation, and frame-by-frame composition, often these effects can appear unnatural. And they are hard to sustain over time, in interaction with other elements and forces in the scene, or in the landscape. It's better to have these motions generated procedurally, based on simulations of real-world behavior. Although real simulations between thousands, or millions, of elements, are out of range for all but the most powerful computers, there are systems which enable some basic physics, such as gravity and collision, to be embedded in models and virtual worlds. Physical linkages between elements also provides a kind of realistic motion.

Another technique to get realistic movement into animated models is to use some motion-capture system. Originally developed for special effects and animation, these systems typically involve a number of sensors which can be placed on a moving object (often a person, such as dancer or gymnast) and a laser-based tracking system which records 3D coordinates of all the sensors in real time, creating a database of the movement of the many points. This data can then be used by special purpose software to decode the motions and apply them to points in the 3D model, generating simulated movement. This could be done with trees blowing in the wind, waves on water, and so on.

3.6.3.1.1 Blowing in the Wind

Some modeling, rendering, and animation systems make provision for *kinematic* linkage between parts of a digital model, such that when one moves, other connected parts move also, but not as a single composition. That is, a leaf blowing in the wind may move its stem, which in turn may move a twig but to a lesser extent, and the twig move a branch but even less, to the point where the entire tree may sway slightly as a result. These *inverse kinematics* can be used to display the appearance of plants moving in the wind (or, when slower, more viscous movement is generated, such as underwater).

The characteristics of wind must be modeled first, however, since it is not ordinarily of a constant velocity, constant direction like a large fan, but has gusts and changes of direction that lead to characteristic wind-blown motion.

Figure 3.38
Image of tree branches in the wind:
a. idle or gentle breeze on the left;
b. gale-force wind conditions on the right.
(See the animation "tree-breeze.mov" on the CD-ROM.)

3.6.3.2 Forest Growth Models

Some visualization software has begun to introduce the notion of "ecosystems" as a way to model the development of plant communities in response to simple terrain variables, such as elevation, slope, and aspect. In these systems, you can specify which plants are to be found in which ranges of elevation, slope, and aspect, and then corresponding images textures are used to generate a rendering.

Forests of course are no more static than their individual plants; they grow, die, change over time. Their growth is controlled by a myriad of environmental variables (climate, soils, nutrients, and others) as well as management practices such as cutting, clearing, fertilizing. To model all of these interactions and effects is still a challenging research project, and well beyond the scope of this book. Some of the techniques described here, however, should be of use in visualizing the results of these kinds of ecological models.

Figure 3.39
Frames from an animation of trees growing over several seasons in competition for space and light; notice how the center tree is crowded out by the two flanking it. Modeled with special research software. Courtesy of Cyril Soler. (See the animation "forest-growth.mov" on the CD-ROM.)

Summary

Whereas terrain is typically the foundation of any landscape model, it's usually vegetation that gives it texture, color, and much of its three-dimensionality. Photographic textures and images of plant materials – from tiny lichens to giant trees – are a necessary component of the landscape modeler's library. Fully developed 3D models are more time consuming and memory-intensive, but offer advantages in the foreground and in interaction with other architectural elements, or when navigating as in a VR model. Using procedural methods to generate vegetation, either textures or 3D models, is the most effective approach when photographs are not available, or when multiple different stages of growth are required. Similarly, adding dynamism in the form of animation, either of growth or motion, as of leaves blowing in the wind, can add realism to the final result.

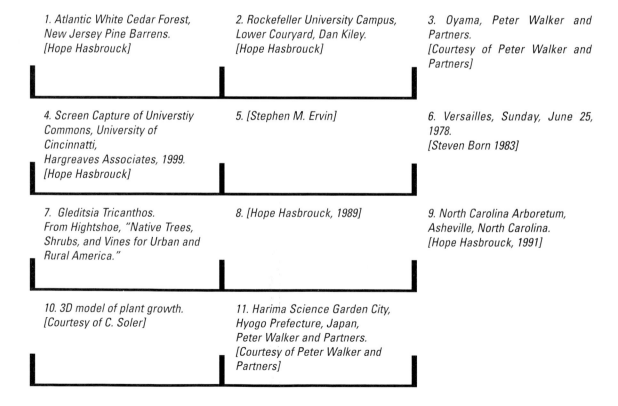

1. Atlantic White Cedar Forest, New Jersey Pine Barrens. [Hope Hasbrouck]

2. Rockefeller University Campus, Lower Couryard, Dan Kiley. [Hope Hasbrouck]

3. Oyama, Peter Walker and Partners. [Courtesy of Peter Walker and Partners]

4. Screen Capture of Universtiy Commons, University of Cincinnatti, Hargreaves Associates, 1999. [Hope Hasbrouck]

5. [Stephen M. Ervin]

6. Versailles, Sunday, June 25, 1978. [Steven Born 1983]

7. Gleditsia Tricanthos. From Hightshoe, "Native Trees, Shrubs, and Vines for Urban and Rural America."

8. [Hope Hasbrouck, 1989]

9. North Carolina Arboretum, Asheville, North Carolina. [Hope Hasbrouck, 1991]

10. 3D model of plant growth. [Courtesy of C. Soler]

11. Harima Science Garden City, Hyogo Prefecture, Japan, Peter Walker and Partners. [Courtesy of Peter Walker and Partners]

References

Carpenter, Philip, Theodore Walker, and Frederick Lanphear. *Plants in the Landscape*. San Francisco, CA: W. H. Freeman and Company, 1975.

Dirr, Michael A. *Manual of Woody Landscape Plants*. Champaign, Illinois: Stipes Publishing Co., 1990.

Hightshoe, Gary. *Native Trees, Shrubs, and Vines for Urban and Rural America*. New York, NY: Van Nostrand Reinhold Company, 1988.

Prusinkiewicz, Premislaw and A. Lindenmayer. *Algorithmic Beauty of Plants*. New York, NY: Springer-Verlag, 1990.

Zion, Robert L. *Trees for Architecture and the Landscape*. New York, NY: Van Nostrand Reinhold Company, 1968.

Figure 3.40

a. Forest scene in southwestern Alberta, Canada; the current conditions of a subalpine forested landscape.
b. The same scene as above illustrating the impact of a very severe fire event.
Courtesy of Doug Olson,
Olson + Olson Planning and Design, Calgary Alberta.
Modeled and rendered in World Construction Set software.
Client: Alberta Environment, Integrated Resource Management.

planar

ripple

fluid

paraline

surface

parametric sol

fountain

pool

system

parbcle system

network

dynamic

Water 4

4.1 Introduction

Water, even when unseen in the landscape, is everywhere, and all-important. Water is never alone in the landscape; it is held and shaped by landform, which is revealed at the edges, banks, and beaches. Vegetation depends upon the workings of the hydrologic cycle, as water moves through the landscape, often underground, and through the atmosphere, giving rise to weather and atmospheric effects including snow, fog, rainbows, and others. Water is sometimes still as glass, placidly reflecting the sky and landscape around it, sometimes barely rippling, giving sparkling glints of reflected sunlight to the scene, sometimes turbulent and tumultuous, as at the beach in a storm, or at the base of a waterfall.

Landscape designers use water in a variety of ways, from the artfully "natural-looking" drainage ways of Frederick Law Olmsted's famous Muddy River improvements in Boston's Emerald Necklace to the carefully designed and controlled water channels and fountains that give comfort and aural/visual delight in the historic Moorish gardens at the Alhambra, in Spain. In the atmosphere, water finds its expression in a wide variety of ways: as rain and snow in precipitation; as fog, mist, and valley haze; as clouds in the sky, and as rainbows in the aftermath of rain.

This chapter covers the basic representational techniques for water: in static form, as flat or rippled "glass," with color, reflectivity, refractivity, and transparency, and in dynamic form, using techniques including particle systems. More examples of moving water are found on the attached CD-ROM.

INTERNAL REPRESENTATION

EXTERNAL REPRESENTATION	2D representation paraline drawings hypsography	3D representation surface: polygon / plane	bump map	parametric ripple
wireframe				
simple color				
texture maps				
diffuse map				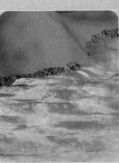
multichannel /procedural				

182

particle motion blur

particle shower

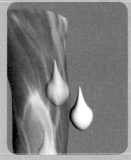

4.2 2D Models of Water

The many forms and properties of water present special challenges to digital modelers. In its most simplified forms, water may be simulated as reflective glass, haze simulated by a progressive lightening and blueing of landscape colors in the distance, and rainbows painted in; but in its more dynamic forms, rippling and forming waves on ponds and lakes, sparkling, splashing waterfalls and fountains, pouring rain and thunderstorms, water requires complex motion control and particle systems.

4.2.1 Paraline/Orthographic Drawings

Water, having no real edges or fixed shape, is hard to represent in a 2D line drawing. Typically, it is only indicated by its effects, such as a shoreline, or surface features such as ripples or waves. Plans and sections may have indications of water's edge, or elevation.

4.2.2 Hypsography

Just as terrain (*topography*) is most simply modeled in 2D by the use of contour lines, water is also described by contours of the underwater basin, or *hypsography*. These contours only represent the shape of the underwater surface, and not the water's elevation, which is naturally slowly changing over time, due to rainfall and evaporation. (Typically, water's elevation is given as an average, or *mean*, as in the case of the average value for the ocean's water, *mean sea level*, or *MSL*, a value taken between high and low tides, and averaged over several seasons, or even years.)

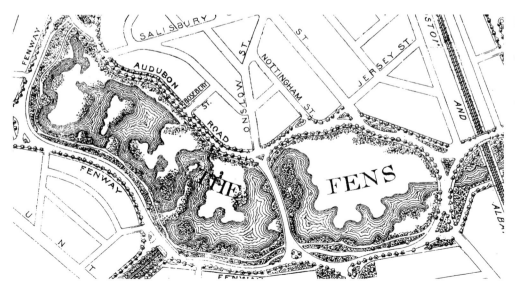

Figure 4.1
From the original plan for the "Improvements to the Muddy River," part of Boston's "Emerald Necklace" by Frederick Law Olmsted. These hypsographic contour lines in the bodies of water are really more cartographic symbols than accurate indicators of subsurface elevation.

4.3 3D Models of Water

4.3.1 Surfaces

In 3D, although water has volume which is important to its visual appearance, it's usually the surface characteristics that are most readily modeled. Starting with a simple flat plane and adding ripples and waves when appropriate, water can be represented most effectively with surface characteristics.

4.3.1.1 Flat Planes

Water has three important physical and optical characteristics which give it much of its appearance in the landscape: it's in varying proportions *transparent*, *refractive,* and *reflective*. Often defined as a clear liquid, water in the landscape primarily takes its color from its surroundings (except when it has other materials — sediment, dye, algae — providing coloration). Blue water is mostly blue from the sky, although, of course, minerals and other underwater conditions add a variety of colorations to water.

4.3.1.2 Rippled Surfaces

Water's liquid surface gives rise to surface irregularities under the slightest effect of wind or other disturbance. These irregularities are most often waves and ripples which have a simple underlying mathematical structure, overlaid with random "noise."

For modeling purposes, a simple *sinusoidal* wave form can be created in modeling software, either radial/concentric, like the ripples generated by a pebble falling into water, or linear, like the waves rolling in on a beach, and often with some control over *damping* or "decay" over distance. Two or more of these wave forms superimposed on a flat surface can generate an appropriately rough, patterned surface for water. The interjection of additional noise, or random perturbation is also often possible, which can add to the variety of effects. Finally some texture maps used for water can have procedural noise embedded in them to introduce the roughness as part of the rendering process.

Figure 4.2
*Water as
a. a flat blue plane,
and
b. a rippled surface.*

4.3.1.3 Lakes and Ponds

Large areas of water, such as lakes and ponds, harbors and marinas, are contained and defined by the landform that surrounds them. (The edge of water is the best example of a "real" contour line!) A model of such waterbodies can be made by creating a detailed terrain model, with contours describing the basin in which the water sits (hypsography), and then placing a simple flat plane or surface of water at the correct elevation. The hidden underground areas of the water surface will be invisible when rendered, and the water's edge will be perfectly described by the intersection of the terrain surface with the water surface. One advantage of this technique is that the water elevation can be easily varied, and can even be animated over time to illustrate, for example, the tidal flux in a marine basin. Often a special surface texture or covering should be used right at the water's edge (sand and gravel, or rocks, e.g.), and should be applied in a band at the correct elevation range, especially if the water's elevation will be varied.

It's important to create an approximately correct hypsographic surface, at least for a range of elevations near the water's edge, if the water condition is to be accurate in its depth; the deep middle or bottom of the basin is naturally less important, except in special circumstances when you might want to visualize underwater conditions, for example.

Figure 4.3
a. Terrain model with blue water surface below it.
b. Water level at normal elevation.
c. Water surface elevation raised above normal, showing flood condition.

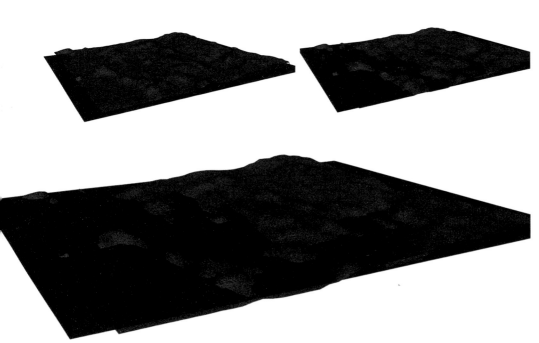

4.3.2 Solid Representations

Using multiple layered surfaces is an effective way of generating depth in water features, but water may also be modeled as a solid volume. This is necessary, for example, to take advantage of refraction in rendering the water volume.

4.3.2.1 Simple Parametric Solids – Prisms

The simplest volumetric/solid form for water is just the solid created by the water-containing shape, a rectangular prism, or cylinder, or half-sphere, etc. When modeling a pool or fountain, this is usually adequate. Often, you can benefit from adding an additional surface layer above the solid volume. Rippling waves are often better implemented on a mesh surface than on a solid.

A single droplet of water, such as dew on a leaf, can be formed from a sphere; adding some deformation, to squash the water droplet under its own weight, adds realism. Either mesh-deforming a sphere or using *meta-balls* is the best approach for this task. A tear-drop shape with a somewhat pointed trailing end can be generated in the same way, or by creating a surface of revolution around a profile.

Water naturally does not take on this "jello-like" form in nature, but often these solids or prisms are required in a model to fill up a basin in a container, especially if there is transparency such that a simple surface will not suffice.

Figure 4.4
Transparent solid volumes of "water": cylindrical, rectangular, and hemispherical.

4.3.2.2 Falling Water

Falling water takes on organic, twisted, irregular forms under the force of gravity, wind, and the effects of surface tension. Modeling these forms is similar to modeling tree trunks and requires the use of twisting, braiding, and other curvilinear distortions. Often, a lofted surface along a smoothly curved arc trajectory is a good beginning. Then some organic deformations, such as twisting, or smooth bumps and swellings, can be added. Getting realistic water forms is difficult, due to the fluid and dynamic nature of real water, but coupled with appropriate textures using color and transparency, and using other visual cues such as structures and containers, the visual effect can be convincing. More effective falling water may be accomplished using particle systems to create a stream of "objects." For most effective modeling of falling water, using animation coupled with sound is required.

Figure 4.5
Images of solid water forms: sheets, cylinders, jets, drops created with solid modeling primitives and warping modifiers such as twisting and tapering.

Figure 4.6
A two-tiered fountain with rivulets of water created using particle systems.

4.3.2.3 Spray, Mist, Drops

When falling or moving water breaks up further into droplets, spray, and foam, particle systems may be the best approach for generating appropriate images. A photographic image map of bubbles or foam might serve for a static image, to be carefully hand applied. Foam is usually best modeled as a texture map on an irregularly shaped blob, set floating on water.

Spray is best simulated by the result of a particle system emitting multiple droplets. Depending on the scene composition, details, and lighting, these can be modeled as tiny spheres or blurred streaks or just white dots.

Mist is best modeled using some built-in fog generation. Ideally, this should be not just haze, applied with a constant density over distance, but should have "patchiness." This effect can typically only be created with some kind of procedural texture. Clouds are almost certainly best managed by photographic textures and environment maps – see Chapter 5 for more on atmospheric water.

Figure 4.7

Images of particle systems:
a. Four different particle emitters: a rectangular area, a solid line, a point, and a cone.
The simple particle streams they emit are like water falling straight down under the influence of gravity.
b. Particle "warping" and "deflection": particles lifted up, as if by a current of air, or a swarm of bees; particles shooting straight out and falling under the influence of gravity; bouncing off a reflective plane; and piling up on and around a spherical defllector.

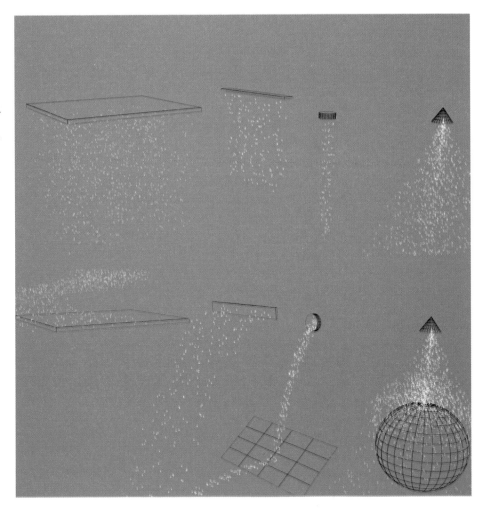

4.4 Textures for Water

Since its physical shape and geometry are so elusive, water's presence in the landscape is mostly conveyed by textures – color, sparkles, reflections– as well as by its secondary effects (depressions in landform and changes in vegetation, e.g.)

4.4.1 Simple Color

Although water as a chemical element is colorless, water in the landscape may well have an inherent color, due to minerals, sediments, and other impurities as well as surrounding landscape conditions. Blue or green hues are common, but so too are brown, depending on whether the water body is the Caribbean sea (many shades of azure), or the Mississippi River (mostly shades of ochre and brown). Lighting conditions, including both the environmental lights (sun, sky, and moon) and artificial lights – including those placed in and under water for effect – have a big impact on the look and color of water. When the digital modeling task is not a literal representation, the choice of water color may also be determined by desired mood and atmosphere, ranging from cheerful and playful to somber and menacing.

Water color is not solid, or pure, but rather tends to be mottled, swirled, and mixed. Creating water colors and textures is a matter of choosing a combination of colors and applying them as textures with appropriate patterns, either taken from nature or created using various software or image processing techniques for mixing and swirling.

Figure 4.8
A pool of water at Hamilton Springs, outside of Austin, Texas. The blue and green colors are variegated by shadows, reflections, depth, and surface ripples.

4.4.1.1 Transparency

All water is to some degree transparent, permitting light to pass through it, enabling the viewer to see into it to the surface and objects below. In a well-maintained aquarium, the water truly becomes a clear medium, revealed only by the motion of fish and seaweed within. Water in the landscape has a limit to its transparency. Even the crystal waters of the sea, sometimes permitting vision as much as 10 meters or more below, has a measurable "cloudiness," measured by scientists as *turbidity*. This gives a diminishing transparency with distance, as with other transparent materials including glass.

Figure 4.9
Water surfaces over a textured pebble surface, at varying degrees of transparency:
a. 10%
b. 50%
c. 90%

TECHNICAL NOTE
In rendering, transparency of materials is often expressed as a parameter varying from zero to one (or from 0 to 255 in an 8-bit data representation), with 0.0 (or 0) being completely transparent and 1.0 (or 255) being completely opaque. This value (often carried in a transparency mask, or alpha channel) is really descriptive of the transparency at a pixel level: a transparent pixel will not obscure an underlying one at all, an opaque one will completely block the underlying, and a 50% transparent one will permit the underlying pixels to be seen through the top one, in some manner (averaging brightness and color values, for example).

4.4.1.2 Reflectivity

In addition to transparency, water also has a degree of *reflectivity*, perhaps its most striking characteristic in the landscape, especially when viewed at a distance. Light rays striking the water's surface both penetrate it transparently, subject to the refraction and diminution with distance, and are reflected at an opposite angle (in simple reflection, "the angle if reflection is equal and opposite to the angle of incidence"). The proportion of the light that is reflected from water is a function of the angle of incidence (light striking perpendicularly is mostly absorbed, light striking at an oblique angle is mostly reflected). When water is perfectly smooth, it may appear much like a glass mirror. Usually though, water has surface ripples which give rise to interrupted and irregular reflections, with highlights which appear as sparkles.

Often, water is used in the designed landscape as a reflecting element, intended to give added depth, meaning, or grandeur to the landscape, or buildings around it. The reflecting pools at the Taj Mahal in India and at the Lincoln Memorial in Washington, D.C. are famous examples.

Figure 4.10
A fountain and reflecting pool at the moorish gardens at the Alhambra, Spain. The channel of water in the ground represents heaven, and appropriately reflects the sky.

4.4.1.3 Refractivity

Refraction is the physical property of bending light rays, due to varying density of the material the light passes through. In a controlled fashion, using curved surfaces of glass or water, refraction is the basis of every lens, enabling magnification and concentration (focus). In a more simple fashion, through a prism, refraction bends different frequencies of visible light by different amounts, giving rise to rainbows and other appearances of spectra. In water, light waves refract as they pass from air into water, giving rise to the appearance of displacement of objects underwater, sometimes accompanied by slight magnification. In the case of a straight pole immersed into still water, the pole will appear bent at an angle of a few degrees.

It is the refractive quality of water that gives rise to rainbow-hued sparkles from dewdrops, and ultimately, to the appearance of rainbows when sunlight passes through water in the atmosphere. (See Chapter 5 for more about atmospheric effects.)

Figure 4.11
a. Diagram of angles of reflection (above) and refraction (below). b. Illustration of the effects of reflection and refraction as a pole passes through a volume of "water." Notice the extra (unrealistic) reflection on the bottom face of the cylinder, an artifact caused by the renderer used to produce this image in 3DStudioMax.

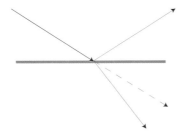 

TECHNICAL NOTE

Reflection and refraction both give visual effects as a result of the angle of a beam of light; in the case of reflection, as it strikes a reflective surface; in the case of refraction, as it passes from one medium (usually air) into another (such as water). For reflection, the rule is simple: $øi = ør$, or angle of incidence = angle of reflection. When there are surface irregularities (e.g. the surface is not perfectly flat) there may be scattering that results giving rise to *specular* highlights and sparkling, when all or most of the light is reflected back in a single direction; or diffuse reflection, when the light beam is scattered into all or many directions. Many rendering systems give fine control over the specular as well as the diffuse component of reflective surfaces.

In the case of refraction, the equation is a bit more complex:

$n_1 \sin ø_1 = n_2 \sin ø_2$ (Snell's Law)

where n_1 and n_2 are the refraction index of the first and second medium, and $ø_1$ and $ø_2$ are the angles of the light beam (from the normal) in the first and second medium.

The index of refraction is related to the speed of light in the medium, so for a vacuum it is 1.0, for air it is 1.00029, for water at 20° C it is 1.33, and for glass, around 1.5

4.4.2 Multichannel Textures

The combination of color, transparency, refractivity, and surface texture makes modeling water a complex task. Combining multiple layers with various levels of transparency and colors is a good beginning. Often, in real water, with a shallow bank, colors are gradated from transparent, revealing underwater stones, sand, and gravel at the shallowest part, to pale blues and greens with less underwater detail visible, to darkest blues and greens (or browns, or black, depending on the lighting and water condition) with no subsurface detail visible at the deepest. This can be modeled by three layered surfaces, each with color and transparency, and possibly an image map at the bottom.

Creating a water surface that has realistic waves is hard to do by hand. Many modeling and rendering systems have plug-ins or built-in functions for generating waves and ripples; but sometimes just using a photographic texture works as well.

Figure 4.12
a,b. Photographic texture maps used for foliage at water's edge and and pebbles in a stream bed.
c. Perspective view showing tilted plane of the ground surface embedded in volume of water, texture maps applied for foliage and pebbles.
d. Final rendering of water and pebbles at stream edge.

Water Surface Textures

Water's surface ranges from glassy smooth to rippling, wavy, and turbulent. Colors range from green to red, and transparency and reflection add to complexity of water surfaces. A gallery of photographs of water in different conditions is a valuable adjunct to the landscape modeler's library.

4.4.3 Underwater Effects

The landscape underwater (*aquascape*) is visually determined mostly by lighting conditions. Three special effects dominate: color, murkiness, and light rays. The characteristic colors of underwater range from bright blue to muddy brown, with corresponding varieties in murkiness. Murkiness can be modeled as very strong atmospheric haze (see Chapter 5).

The refractive (focusing and bending) characteristics of water give rise to unique underwater lighting conditions. Sometimes, rays of sunlight passing through still water illuminate particles in the water and create the effect of visible shafts of light (sometimes called "God rays"). The other condition comes from ripples and small waves on the surface creating braided, curving patterns of light, called *caustics*. Modeling these is best undertaken with special texture maps; some special-purpose software or rendering "plug-ins" have also been developed just for modeling underwater effects.

Figure 4.13
a,b. Images of caustic light patterns.
c. Underwater scene with "God rays" in ocean water; caustics on top surface of whales.
Courtesy of Rodney Hoinkes, Immersion Studios Inc.

4.4.4 Wet Objects

Water occurs not only on its own in the landscape, but it can color and change other elements. Wet objects have a combination of shininess or slickness in appearance, as well as often a physical change in shape as well (drooping under gravity from the added weight of the water, for example, and with sharp edges softened, as with wet fabric). Water also tends to darken colors of materials such as paving. Since water evaporates, and is fluid to begin with, the outlines of wetness are usually irregular and patchy. Wet surfaces are best modeled with a combination of color, shininess, and photographic texture.

4.4.5 Puddles

Puddles occur in the landscape as a result of irregularities and depressions in the terrain. Even the most carefully leveled paved parking area has small, local imperfections, and water finds and highlights them, from its tendency to run to lower elevations, and to "seek its own level," forming small local perfectly flat areas which contrast with the surrounding terrain. On brick, asphalt, or concrete, often these puddles, over time, form a kind of "bathtub ring" of stain or discoloration that extends around the perimeter of the puddle. Modeling puddles can be done in the same way as described for lakes and ponds earlier: a flat surface of water is superimposed over the slightly irregular terrain of bricks or paving. Where the water is exposed is the puddle.

In some cases, built surfaces will be modeled as smooth and flat, without surface imperfections, and these may be difficult to introduce. In this case, you can use a slightly irregular warped water surface; when it is overlaid on the smooth paving surface, the same effect is achieved: only those parts of the water surface raised above the paving surface will be visible. It may take some tinkering with the geometry and surface irregularities to achieve the desired effect. Reflection and transparency are important for this kind of very shallow water.

Figure 4.14
Puddles simulated by an undulating water surface overlaid on a flat paving surface. Modeled and rendered in 3DStudio Max.

4.4.6 Snow and Ice

Water in its frozen form – as snow or ice – can cover and transform the landscape, at least in temperate and colder climates. In its simplest form, snow covering is just a whitish surface on terrain, with various colorations, textures, and reflective qualities. Frozen water, such as ice on a lake or pond, may take on a variety of colors and textures, from shiny transparent black ice to matte white or dull gray. Often, entrapped air and other impurities cause ice to become cloudy and opaque, but because it retains some of the water's transparency, refractivity and reflectivity, it can have a wide range of visual appearance.

One form of icy water in the landscape occurs after a freezing rain, or hail storm, which results in ice layered and encrusted over all elements in the landscape, notably the branches of trees. This crystalline world is full of tiny reflections, refractions, sparkles, and rainbows. A simple geometric modeling approach is to take selected branches and twigs, make a duplicate object, scale it to slightly enlarge it, center it on the original, and set the material properties of this casing object to ice-like (transparent and shiny, at least).

Figure 4.15
a. A field of snow, on rolling terrain, with bright direct lighting to match the background sky image.
b. Ice "cubes" on an icy surface.
Modeled and rendered in 3DStudioMax.

Figure 4.16
a. A forested hillside covered in snow.
b. Tree branches covered in snow.
Modeled and rendered in Blueberry3D. Courtesy of A. Ogren, Blueberry3D.

4.5 GIS-based Hydrologic Models

At the scale of the larger region, you can use GIS data and software to create representations of water in the landscape. In addition to digital elevation models (DEMs) from the USGS, you can obtain hydrologic features maps, which show streams, rivers, and lakes in vector format (lines and polygons). You can use these maps, along with other features such as vegetation, or aerial photography, to create a geospecific texture map, with enhanced blue colors for water, to drape over the terrain. You may have to widen the streams and rivers to have them show up, depending on the scale and the angle, amount of vegetation, and other factors in the visualization.

Figure 4.17
a. Streams and lake show as blue in landcover GIS map.
b. The water level in the lake is artificially elevated by inserting a flat blue plane at a new higher level in the 3D perspective view, to visualize the effect of raised water level.

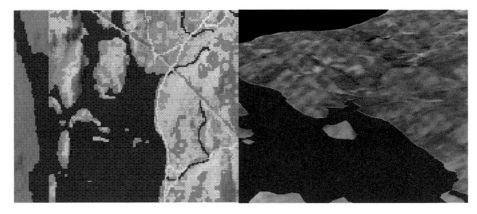

Often, the degree of precision in the DEM is pretty coarse, compared to the linear water features, and you may need to slightly exaggerate the relief in the vicinity of the water. This technique, which has been called "burning in" the hydrologic features in to the DEM, consists of just lowering each grid cell in the DEM by a specified amount – usually just a few feet, or less than a meter – underneath the water features. This helps to emphasize the way the water sits in, or cuts into, the landscape.

You can also use GIS software to determine some hydrologic characteristics from the DEM. One common use of GIS is to delineate *watersheds* – regions of land which all drain to a common outflow, usually a stream or river – for purposes of planning or natural resource management. For example, a logging operation upstream in a watershed may have some soil erosion or pollution implications in the waterways below, and identifying which areas of land drain into which bodies of water is an important step in making these simulations or analyses. GIS software often can also perform an analysis of *flow accumulation*, for example, to predict how much water will run off the surface and into the streams and rivers, and at what points, in the process of simulating floods or changes in water levels with changes in precipitation, or of built and natural surfaces.

In nature, water is moving through the ground and through the atmosphere all the time, in the course of the hydrologic cycle, through evaporation, condensation, precipitation, and surface and underground flow. Modeling the dynamics of this cycle is a complex undertaking, involving physics-based formulas and techniques beyond the present scope. A number of software packages are in use for civil engineering calculations of runoff, hydraulic head, and other hydrologic functions. You should be able to use some of the techniques presented here to visualize different stages in, or aspects of, the hydrologic cycle as calculated by these other programs, especially when linked to GIS to give a spatial georeferenced component.

GIS systems can also be used to visualize subsurface water. Here, the issue iss ordinarily not photorealism, since the water can't be seen at all normally, but some sort of coloring and transparency which highlight the rise and fall of water levels, often around wells or other subsurface features.

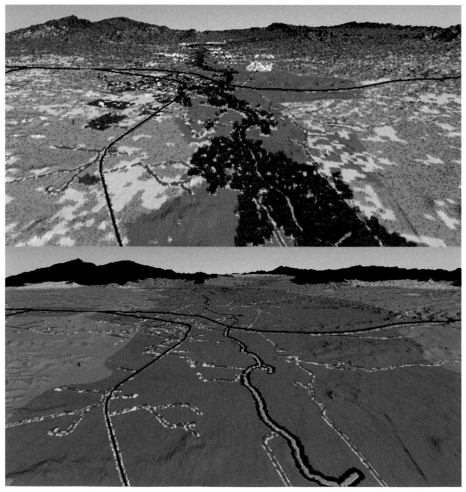

Figure 4.18
Images from GIS study of the effects of regional growth plans on subsurface water supplies in the region of the San Pedro River, Arizona.
a. Aerial view of development pattern.
b. False color view showing subsurface water levels, dropping due to aquifer depletion from water supply wells.
Modeled in ArcInfo and rendered in World Construction Set.
Courtesy of Michael and Tereza Flaxman, Carl Steinitz, et al, Harvard University Design School.

4.6 Water Dynamics

Figure 4.19

Images of physics-based water simulations, in which water splashes and waves are simulated as multiple tiny droplets interacting according to the laws of physics and hydrodynamics.
Courtesy of Jessica Hodgin, Georgia Tech Animation Lab Water Simulation Project.

Beyond its visual characteristics, perhaps the most important characteristic of water is its fluidity, which enables it to flow and to alter its surface form in myriad ways, from mirror flat to rippling waves to roiling turbulence, and to change its form from ice to steam. These dynamics are of course impossible to truly represent in still images or solid geometric models. There are, however, some basic techniques for starting to model the forms characteristic of moving water, including waves, ripples, bubbles, streams, so that elements such as fountains and waterfalls can be introduced into your landscape model.

The best techniques for modeling water dynamics employ so-called *physics-based* models, and are not ordinarily available in basic modeling and rendering packages. These physics-based models use complicated systems of multiple interacting particles, coupled with physical laws and descriptions of such characteristics as viscosity, surface tension and others to simulate the micro-behavior, and then appearance, of water.

These kinds of techniques are absolutely necessary for realistic interactions with water, or when modeling splashes or waves from virtual interactions, where real forces should be at work. For many illustrative purposes, such physics-based models are not necessary, and understanding the desired appearance of motion or dynamics may be good enough.

 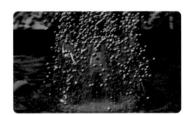 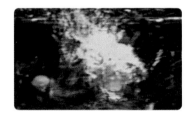

4.6.1 Movement through Water

Choreographing an animation through water (swimming?) is similar to animations in thin air; except the motion should be slower and more fluid. A boat smoothly sailing over a body of water is most likely to have a smooth spline path, with no abrupt changes in motion of viewpoint. A creature (heron, or human, etc.) splashing through water is likely to have motion characterized by regular short stops, and possibly abrupt changes in motion. Swimming underwater is getting rather far from the landscape experience, and scope of this book, but can best be modeled by smooth motion coupled with appropriate cues (bubbles, splashing surface, possibly a face mask, etc.) Subdued lighting and heightened distance haze, or murkiness, can also add to an underwater feeling.

Figure 4.20 *Simulated Flooding of the Willamette River in Oregon*

Frames from an animation of simulated flooding of the Willamette River in Oregon, using GIS data and aerial photography. These images illustrate the spatial and temporal pattern of floodplain inundation of a 1000-acre site, showing the changes to both the timing and amount of inundation with historic side-channels reconnected to the main river channel.

Courtesy of Maureen Raad and David Diethelm, University of Oregon, Eugene. Modeled and rendered in ElectricImage.

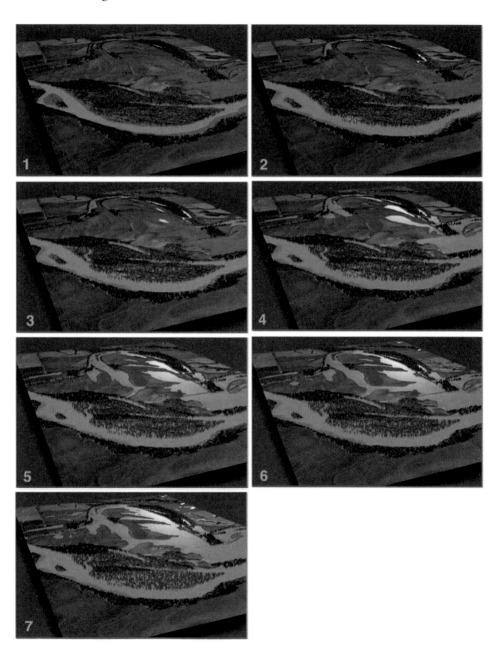

4.6.2 Movement of Water

Effectively modeling the motion of water requires either a very good "painterly" approach to capturing the essential visual qualities of moving water, or some computational tools that actually use physics-based simulation techniques, whether simple or extremely sophisticated, to create waves, turbulence, eddies, and the other characteristics of fluid dynamics. Some modeling and rendering software has various "special effects" for water motion embedded, which can be used for both animation and captured still images of moving water.

Figure 4.21
"Alaska": rendering of a river scene with floating logs and water turbulence. Modeled and rendered in Animatek World Builder. Courtesy of Igor Borovikov

Figure 4.22 *"Sea Gull"*

Several frames from the animation "SeaGull," on the CD-ROM, showing animated ocean waves, as well as wind. Modeled and rendered in Animatek World Builder. Courtesy of Igor Borovikov.

4.6.2.1 Ripples and Waves

The complex forms and patterns made by wind passing over water, which we perceive as waves, small or large, follow a basic mathematical structure: all waves can be characterized by *amplitude* (height) and *frequency* (horizontal spacing), and under physical conditions, some *decay* of these two over time or distance. Under normal conditions, these are fairly regular, so basic waveforms have a repeating, regularly-spaced characteristic. This regularity is ordinarily modulated by local variations and randomness, so that mathematically pure waveforms are usually not found in nature. Also, waves in fluids travel, reflect, and intersect, so that in a contained volume, there are many and complex interactions of waveforms at work.

Using the built-in ripples and waves of many modeling and rendering packages to create animations is in most cases a simple matter of setting the parameters of the wave forms over time. Typically some decay or damping over time should be applied, as real waves lose their force with age, and eventually fade out. Special-purpose simulations or rendering plug-ins are available for simulating the complex surface of the ocean, whose waves are created by interactions of tides, currents and winds, leading to many smaller waves on the surface of larger "structural" swells.

Creating a vortex, or whirlpool, is not something you can do with ordinary modeling packages; rather some more sophisticated physics-based modeling is usually employed. You may be able to make an interesting mode of a vortex using some twist options, if they are available. This is more likely to work for a static, rather than a dynamic model, since a vortex has real circular motion of the water at the surface, not just spiral twisting.

Most simple modeling/rendering software is not sophisticated or powerful enough to model wave reflections, when the wave hits a wall or surface, as such simulations depend on a detailed physical analysis and complex energy equations. For most ordinary visualization purposes, this is not a major drawback.

Figure 4.23
a. A complex series of waves, with higher and lower frequency waves superimposed, makes a realistic ocean surface.
b. A simple ripple in a flat surface.

TECHNICAL NOTE

Waveforms can be smooth or jagged: sawtooth, and square-wave forms are encountered in electronics, but in nature mostly it's the smoothly curved ones we are interested in. The *sine wave*, which has the form

$$y = \sin x \text{, in 2D, or}$$
$$z = \sin (\text{distance}(x,y)) \text{ in 3D}$$

is used universally to create many different natural phenomena, and has characteristic peaks and troughs.

All waveforms can be described by four quantities: frequency, amplitude, decay rate, and phase.

Frequency refers to the spacing of the peaks, or troughs, one to the next. A low-frequency wave has a longer time between peaks; high-frequency, a shorter time.

Amplitude is the height of the peak (or depth of the trough), measured from the adjacent trough (or peak).

Decay rate is a ratio, or speed, with which the amplitude decreases over time.

Phase refers to the alignment of the wave, whether a peak or a trough is over the origin. For trigonometric functions, this varies from -1 to +1, over a distance of pi (3.14) units.

A simple animation of a wave can be created by setting the phase to change over time, so the wave appears to roll; the higher the phase change, the more sequential peaks and troughs will appear over time.

4.6.2.2 Waterfalls

In nature, water usually finds its course embedded in the terrain, from rivers and streams to the deep chasms of the Grand Canyon, with extremely gentle, often nearly horizontal, slopes. Sometimes, however, when the underlying geologic surface is hard enough, water falls over rocks, creating cascades and waterfalls. Under the influence of obstacles and gravity, water loses its placid and flat surface, and becomes undulating, ropy, streaming, and tumultuous.

Modeling a waterfall in a static 3D model is a matter of choosing surfaces and solids with appropriate forms (rounded, perhaps multiple intersecting) and carefully controlled colors and textures. The biggest obstacle is overcoming the tendency for the water to look solid, or frozen. Transparency and "noisy" texture are both necessary. Adding sparkles and highlights adds to the watery effect, as do bubbles and foam. The best approach, however, is to use particle systems and create an animation, possibly with sound. With this method, you have less control over color and reflection, but more control over flow parameters and the effects of gravity, and the trace left by the particles is more realistic, especially over obstacles or "deflectors."

Figure 4.24
a. A waterfall in nature.
b. A model of a waterfall, using particle systems for the falling water and deflectors, reflection, and transparency in the pool below. Modeled and rendered in 3DStudio Max.

4.6.2.3 Fountains

Artificial fountains are sometimes designed to look and behave just like natural waterfalls, so all of the same techniques apply. Often, however, built fountains have strongly architectural details to them, and unnatural waterforms, such as spouts and sprays, which benefit from other modeling techniques.

Built fountains are often contained in architectural structures, from basins and channels to walls, within, through, or over which the water flows. In this case, getting the base structure right is the first step. You can use boolean operations to create cavities and basins (subtracting a rectangular solid from another larger rectangular solid, or a sphere from a larger block, for example) and use bump maps, textures, and surface warping to create rock, concrete, or other textures.

Then you can add the water. Using a combination of solids, surfaces, and particle systems may be required. For water that you can see through, volumes or surfaces with appropriate coloring, transparency, and refraction are best. The techniques for making solid falling water discussed above can be useful. For falling or spraying water, particle systems give best results. Rippled water surfaces or waves can be added for increased realism. In animations, the parameters for the rippling, bending, twisting and so on can be set to change slightly over time, introducing the kind of dynamic variability that typifies moving water.

Figure 4.25
Model of a fountain with water falling from a channel in a brick wall into a basin. Modeled and rendered in 3D Studio Max.
(See also the "fountain.mov" animation on CD-ROM.)
Inspired by water fountains of the landscape architect Luis Barragan.

MAKING A WATERFALL OR FOUNTAIN

Objective:
To produce a rendered image of a water feature with flowing/falling water, such as a fountain or fall.

Inputs:
- 3D geometry of basin, container, or topography
- Digital images of textures for surfaces, including water
- A particle animation system

Step 1.

Assemble source material.

a. Acquire or generate 3D geometry. For natural water features, this is just the topo map or grading plan, but it may be augmented with cross sections or specific 3D models of boulders, basins, cast-concrete features, etc.

b. If the water feature involves a basin or pool, etc., you should be careful to generate the void, possibly by using boolean subtraction operations. You will also want to create a solid volume of water to fill the basin. This may also be done with boolean operations. You will have to specify the top elevation of the water volume, keeping it at a specific depth, just below the lip of the basin, or as needed.

c. Acquire digital images of textures by scanning or by capturing with a digital camera, etc. Water images may be useful for textures of water surfaces.

Step 2. Apply textures to geometry for all the non-water elements.

Step 3. Apply water textures, colors, transparency, and reflectivity to water elements. Reflection is an "expensive" (time-consuming) operation in ray-tracing, so it is best to limit its use to those areas or elements where its visual effect is essential, such as the basin or pool at the bottom of a fountain or fall. Two-layer surfaces may be effective for water surfaces, with a top layer more transparent, revealing a second more colorful layer.

Step 4. Make a test rendering, and adjust eye position, camera, and lighting parameters for best visual effect, highlighting desired features and providing sufficient detail in areas of interest.

Step 5. Adjust 3D geometry if needed, to align surfaces, obscure or reveal views, etc. Often the addition of a few boulders at the foot of a natural water feature adds realism.

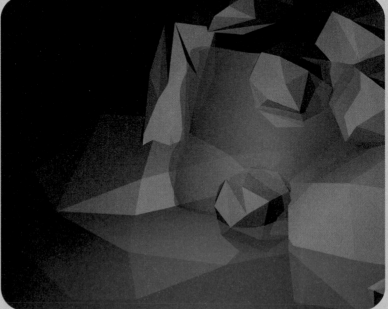

Step 6. Add falling water. This may take the form of solids and/or particles.

a. Solids. Use cylinders, sweep operations, and various 3D modifiers to add bends, twists, and taper to create realistic rivulets, streams, or sheets of water. Multiple layers and intersecting objects can add realism. Add water textures and transparency.

b. Solids/Animation: For animations, vary the parameters of twist and taper over time, to give the effect of undulating water.

c. Particles: Use available particle system to create a stream of particles alone, or in combination with transparent solids. Create several emitters of correct shape and position to generate particle stream, whether a focused spray, or sheet, etc. Use available deflectors or trajectory controls to simulate effect of gravity, pulling stream down. Vary the settings of particle generation and force to achieve desired effects. For most water features, very dense particle generation is appropriate.

d. Particles/Deflectors: Use deflectors located along with 3D geometry to cause rocks, boulders, ledges, and basin lips to splash or deflect water for most realistic effects.

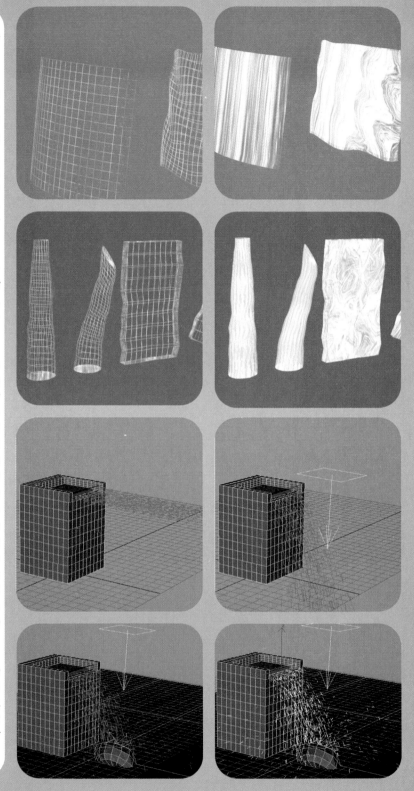

e. Particles/Animation. Use available particle generation parameters, varied over time, to give realistic effects of undulation. Use random emissions if possible, and take advantage of any special water effects such as pulsing or swirling, etc. Some particle systems may have additional effects such as motion blur which can be added.

Step 7. Add ripples and waves. You may want to add rippling or wave characteristics to surfaces and solid streams of water, to add to their dynamic appearance over time in animation. Any sheets of water, or pools, etc., should have some surface undulation. You should add one or more concentric waves emanating from the point of contact of any water falling into the pool.

Step 8. Add bubbles and foam. You may be able to use particle systems for bubbles, associated with the streams of water or their point of impact. Foam can be added as a photographic texture on organic-shaped blobs near the point of impact, or along the edges of pools or basins.

Step 9. Add background imagery as desired and, after creating animation, add water sounds if appropriate.

A two-tiered fountain with curved basins created by solids of revolution; surfaces of water in the basins; and particle system sprays falling from upper basin to lower.

A fountain with a large rectangular basin below, and a water spout coming from a channel set into a brick wall above. The water stream is a modified cross-sectional sweep; the water in the basin below is several layers with transparency and rippling.

Waterfall created with large boulders and solid water; water is created as a curved NURB surface, with a streaky water texture map applied. Water in the pool below is a simple surface of transparent blue, with reflectivity, foam, and ripples.

Waterfall created with a particle system providing three separate streams falling from a rocky precipice above; deflectors around several boulders at the base cause the water stream to separate and splash.

All these fountains and waterfalls modeled and rendered in 3DStudio Max.

See the CD-ROM for an animation of the bottom particle-system waterfall.

4.6.3 Multimedia – Sound

Water makes sound – almost musical in some cases. Synchronizing sound to images is an art beyond the scope of this text, but there are many multimedia software systems designed for production of mixed sound and video. Adding sound to a landscape model is tricky to do in an effective way, but can often add depth and expression to models with water elements if done well. Modeling and rendering software needs to be augmented with special multimedia or video-editing software in order to be able to handle sound files, and cutting and mixing soundtracks. Creating sound is also a domain for specialized software; in most cases it's easier to capture sound with a microphone and tape receder (or digital recorder) in the field, and use the software to manipulate and modify the sounds with digital effects as desired. Many prerecorded sounds in digital format (.AIFF and .WAV files) are available on the Internet and on CD-ROM.

Adding a music track to an animation is attractively easy, and so has become a common convention, but more often than not the music distracts from the message of the animation, rendering the whole product more like an MTV music video, but without the content or production values! "Silence is golden" is probably good advice for most animations, but when special circumstances – such as the sound of a fountain or waterfall – warrant it, judicious use of sound can be effective. Often, a simple narrative voice-over soundtrack can add valuable information.

Note that sound is inherently an "immersive" experience; we usually hear in stereo, with both ears. Thus, it can be that sound added to a landscape model, whether still or animated, is best achieved in an immersive display environment of some sort (see Chapter 6), where stereo sound can be projected.

Moving water is not the only landscape phenomenon that can benefit from the addition of sound – leaves and branches rustling in the wind are equally evocative. But water effects, from crashing waves to whispering streams to musical fountains, are a good place to try out some multimedia techniques.

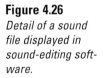

Figure 4.26
Detail of a sound file displayed in sound-editing software.

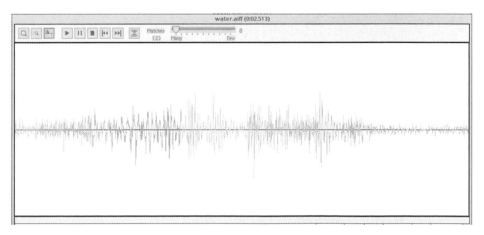

4.7 Summary

Water is best modeled in the landscape using some combination of color, reflectivity and transparency. Water surfaces may be flat in early morning, but are more likely rippled by wind and other actions, which can be modeled by a series of algorithmically controlled sinusoidal ripples or waves. Moving water can be animated using a combination of rippling, twisting, morphing, and other effects, especially particle systems. Particle systems are especially effective for sprays or gravity-controlled water. Digital models of water are especially enhanced by multimedia technology, adding sound to the presentation, whether still or animated.

Chapter Matrix Picture Credits [Page 180]

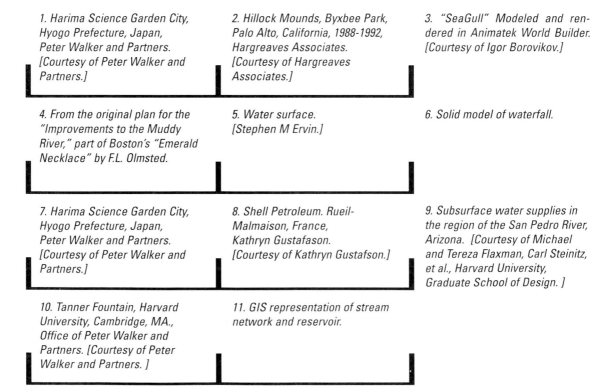

1. Harima Science Garden City, Hyogo Prefecture, Japan, Peter Walker and Partners. [Courtesy of Peter Walker and Partners.]

2. Hillock Mounds, Byxbee Park, Palo Alto, California, 1988-1992, Hargreaves Associates. [Courtesy of Hargreaves Associates.]

3. "SeaGull" Modeled and rendered in Animatek World Builder. [Courtesy of Igor Borovikov.]

4. From the original plan for the "Improvements to the Muddy River," part of Boston's "Emerald Necklace" by F.L. Olmsted.

5. Water surface. [Stephen M Ervin.]

6. Solid model of waterfall.

7. Harima Science Garden City, Hyogo Prefecture, Japan, Peter Walker and Partners. [Courtesy of Peter Walker and Partners.]

8. Shell Petroleum. Rueil-Malmaison, France, Kathryn Gustafason. [Courtesy of Kathryn Gustafson.]

9. Subsurface water supplies in the region of the San Pedro River, Arizona. [Courtesy of Michael and Tereza Flaxman, Carl Steinitz, et al., Harvard University, Graduate School of Design.]

10. Tanner Fountain, Harvard University, Cambridge, MA., Office of Peter Walker and Partners. [Courtesy of Peter Walker and Partners.]

11. GIS representation of stream network and reservoir.

References

Campbell, Craig S. *Water in Landscape Architecture*. New York, NY: Van Nostrand Reinhold Co., 1978.

Halprin, Lawrence. *Cities*. Cambridge, MA: MIT Press, 1963.

Litton, Jr., R. Burton, and Robert Tetlow. *Water and Landscape: An Aesthetic Overview of the Role of Water in the Landscape*. Port Washington, NY: Water Information Center, 1974.

Figure 4.27
*"Pine islands"
an imaginary land-
scape with stone
islands and dra-
matic pine trees.*
Modeled and ren-
dered in Animatek
World Builder.
Courtesy of Igor
Borovikov.

Figure 4.28
*"Ops Pool"
an imaginary pool
in a forest setting.*
Modeled and ren-
dered in
3DStudioMax.
Courtesy of Olli
Pekka
Saastamoinen.

illumination
sunlight

illumination
moonlight

artificial light
sources

shadows

sky

fog fountain

rain

wind & dynami

Atmosphere 5

5.1 Introduction

Landscape modeling and visualization requires attention, beyond the constituent elements (landform, plants, and water) to the two essential ingredients that shape how the landscape looks and feels: the *atmosphere*, and the *light* that passes through it. Sunlight, moonlight, or streetlights (or the lack of them) have everything to do with how we see the landscape and its elements. Horizontal rays of golden sunlight on waving fields of grain; leaden gray clouds over rolling hills of heath and moss, enveloped in hazy gray fog; moonlight reflected beneath a stone bridge over a still pond; fluffy white clouds in a clear blue sky – these are all images whose metaphorical "atmosphere" depends on the literal atmospheric and lighting conditions which produce them.

The combination of water in the air, which makes clouds, fog, haze, rainbows and other atmospheric effects, and lighting conditions, ranging from harsh noon sunlight to diffuse overcast mornings, makes all the difference in a rendered scene, after the landscape elements are modeled. In addition, *motion* of the atmosphere, as wind, gives rise to some of the most obvious dynamics in the landscape, other than flowing water: the waving and rustling of foliage in the wind.

This chapter explores the techniques and conditions for using atmospheric effects and lighting in rendering your digital landscape models, and using dynamic techniques to model the effects of wind.

5.2 Illumination

The overriding factor in any computer rendering – as in painting, or photography – is use and control of lighting. In the natural landscape, most lighting, most of the time, is provided by the sun, modulated by clouds and filtered by vegetation. Light, or its absence, creates or prevents shadows in the landscape, which constitute an essential depth-cue and textural element in any scene. In built landscapes, including urban scenes, natural light may well be augmented by artificial lights, spotlights and floodlights, streetlights and reflected neon signs, which create emphasis and color. Moonlight has different qualities yet – colder, bluer, less intense, because of its essential reflected nature. Cloud conditions vary from none, in completely clear skies, with their attendant crisp shadows and high-contrast lighting conditions, through a wide range of cloud forms and textures, casting moving shadows and dappled sunlight on the landscape below, to completely overcast conditions, giving rise to shadowless, low-contrast, almost monochromatic landscape conditions. Lights in the landscape sparkle and reflect around water, gleam and disappear through the branches and foliage of trees and shrubs, disappear altogether into deep fog on the seashore or in river valleys.

Figure 5.1
Sunlight diminished by clouds and haze encircling distant mountains gives rise to strong silhouettes of trees in foreground, in a landscape outside of Athens, Greece.

Controlling these lighting conditions in modeling/rendering software is a challenge. Most beginning renderers have had the experience of pressing the "render" button only to be confronted by a pitch black screen, or window – due to having neglected to place any lights at all! The vast majority of landscape scenes produced by computer have the artificial and somewhat disturbing quality of being lit entirely by bright, diffuse light, often not casting any shadows on the ground. Casting shadows itself is a computationally demanding task, requiring various sorts of ray-tracing and physically/optically inspired procedures, which are sometimes not even available at all, or require special attention, such as choosing shadow-casting lights on shadow-generating objects sitting on shadow-receiving surfaces! Shadows themselves come in a variety of forms, from diffuse, blurred, soft zones of darkness to crisp, dark, hard silhouettes and shapes, depending on the quality of light, fuzziness of object, smoothness of shadow-receiving surface, and last but not least, the various settings and options in the rendering software used.

Two essential types of light control the appearance of the landscape: *diffuse*, or *ambient* lighting, which comes from all directions at once, and *directional* light, which has a positional source and angle of radiation. In the landscape, ambient lighting comes from scattering of the sun's directional rays through atmosphere, dust, and clouds, and reflections from and among landscape elements. Some combination of these two kinds of light is almost always required in landscape rendering. (In the landscape, except in the dark of night, there is almost always some ambient light, rendering objects even in deep shadow still visible. Only in the inside, in closed architectural spaces, is purely directional light usually found.) Directional light increases the strength of shadows and *contrast* in scenes; ambient light reduces the contrast.

Figure 5.2
View of University Commons landscape produced with:
a. Ambient light only, no directional light;
b. Direct light, with shadows (note that steps and other features become visible with directional light).

5.2.1 Sunlight

The primary source of light for most landscape images is *Sol*, the earth's sun. Often naively drawn as a yellow ball, the light from the sun is naturally white, a combination of all colors, which are revealed when broken up by a prism into a rainbow, or spectrum. The sun is sufficiently far away from the earth that its light rays are essentially parallel when striking the landscape. The sun's position in the sky (to the south, in the northern hemisphere, and to the north, in the southern hemisphere) is determined by the viewer's location on the planet (in latitude and longitude), by the season, due to the annual revolution of the earth around the sun, and by the hour of day, due to the daily rotation of the earth on its axis.

When the sun is high in the sky – more than about 30° above the horizon – its light is brightest and whitest. Closer to the horizon, either at sunrise (in the east) or sunset (in the west), the increased thickness of atmosphere that the light rays pass through, and the aerosol particles therein, mostly dust, give rise to yellower, oranger, then redder light. This orange-red light at sunrise or sunset permeates the sky, and is reflected by clouds near the horizon. Further from the sunlight, the sky is still blue, and there may be bands of colors including yellow, gold, and green in between in a particularly colorful sunrise or sunset.

In a rendering system, a single bright white parallel light source can be used to simulate the sun, in combination with some percentage of ambient lighting. For ordinary daylight conditions, no additional coloration is required. For special conditions, such as sunrise or sunset, adding orange-red coloring to the light may be appropriate, as well as using some environment settings – such as a gradation from blue or purple to yellow – and/or background image maps with clouds.

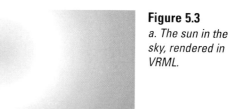

Figure 5.3
a. The sun in the sky, rendered in VRML.

TECHNICAL NOTE

The actual position of the sun in the sky, and hence the direction of its parallel rays on a landscape scene, is controlled by celestial mechanics and the combination of daily rotation, annual revolution, and tilted axes of the earth. Given the latitude and longitude of the landscape project, and the date and time of day, the sun's position can be simply calculated in terms of azimuth (compass degrees, from 0° or 360° north through 180° south) and elevation (in degrees above the horizon, from 0° at sunset or sunrise, to 90°, at noon on the equator). These values can be found in printed tables, computed by simple trigonometric formulae or special software, and are often built-in to modern rendering software packages.

(See also the note in the next section, on Shadows.)

5.2.2 Moonlight

Absent the sun, the landscape may be illuminated – on some nights each month, anyway – by light from *Luna*, the earth's moon. This is just sunlight, reflected by the reflective surface of the moon, and is most visible and effective in the landscape when the moon is full or very nearly full. Then it casts light strong enough to cast shadows, and bright enough to see by. The light is much cooler, and bluer, than sunlight, because of scattering of the long wave (reddish) frequencies of the light. (In fact, the moon's surface is a slightly brown color, but that is only revealed through a telescope.) The full moon on a clear night provides only about 1 millionth as much light as the sun on a day (less than 1 lux – lumens per square meter – for the moon, versus over 100,000 lux for sunlight), and there is far less ambient light at night as well. (It's remarkable testimony to the sensitivity of the human eye that you can see well enough to read by over a range of one million to one!)

Under very low light, such as in moonlight, human visual perception is dominated by the *rods* in the eye's retina, which are extremely sensitive, but provide only monochromatic (black and white) images, at coarser resolution – so-called *scotopic* vision. Color, and finer details, are enabled by the *cones*, which work best in brighter sunlight. So, perceptually, nighttime images have muted colors and may be somewhat grainy in resolution.

You can simulate the moon's light with a parallel spotlight, like the sun, with a lower intensity, less ambient light, and possibly a colored filter (slightly bluish). Whereas the sun is hard to include in an image, since it is so bright, a visible moon in the sky can add atmosphere as well as light – especially if reflected in water, gently rippling.

Under certain atmospheric conditions, such as haze or smoke in the sky, or when the moon is very close to the horizon, the disk of the moon may appear to be orange, or sometimes blue, gray, or even greenish. These colors on the surface of the moon can add drama and effect to a nighttime landscape rendering.

Figure 5.4

a. Image of the full moon, from the Lick Observatory. b. Rendering of a 3D model of the moon, reflected in a pool of water under a bridge.

5.2.3 Night Lighting

Landscapes are seen and experienced at night, even without moonlight, by the aid of artificial lighting. Accurate rendering of artificial light conditions, depending on the style of fixture(s), type of bulbs, down to manufacturer and model number, is possible only with suitably advanced and specialized illumination software. Most rendering systems are not so specific, nor so accurate, and instead may merely enable you to specify materials as *self-illuminating*, so that they appear like lamps. This can be quite satisfactory for some night lighting images; sometimes, you will want to insert small lights into these objects in the model, so that they actually cast light, and so can cast shadows.

Shadows from artificial lights, which come from nearby sources, are not made by parallel light rays, as from the sun or moon, and so appear to diverge quickly at an angle away from the light source. Often night lighting is provided by spotlights or floodlights, both of which produce visible cones of light in the landscape. Spotlights are more narrowly focused, floodlights have a wider beam. Both can be found outside, either mounted high up, in a tree or on the side of a building, or low down, set into the ground, in a clump of shrubbery or just as a fixture attached to the ground.

Outdoor lights may also be found illuminating pathways. Typically these are smaller fixtures, with less bright bulbs, casting an even, or sometimes directional light, on the nearby ground and plant material.

Figure 5.5
Rendering of the University Commons landscape at night, with up-lighting in the trees at the apex of the spiral mound.

5.3 Shadows

Shadows are really just the perception of unlit areas, in contrast with lit areas, from differential illumination and from one object obscuring another's light. A bright light source casts a shadow of an opaque object because a zone behind the object – called the *umbra* of the shadow – intersects some shadow-receiving surface. The outline of the shadow is the profile of the object, seen from looking back directly at the light source; the size of the shadow grows with distance between the shadow-casting object and the shadow-receiving surface. Technically, only bright point lights, like a small lightbulb, create pure umbras; distant light sources, like the sun, or continuous ones, like a bank of lights, create intermediate zones of partial darkness – called the *penumbra* – giving rise to shadows with soft, or fuzzy, edges.

Since we rarely look up into the sky, or into the sun, its presence and position are more often indicated indirectly, by the lighting conditions, especially shadows in and on the landscape around us. Bright sunlight leads to high contrast in the visual landscape: extremely bright areas, such as the tops of trees, open areas, and reflective surfaces such as painted metal and concrete, coupled with dark zones in full shadow. These shadows often overlap and run together, so their constituent shapes and forms are lost, but the overall effect of a dark zone remains, as inside the foliage of a tree, or on the floor of a forest. Even in shadow, objects are lit by the ambient light, or skylight, and so may have a slightly

Figure 5.6

Photograph of the ferry quay, Rapperswil, Switzerland. The dramatic forms of the "coppiced" linden trees is emphasized by lake fog (giving bright white background) and direct sunlight, casting strong shadows on paving in foreground.

bluish tint. This is most visible in shadows on snow, which is a highly reflective surface and so even objects and areas in full shadow are reflecting some ambient light and sky color. Often, in rendering systems, you may be given control over the absolute value of the darkest shadow areas, as a percentage. At night, or on the moon, you might set this to zero, but otherwise it should be 10% or 20%, at least.

In areas with simple, smooth surfaces such as paving, or clipped lawn, isolated objects such as trees and shrubs, flagpoles and fences, etc., cast distinct shadows whose patterns and shapes are distinguishable, and often add to our understanding of the geometry of the objects. These shadows run over undulations, breaks, and vertical walls in the landscape, creating their own patterns, which may be used for specific effect by designers.

In areas with coarser ground texture, such as taller grass and weeds, the shadows of vertical objects may be all but invisible when viewed from the side, from eye level, and only visible when viewed from well overhead. Shadow casting is a computationally expensive task, so if you can get away without shadows, or if they won't be seen anyway, you can render without them.

Sometimes, features of a landscape can be indicated by shadows, even when the object is out of the scene. A long tree shadow cast on the ground in front of the viewer can suggest a tree, almost as vividly as if the tree were visible. Since the actual shadow casting object can't be seen, there's no need for the shadow to

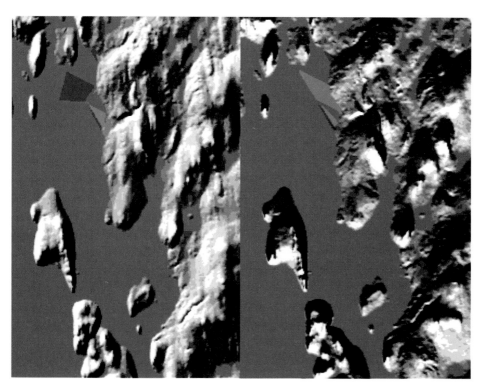

Figure 5.7
*Landform rendered with
a. Sun from the north;
b. Sun from the south.
To many people, the image on the left seems "correct," in the image on the right the terrain appears inverted, like a plaster mold of the real terrain.*

match it, and so an image of a shadow, added as a texture map, or as a projector mask on a light, can be used instead of an actual rendered shadow. Whenever texture-mapped or projected shadows are used, you must take care that their direction and magnitude match the lighting condition in your scene, especially if they are mixed with actual rendered shadows.

Figure 5.8

University Commons landscape, perspective views with plan superimposed in background, showing:
a. shadows cast in mid-afternoon;
b. elongated shadows in late afternoon, emphasizing the rolling landform.

5.4 The Sky

Just as every building is surrounded by landscape, so every landscape is surrounded by sky. Sometimes referred to – and modeled as – a bowl, or hemisphere, the sky is visible directly overhead, unless obscured by building or tree, and in 360° around, at eye level, unless blocked by landscape elements, such as landform, buildings, or vegetation. Although ordinarily thought of as "blue," the sky in fact is capable of many appearances, depending on atmospheric conditions. The blue of the sky, which arises because of differential refraction in the atmosphere, which scatters blue light more thoroughly than other frequencies, has gradations and mottlings, modified by the position of the sun, and the quantity and form of water vapor in the air.

In a digital model, the sky is usually not a distinct object; far more often it is just a background color, or bitmap image. When an animation, or virtual tour, is desired, it may help to model a sky-dome, or inverted half-sphere, on which the image of clouds is projected, since this will enable the clouds to move slightly, overhead, as the viewer moves through the model.

Figure 5.9
a. The clear blue sky, with some brightening towards the horizon.
b. A hemispherical dome used as the sky in a 3D landscape model.

5.5 Clouds

The appearance of the sky is in large part determined by the presence or absence of clouds. A clear, blue, cloudless sky, a blue sky with fluffy white clouds, a leaden, gray sky with layered dark stratus clouds, or a bank of fog reducing visibility to tens of meters or less, are all variants that arise from clouds. In nature, clouds are aggregations of water vapor and ice crystals suspended in air, held (loosely) together by their humidity and the tendency of air masses to move as a unit. Their edges are ragged, where the water can move back into vapor in the air, but seen from afar, from the ground, may appear quite smooth, bulbous and fluffy.

Meteorologists categorize clouds by their form, their usual altitude in the sky, and their propensity to bring on precipitation. Familiar cloud types include *stratus* (flat), *cumulus* (fluffy), and *cirrus* (feathery); these may appear with modifiers, such as *alto-stratus* (*alto* meaning appearing high in the atmosphere) or *cumulo-nimbus* (*nimbus* meaning the cloud may cause precipitation).

Though made mostly of water, clouds appear white, because of the tendency to scatter light waves of all frequencies in all directions far outweighs the slight blue tint leant by their water content; when full of water, about to precipitate as rain, or hail, or snow, they appear dark, gray to almost black, because the water content is so high it absorbs, rather than reflects or scatters, light, especially in the dense middle. Clouds in the sunset or sunrise sky may be colored brightly – pink, orange, purple, red – by the long horizontal rays of the sun. Clouds may

Figure 5.10
a. Clouds seen from overhead, from an airplane. b. Clouds at sunset.

also block the sun, causing halo effects around their edges, and casting shadows in the ground below; in general these shadows are not noticeable in eye-level views, except as a general darkening of the landscape, and the disappearance of other direct shadows.

In digital models, clouds are almost never objects in their own right. Most typically, they are simply applied as bit map images to a background sky color, or a picture of a cloudy sky is used as an environment map. Sometimes, in more advanced systems, clouds may be generated procedurally, usually as a texture applied to the sky, or sky hemisphere. These cloud-generating procedures mostly work on the basis of creating some random noise, for variable densities, coupled with some method of producing "clumping." A sphere, or elliptical solid, can serve as the approximate bounding volume for the procedure, and the clouds take on a volumetric appearance. Then, in rendering, they are colored white, or gray, as determined by the procedure, possibly modified by the sun color or other lights.

Choosing appropriate cloud images for your landscape model is part of the process of establishing a feeling, or atmosphere. The choice of sky, and clouds, needs to be coordinated with lighting conditions. A bright sun casting shadows is incompatible with a gray sky with low-lying stratus clouds; an ambient lit scene with no shadows or direct light is generally incongruous with a bright blue sky. The combination of sunlighting and cloud conditions can make a huge difference to a scene.

Figure 5.11
Various photographic cloud images are an essential element in the digital image collection for landscape modelers.

Figure 5.12
This photographic sky image, included with the popular 3DStudio rendering software, has been used in hundreds or thousands of landscape and architectural renderings worldwide.

Figure 5.13
Procedurally generated clouds:
a. fluffy cumulus cloud form;
b. orange-tinted alto-cumulus clouds.
Courtesy of David Ebert, University of Maryland.

Figure 5.14
Computer-generated clouds over a terrain texture-mapped with a satellite image.
Courtesy of the Remote Sensing Laboratory, University of Zurich.

5.6 Weather

Models of landscape cannot really incorporate weather; and models of weather are orders of magnitude more complex than the most complex landscape. Nonetheless, the most visible artifacts of weather, fog and rain, haze and rainbows, can appear in the landscape and can be used to add depth and realism to renderings.

5.6.1 Haze and Fog

The real atmosphere is full of *aerosol* particles, including dust, ice crystals, water vapor, and air pollution, which under varying conditions give rise to a range of visual effects that affect the perception of the landscape. Perhaps the most common is *atmospheric haze*: the apparent blueing and fading of objects further from the viewer. This *aerial perspective* is seen most vividly in long distance landscape views over several miles, or more. In nature, it is due to the effect of *airlight* – sunlight that is scattered, and made bluer, by water molecules in the air – through which the distant mountains are seen. Additional particles, such as fog, or smoke, add additional opacity, although usually of a whiter, or grayer (or yellow-brown, etc.) color.

In rendering systems, this effect is simulated by some amount of additional blueing, and diminished brightness, of objects in the distance. Usually this is just a linear falloff, although that may not always be the most accurate for various real landscape effects. Most systems allow some control over the beginning distance at which the haze or fog effect is applied, and the minimum and maximum densities. Some may also have procedural or "volumetric" fog, which will have "patchiness" to it, more like real fog.

Figure 5.15
A mountainous terrain, rendered with fog and haze Constant fog fades to white in the background; "volumetric" fog appears in midground and settled in the valley in center.

5.6.2 Rain

Landscapes are often represented under bright blue, sunny skies, but there are both times and places for which that is not the most appropriate. All living landscapes need some rain – even deserts – and some landscapes are the more beautiful for it. Rain tends to be associated with overcast skies and gray clouds, naturally enough, but it can also bring a luminous quality to the landscape, because of the increased reflectivity of wet surfaces.

The rain itself, or sleet or hail, is usually not visible enough to attempt modeling. Individual raindrops are rarely seen. Rather, rain tends to appear as a gray haze over the entire landscape. Raindrops falling into water are visible, as concentric rings of ripples, and this can be used as a visual cue. (Snow, by contrast, normally does have visible flakes in the visual field. These can be modeled as particles in a particle system, or perhaps added in by image processing afterward, using a mask of randomly distributed dots, of various sizes and shades of gray, which is overlaid on the image.)

Rain is also responsible for the appearance of rainbows, due to the refractive effect of the water drops in the sky. Rainbows always appear when the sun is to the back of the viewer, and their size is a function of the position of the sun above the horizon. No rendering system that we know of has the ability to create a rainbow from the refraction of modeled water in the atmosphere; rainbows in landscape images, if they occur at all, must be painted and placed by hand. Note that a rainbow has no real location in space – it's an optical effect dependent entirely upon the position of the viewer and the sun – and so can be hard to place convincingly.

Figure 5.16
Simulation of rain by particle system producing "droplets" from overhead; also graying of sky and thickening of fog.

5.7 Colors in the Landscape

Landscapes, and landscape representations including digital renderings as well as sketches, photographs, and paintings, can range in their coloration from monochromatic and muted to polychrome and exuberant. Choosing colors in a model is a matter of considering the purposes and uses of the renderings to be produced. If "realism" is important, then a careful selection of colors, usually from accurate photographic sources, is essential. If "expression" is the goal, or "atmosphere," then choosing colors is at first a subjective exercise, followed perhaps by some consideration of basic color or perceptual theory, choosing harmonizing, or contrasting colors and color combinations.

Using solid colors from a computer's color picker is bound to give flat, artificial looking images, like a comic book or cartoon. Adding in textures and ray-traced effects such as transparency and reflections can give a more physically believable – but not necessarily realistic – effect. In fact, many digital landscape models have been made for fantasy-based landscapes, as settings for video games, or science fiction movies, or book covers. These uses are important, but so are the communicative purposes of designers such as landscape architects, architects, and others, as well as illustrators, who walk a fine line between photorealism and abstraction for the purpose of making a point, or telling a story.

Given the point, or the story, then an appropriate level of color and texture, as well as other modeling and rendering decisions, can be made.

Figure 5.17
a. Colors of fall foliage in a New England wetland landscape.
b. The same image in grayscale.

Figure 5.18
A synthetic snowy, mountainous land-scape under vary-ing lighting and atmospheric con-ditions:
a. Clear blue, no shadows;
b. Clear blue, directional shad-ows;
c. Overcast and hazy;
d. Overcast, red/orange sunset sky color.
Modeled and ren-dered in Natural Scene Designer.

5.8 Atmospheric Dynamics

Like the rest of the landscape, the atmosphere is dynamic, constantly changing, on time scales from second-to-second, through diurnal, to yearly and longer. Modeling these changes in any realistic physical way is a complex task, well beyond the scope of most computer systems, and this book. The interactions of molecules of air and water are far too numerous and complex to begin to simulate without enormous computational resources and scientific knowledge.

Nonetheless, you can substitute some amount of "looks like" for "works like," and capture some of the simpler dynamics of atmospheric change using ordinary modeling and rendering systems. A simple approach is to animate one or more of the parameters of some atmospheric effect, such as sunlight position, fog density, or sky color, so that they change over time. The sun setting into the ocean, for example, can combine motion of a red disk, the sun, with changes in sky color and cloud configuration.

5.8.1 Solar Motion

The sun's position in the sky is changing all day long, along a mathematically controlled circular arc, giving rise to long shadows from the east in the morning, small shadows directly underneath at noon, and long shadows again at sunset, from the west. Sometimes it can be useful to animate the shadow conditions over the course of a day, to study their impact on playspaces, gardens, etc. This can be done in any system which provides parametric control of the sun (light) position; otherwise, you might have to manually set up a series of positions (*keyframes*) along the arc, and have the system linearly interpolate between them.

(See the example animation "uc-light.mov" on the CD-ROM.)

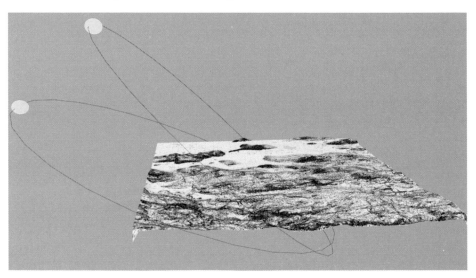

Figure 5.19
The arc of the sun shown in the summer time (higher) and winter time (lower) over a draped terrain model.

5.8.2 Wind

An important contributor to apparent motion in the landscape is the motion of the atmosphere itself, in the form of wind. Not visible by itself, the wind's effects are most apparent on vegetation and foliage, causing leaves to sway and rustle, and larger limbs and trunks to move visibly, rhythmically, when the wind is strong enough. Snow and rain may also reveal the motion of wind.

The mechanics of wind motion are complex. Sometimes a constant force from a single direction, wind may also suddenly shift direction and speed, giving rise to gusts and unpredictable effects. The interaction of winds and breezes with objects in the landscape, such as buildings, vegetation, and even landform, are also complex and hard to predict. Only sophisticated, physically-based models could ever give real wind effects, but some fairly realistic effects can be had by using a simple model of wind, and either [article systems effects, for snow and rain, or some basic *inverse kinematics* ("IK") in tree branches, limbs, and leaves.

The basic idea of IK motion is that leaves are the primary wind catchers; they in turn move the branches to which they are attached, to a lesser degree, and the branches in turn move the larger limbs. These limbs and branches are *elastic*; that is, they will bend a certain amount, but then tend to spring back to their original position. The combination of these motions gives rise to a characteristic wind-blown look to leaves and branches, and can be animated with some advanced modeling and rendering systems. Some may even give specific control over wind parameters, such as gustiness, prevailing direction, and so on; otherwise, these wind parameters may have to be animated using some built-in particle systems or other warping modifiers.

Figure 5.20
The right-hand portion of this image illustrates the parametric tree under a severe wind condition compared to the left-hand portion of the image which shows the parametric tree in an idle state. (Note: The wind condition is exaggerated for the purposes of the illustration. The animation "breeze.mov" on the CD-ROM mimics a gentle breeze.)

235

5.9 Summary

Atmospheric effects – lighting, sky and clouds, wind motion – can give life and a sense of realism to landscape models and renderings. Getting them physically, environmentally, and meteorologically correct is too hard for most systems, but getting them convincing, and expressive, is just a matter of taking time to adjust parameters. Often observing carefully in the real landscape is the best way to get ideas and visual precedents for modeling and rendering the atmosphere.

References

Birn, Jeremy. *[digital] Lighting & Rendering*. Indiana: New Riders Publishing, 2000.

Lynch, David K., and William Livingston. *Color and Light in Nature*. Cambridge, England: Cambridge University Press, 1995.

Chapter Matrix (Page 216) Picture Credits

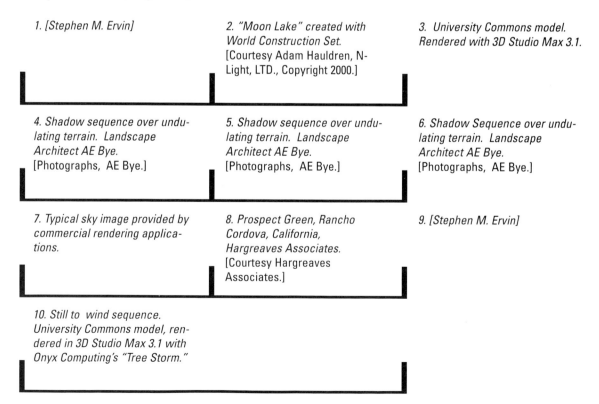

1. [Stephen M. Ervin]

2. "Moon Lake" created with World Construction Set. [Courtesy Adam Hauldren, N-Light, LTD., Copyright 2000.]

3. University Commons model. Rendered with 3D Studio Max 3.1.

4. Shadow sequence over undulating terrain. Landscape Architect AE Bye. [Photographs, AE Bye.]

5. Shadow sequence over undulating terrain. Landscape Architect AE Bye. [Photographs, AE Bye.]

6. Shadow Sequence over undulating terrain. Landscape Architect AE Bye. [Photographs, AE Bye.]

7. Typical sky image provided by commercial rendering applications.

8. Prospect Green, Rancho Cordova, California, Hargreaves Associates. [Courtesy Hargreaves Associates.]

9. [Stephen M. Ervin]

10. Still to wind sequence. University Commons model, rendered in 3D Studio Max 3.1 with Onyx Computing's "Tree Storm."

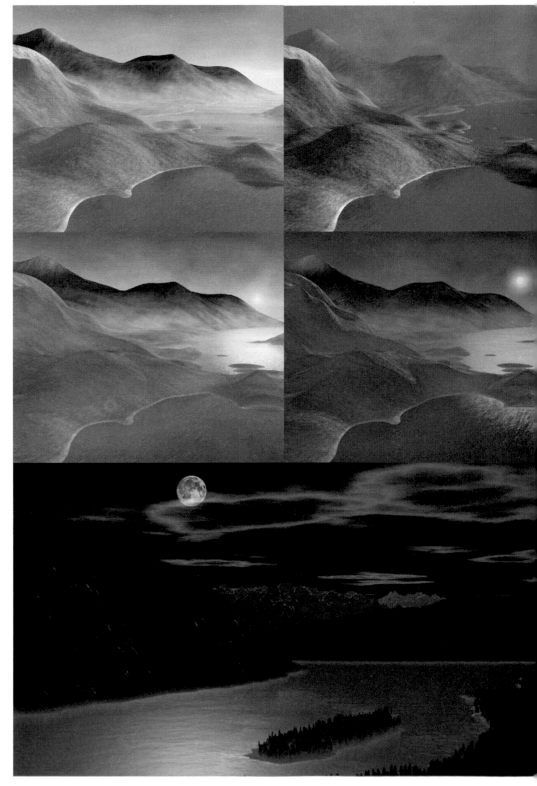

Figure 5.21
Four images of an artificial landscape under different lighting and atmospheric conditions. Modeled and rendered in RealSoft3D, courtesy of Damian Sainsbury.

Figure 5.22
"Moon Lake" created with World Construction Set. Courtesy of Adam Hauldren, N-Light Ltd., Copyright 2000.

Synthesis 6

6.1 Introduction – Putting It All Together

Previous chapters isolated and emphasized the individual elements of landscape – landform, vegetation, water, and atmosphere. But in real landscapes, and most modeled ones, these elements are combined and interact. Water in the landscape is inherently related to the landform, whether held in a basin, like a pond, or running in a channel formed by sloping banks. Trees and other plants in the natural landscape are located partly by preferences for sunlight, slope, aspect, soil type and moisture, and other plants. In a designed landscape, these elements are carefully composed to reinforce design ideas, visual effects, and choreographic sequences. Animals, including people, inhabit and add life to these landscapes.

Analyzing landscapes often starts from the "ground up," with subsurface geology forming the basis upon which soil, water, and plants develop and are understood. Similarly, in building a digital model it makes sense to begin with terrain, as that will set the surface elevation for the other features. When using ecosystem relationships, in GIS or other software, it may make sense to locate the water elements next, as plants will respond to water's presence. Next, before vegetation, any architectural elements (buildings, e.g.) and hardscape (paving) need to be located, as the vegetation must be placed in relationship to, and so as to avoid, these elements. Last, decisions about lights, cameras, and atmospheric effects, as well as output media and formats, come in the rendering and visualization stage. Choosing these rendering parameters raises both aesthetic and sometimes ethical questions, related to the purposes of the modeling. Sometimes, these different processes or decisions are undertaken by different individuals as part of a project team, making the need for convention and communication paramount.

The rest of this chapter is about the process of "putting it all together," including details of presentation media and formats. Finally, the appendices include a glossary of landscape modeling terms and a listing of some of the software systems that the authors know about at the time of writing, and of data sources and other useful resources for landscape modeling.

6.1.1 Structures, Vegetation, and Water on Landform

Getting landscape elements to sit properly on the landform – at the right elevation, without visible gaps or discontinuities where they touch, or grow out of the terrain – is an essential and often difficult task for landscape models. Some CAD modeling systems have snap settings that will let you position new elements so they touch the terrain object (or objects); in others you may have to invoke some batch operation to move the already placed elements to the surface. Oddly, and sadly, this is not the case in all systems, and not all landform modeling objects (tins, meshes, NURBs, e.g.) can be used for snap operations. Sometimes you may be able to use associated database technology to compute, or store, a spot elevation value for landscape objects and use that to set them on the terrain. For numerous and multiple objects, like the trees in a forest, some automated special-purpose system is usually the only feasible approach.

Buildings offer a special case, since they touch over an area, typically rectangular, or polygonal, rather than at a point. On anything other than a flat site, this means the terrain will have a range of values around the perimeter of the building, at the foundation level. One solution taken by unimaginative builders is to simply clear a flat "pad" for every building, which forces some landform grading all around the building, cutting and filling to create the pad, and channeling to prevent water from flowing into it. A more sophisticated approach is to vary the levels of the building to fit more closely the levels of the terrain, and then use grading and paving to clarify the transitions, especially at building entrance points. If you have access to detailed building plans, they should show spot elevations or even contours all around the building. Rather than actually model the landform with a hole, or excavation, for the foundation of the building, you can just make the terrain continuous over the building footprint, and then set the building in on top of it; letting the rendering system hide the earth inside. (Of course, if you are building a detailed model of the interior spaces as well, as for a VRML model, this technique won't work, and you'll have to actually excavate the virtual terrain).

A simple technique for making a building, or other object, appear to sit perfectly in uneven terrain, is to model the building or other object with extra depth below ground level – in essence, make an extra deep basement on the building. Then when the building is set into the terrain (at a subterranean level), when

rendered, the landform will appear to flow seamlessly all around the object. This same technique can be used with tree trunks, or telephone poles, or other embedded objects.

Modeling buildings as part of the landscape scene is something that this book has not addressed, there being many good references for 3D architectural modeling. It's important to point out some of the more important issues for the landscape modeler, however.

Most architectural models are not created in any geographic coordinate system; usually they are just in some arbitrary 2D space, often (but not always) with the origin (0,0) being in the lower left corner so that all coordinates are positive. Locating such a building model in the landscape model may require shifting and rotating all coordinates, or the model may be simply inserted at a specific location, with an optional rotation, if the modeling software supports that.

Sometimes, this can be acceptably performed approximately "by eye," but if critical site relationships such as building entrances and terrain elevations are being modeled, then precise and accurate control of placement is required.

Many architectural models are themselves rather complicated, with many polygons, and often much invisible detail. In a larger landscape model, it may not be practical to use the building model in its entirety, and some simplification will be necessary. Sometimes, basic massing of buildings – solid color blocks showing the basic geometric form and proportion – are sufficient. Sometimes, architectural details such as materials or colors are important, and should be represented. In this case, using photographic textures to convey detail, rather than modeling every individual window or brick, is a good technique.

6.1.2 People and Other Animals

The four constituent elements of landscape – landform, vegetation, water and atmosphere – that were covered in the previous chapters are the essential elements to be sure, but landscapes are inhabited by animals too, who often play an important role in shaping the landscape. That is certainly true for people, and indeed often the reason we want to model, analyze, or represent landscapes is because of some human (or, in the case of science-fiction, perhaps non-human!) purpose. Modeling animals, including people, in the landscape is like other elements: in lieu of actual dynamic models of animal or human behavior, such as landscape ecologists and urban dynamics researchers might provide, the choice is between some form of polygonal solid models, or simple bit-mapped billboards. A number of sources exist for 3D models of human forms, which can be incorporated into your landscape model, at the cost of a relatively large number of polygons and or NURB surfaces; alternatively, photographic images can be artfully cut and pasted as needed, and texture-mapped in your scene. Adding even a few people can often add an element of interest and scale to your landscape models.

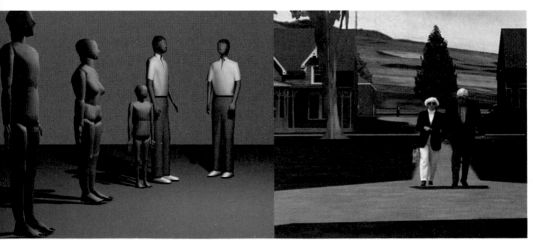

Figure 6.3
a. 3D solid models of people, modeled and rendered in 3DStudioMax. b. "Billboard" people in model (note rectangular shadow).
Modeled and rendered in Evans & Sutherland RapidSite.
Courtesy of Evans & Sutherland.

Figure 6.4
Model of the campus of University of Toronto, with photographic texture-mapped buildings and central green space shown with texture-mapped trees and landform.
Modeled and rendered in PolyTrims software.
Courtesy of John Danahy, the Centre for Landscape Research.

Figure 6.5
Model of proposed residential development.
Modeled and rendered in Evans & Sutherland RapidSite.
Courtesy of Evans & Sutherland.

6.2 Professional Practice

Some digital landscape modelers will have the freedom of painters, to invent landscapes without constraints, perhaps exploring scale-free, fantastic landforms and plants, subject only to aesthetic criteria. For these, digital tools are just another expressive medium. For others, such as landscape architects and other professionals, digital modeling tools are more than just expressive; they are controlled instruments of technical representation, and are most often used in the context of real-world, or design-world, constraints and limitations in which measurements count and some elements may be fixed. The broad continuum from freehand sketching and eyeball adjustment to mechanical drawing and precise alignment is familiar to designers, and most digital landscape modeling tools can be used in both modes.

6.2.1 Accuracy, Precision, and Conversion

Computers are notorious for their precision, but precision is not the same thing as accuracy. *Precision* simply refers to the detail in measurement – for numbers, the number of decimal places, for example, so that 3.14159262738 is a more precise value than 3.14. In landscape context, this may refer to the choice between 10 cm, 1 m, or 3 m contour lines, which give respectively less precise landform descriptions. 3 m contours are typically found on USGS topographic maps; good site surveyors can produce elevation measurements to within 10 cm (4 in.) with ease.

Accuracy, by contrast, describes how close a measurement is to the truth, or the correct value. It is very easy to make a very precise, but totally inaccurate, measurement (for example, using a tape measure which has some amount broken off the end of it). In the digital medium, every number is potentially as precise as desired (up to the limits imposed by the underlying digital chips and software, which for most modern computers is about 100 decimal places), and it is a user choice to limit the precision, for example by setting up a grid snap so all distances are integers, or whole feet or meters, or using a finer grid so that distances are rounded to the nearest inch, or centimeter, say. For many simple, rectangular designs, integer values may be fine; for more complex, curved, or jagged forms, finer precision is often required to avoid "rounding off" errors. Whether these values are accurate or not depends on the application, and the requirements.

Often early schematic design is done without respect to detailed dimensions (i.e., at a low precision), but overall proportions, and some basic dimensions, are already set. For detailed construction drawings, the level of precision will often be determined by the actual construction technology that will be used, and the constraints of that technology. A large bulldozer, for example, can move earth to within a foot or two; a person with a rake can get levels to within a centimeter or so. Similarly, the dimensions of a brick are fixed and well-known, but the size of a shrub is harder to measure or predict with the same precision.

If you are using digital tools, you can mix and match the degrees of precision as desired. For example, an existing site and buildings may be determined and plotted with great precision, and then alternative designs sketched freehand within those constraints.

A major difference between digital models and other more traditional drawings in this regard is that almost all drawings are made at some predetermined *scale*, 1:100 for example, in which 1 drawing unit represents 100 actual units on the ground. This scale together with the drawing technology sets some limits to precision, since the thickness of a pencil line, say 0.1 mm, already represents some distance (at 1:100, 1 cm) on the ground, and no distance smaller than that can really be represented. This is why a number of drawings at different scales are typically used together for all but the smallest projects. By contrast, digital computer models are not inherently at any scale, or more correctly, they are at full scale, since the units of measurement are arbitrarily precise, and any dimension or distance can be specified. Only when the model is plotted out, or made visible on a screen, does the representation take on a "scale." Thus, it's easy to create a model which has no identifiable scale – units could be inches, or kilometers, and are unspecified – using computer drafting and modeling tools.

This freedom from scale is fine for individual projects, but can be disastrous when several different models are put together, or pieces come from different modelers or modeling environments. In this case, when parts must match up, and when the overall model needs to fit within a specified geography, both scale and coordinate systems, including projections for larger projects, must be carefully controlled. Establishing agreed-upon units (inches, or meters, etc.) and standards for precision is essential.

Figure 6.6
A scaleless imaginary landscape, created in Bryce software.

6.2.2 Digital Modeling Project Management

Modeling the landscape is just complicated enough, even with the best software and good data, that even the simplest rendering may take on qualities of a larger more complex project, requiring attention to process details and careful management. Even if the scope of the proposed modeling project is modest, management of files, folders, conversions, intermediate steps, alternative settings, and final products requires a systematic approach.

Typically, a landscape modeling project has three important phases: management of the base data, such as terrain model and planting plans; construction of the 3D model; and preparation of final output, such as renderings or animation. In each of these phases, file-naming conventions, and careful note taking are important.

Base data are almost never acquired in their perfect or final format. Instead, for example, often the regional terrain model is acquired at one scale in one map projection, contextual photographic images are collected in various formats, the site grading and planting plans are acquired or digitized in different programs, and a sketch showing desired views is made available on a scrap of paper. The first step is to bring all the site data together into a common coordinate system, which may require shifting of projections and units. Then the various images and textures need to be cataloged. For each file, some basic information such as its lineage – where and by whom and when was it made, what format and how big is it, any other useful information such as scale, or resolution, etc. – should be kept. This information is called *metadata*, literally, data about the data. Whether kept digitally, or in a project notebook, this information is essential, especially if a project is to last for more than a few days or involve more than one person. Whenever conversions are performed, some record should be kept, in order to answer questions, or correct problems later in the process. As tempting as it is to skip this record keeping, or try to keep it all in your head, these steps are essential project-management tasks.

For images, some kind of image catalog program is invaluable, as it can be used to print out contact sheets, with thumbnail images and associated information such as filename, size, resolution, format, etc.

No matter what operating system or computer software is being used, some kind of file folder system for each project can be very useful as a basic organizational system, for example:

- ORIGINALS   original files, including metadata
- BASE_DATA   converted files, in common coordinate system
- IMAGES   image files, for textures, views, etc.
- MODELS   the main model, or sub-models
- RENDERINGS   output images
- ANIMATIONS   animations – note, these may be very large!

Within these folders, subfolders may be useful, depending on the details of the project, for example "RASTER" and "VECTOR" base data, or "LOW_RES" and "HI_RES" images may be segregated. This system makes it easier to backup and archive (for example, by saving all files on a CD-ROM) and to find necessary files as needed. Some software may assist by enabling you to specify certain directories or paths as the default location for kinds of files, such as texture maps, where it will automatically look when loading files. Other software may use some kind of file-naming convention, requiring that all related project files have a common prefix, or some other system.

Most computers automatically record the time and date when files are created; this can be very useful in managing a project, so long as the computer's internal clock and calendar are correctly set! Some systems may even have some kind of revision control system, so that backup copies of all files are made whenever they are opened, or subsequent versions get a version number appended to the file name. If not automatic, it's a good idea to manually establish a convention for naming subsequent versions of files, perhaps also encoding the name of the author if more than one is involved, such as PROJECTA_V6_SME (Version 6 of the Project A file, made by the modeler with initials SME).

If built-in project-management and file-management tools are not available (and for many desktop systems, they will not be), it's important that every member of the modeling team, even if there is only one, stick to these conventions. Also, a systematic back-up system should be established, unless this is automatic, so that precious work is not lost due to minor mechanical or magnetic failures (such as are bound to happen on any computer system!)

Figure 6.7
A useful file folder hierarchy for digital project management.

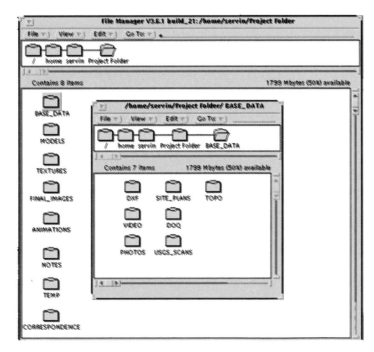

6.3 Presentation and Output Media

The final goal of every digital landscape model is some sort of presentation, whether formal or casual, public or private, scripted or impromptu. Choosing the presentation format and media is as much of a design decision as anything else in the process. Many times the circumstances or conventions dictate the form, but often there are choices to be made. Recognizing the values and limitations of various output media, and different modes of presentation, is critical. A presentation is really a narrative, a story, and so it embodies a point of view, which is most often directly suggested by the choice of camera and literal points of view of, and from within, the landscape model.

6.3.1 Camera and Viewpoint

The choice of viewpoint makes a great difference in the perception of a landscape. A traveler walking through deep woods, along a sinuous path, and finally reaching an open overlook forms multiple reinforcing impressions of the landscape. In digital rendering, you can control the same kinds of impressions by choice of camera angle, position, and other parameters. Three different viewpoints are in common use, and have very different effects: directly overhead (plan), aerial oblique, and eye-level perspective.

Figure 6.8
View inside the University Commons landscape model, looking towards the grove of Carpinus trees.

6.3.1.1 Plan View

The first view, directly overhead, gives a *plan* view, or a "bird's eye" perspective. This is a view rarely enjoyed by humans, except in airplanes looking down, and so is the most detached and perhaps indifferent view. It is omniscient, seeing everything, but often objects are seen in unusual ways (trees almost as plan view symbols, buildings dominated by roofs, and so on). In this way, layout and spatial proximity relationships can be best visualized, but the visual aspects of the landscape portrayed may be lost. Ordinarily, a plan view is taken from a sufficiently high altitude that perspective effects of objects on the ground are minimal (although some haze, or blueing of more distant ground, can be seen in areas of high topographic relief). However, when the viewpoint is brought closer to the ground, the perspective can be dramatic, especially when looking straight down into tall vertical elements such as conifer trees, or telephone poles, etc. Direct overhead views have rather special illumination qualities as well, since the tops of all the landscape elements are always in full sun, and shadows tend often to be hidden underneath canopy.

Figure 6.9
Plan view of University Commons landscape model.

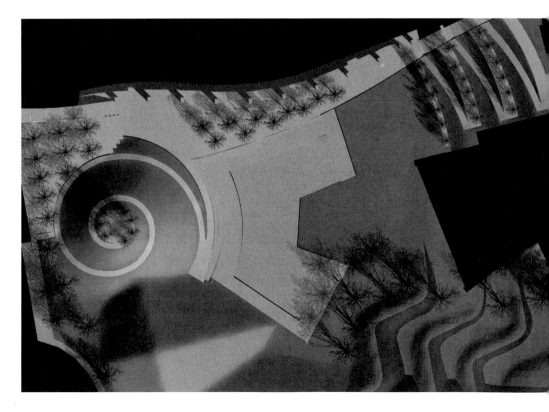

6.3.1.2 Plan Oblique

The plan oblique is a type of projection drawing that has a high angle of view where one vertical plane has more visual emphasis than the other. The advantage of the plan oblique is that it provides a dimensionally correct or true orthographic plan with the height of elements such as landform, vegetation, and built structures. Temporal or phenomenal conditions can be layered into the drawing through the casting of shadows, emphasizing the play of light amongst the plan elements. With one vertical plane receiving greater visual emphasis, some elements may be lost or hidden while others are more visible or foregrounded. The selection of the point of view must be deliberate so as to highlight specific spatial relationships or temporal conditions. The oblique drawing or view is a constructed projection for the purposes of illustrating specific plan and sectional relationships, and is not intended to simulate human vision like the perspective projection.

Figure 6.10
Aerial oblique view of University Commons landscape model.

6.3.1.3 Eye-level Perspective

The most engaging viewpoint is the eye-level perspective, in which landscapes are seen as they would be from a typical (adult) eye-level view (of about 5'6", or 1.7 m off the ground). In this view nearby elements obstruct further ones, and the view is limited to a cone of vision about 60 degrees wide, so that most of the landscape is not seen at any one time. This is the view most likely to resonate with viewers, inducing emotional feelings – of beauty, awe, mystery, suspicion, etc. This view is also the one most influenced by lighting, shadows, and atmospheric effects.

From a modeling and rendering perspective, the eye-level view allows the most potential economy, as only visible elements need to be modeled, and selective levels of detail can be employed. Naturally, one would usually model a bit extra – if not the whole scene – so as to be able to shift the viewpoint around to find the very best. Often lighting and shadows might need to be adjusted in combination with setting the viewpoint, to achieve the desired results (either more dramatic and obscuring shadows for atmosphere and mood, or fewer, for clarity and communication).

Figure 6.11
Eye-level perspective view of University Commons landscape model.

6.3.1.4 Animation Cameras and Viewpoints

The same basic views used for static visualization – plan, oblique, and eye-level – can be used alone or in combination, in dynamic animations as well. Many landscape scenes are large enough that an animated view (a walk-through or flyover) is the best way to illustrate all of the landscape. In addition, landscapes are often experienced in motion and these representations can be used to simulate that experience. In the case of a virtual environment, such as VRML, the viewer will control the camera, and so all you can do is define pre-set camera "viewpoints" which may be used, but you don't control the path through the model. In a pre-canned animation, where you control the view, the choice of camera parameters and path is crucial. You may choose to start with an aerial view, then zoom into eye level, or stay at eye level the whole time, or even use unconventional views, such as from underground, or sideways, in a cinematic way to emphasize perceptions of the landscape space. In animations, you control both the viewer's position, and also the camera's "look-at" direction and other parameters such as angle-of-view; controlling these is the key to making everything from simple documentary walk-throughs of a landscape model to impressionistic and even fantastic cinematic experiences.

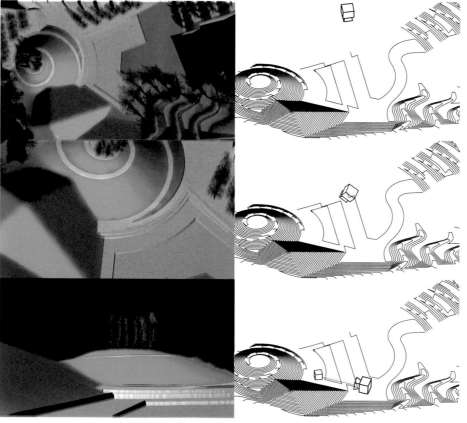

Figure 6.12
Plan, oblique, and eye-level views with their associated camera positions in relation to the model's geometry.
a. Plan
b. Oblique
c. Eye-level

6.3.2 Media

The final medium for the visualization of any landscape representation will also determine the modeling approaches and techniques. Choosing an output medium and format early on is essential to make sure that work is efficient and effective in preparing material for your final presentation.

6.3.2.1 On-screen

Figure 6.13

*The four most
common screen
display sizes:
320 x 240
640 x 480 (VGA)
800 x 600 (SVGA)
1024 x 768 (XGA)
Not shown:
SXGA (1280 x 1024)*

Most digital modeling work is done interactively in front of a computer screen, normally limited to 72 - 100 dpi, and less than 2000 x 2000 pixels, in full (24-bit) color. Having two screens, side by side, can be a very great convenience, but requires special hardware setup. Work that is to be presented over the Internet, or the World Wide Web, is usually confined to screen size or smaller (800 x 600 is a common compromise), for transmission efficiency, and often smaller, low-resolution "thumbnail" images are made as a preview, so that the viewer can choose among several images without downloading each in its entirety.

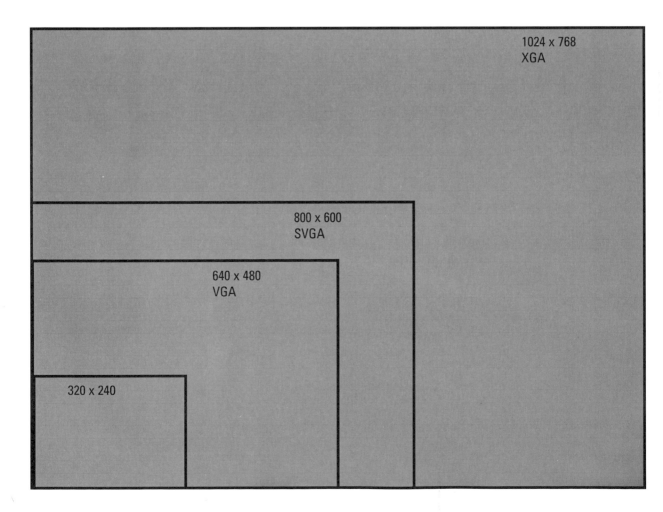

6.3.2.2 Printed Output

For printed output, either letter-size (8.5" x 11") or tabloid size (11" x 17" or 12" x 18") is most common for color laser printing, at 600 - 2000 dpi. Larger sizes, up to 36" wide by 20' long, are produced on ink-jet plotters, typically at around 600 dpi. Printers and plotters always use CMYK, rather than RGB, printing techniques, and some color changes can occur when converting between them, so careful calibration as well as trial and error are often required for color matching. File formats for all of these vary, but Postscript format is a common standard. Postscript can encode linework as well as raster images, and can include text in specified fonts which can be scaled without loss of detail or introduction of jagged edges. Pure photographic images, including screen-snapshots, are recorded as raster files, and may be in TIFF, BMP, or JPEG format (or a wide range of others, but these are the most common). Low resolution photographs may look coarse, grainy, and jagged when enlarged to very large sizes, and so are best printed in the smaller formats.

6.3.2.3 35 mm Slides or Photographs

If 35 mm slides are to be made, then the 3:2 aspect ratio (or smaller) should be respected. Slide-writing hardware and software can generally take a combination of file formats, like those listed above, and can handle a range of resolutions up to 4000 dpi or higher. Slide recorders typically employ RGB, rather than CMYK format. The newer APS (or IX240) system allows for three different standard sizes of exposures:

"H" format 30 x 17 (close to HDTV 16:9 ratio)
"C" format 24 x 17 (close to 35mm 3:2 ratio)
"P" format 30 x 10 (Panoramic 3:1 ratio)

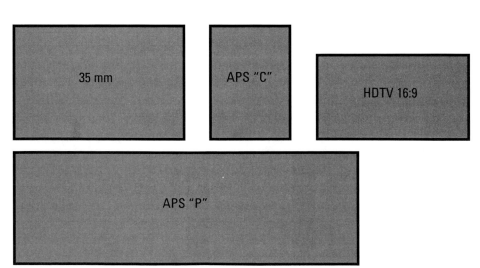

Figure 6.14
The four common photographic film formats: 35mm and the newer APS film sizes. Many digital slide writers have removable camera backs, and so can create output for many different formats.

6.3.2.4 World Wide Web

The *World Wide Web* (WWW) – or more generally, the Internet – provides opportunities and constraints all its own for presentations. The distributed nature of the Web means that it is often the best choice for sharing models and other information with multiple parties, especially if they are geographically remote, but also even if they are in adjoining rooms. The set of graphical format standards that make the Web work (HTML, XML, and many others, constantly evolving) are of necessity well documented. Many commercial and open-source computer programs are available for creating and manipulating Web content (individual pages and complete sites). The format requirements are generally the same as those of on-screen presentations, but in many cases an additional effort is required to minimize graphics complexity in the interest of transmission time (time for the remote viewer to download the images). Many compression schemes, and special image formats for the web, both proprietary and open-source, are in constant evolution. This is an area of technology changing rapidly, so be sure to consult an up-to-date reference (on-line on the Web is often best!) about current Web publishing standards and techniques.

6.3.2.5 Animations

Animations require enormous file sizes, since anywhere from 15 - 30 frames are required per second. Consequently, they are usually produced at small image resolutions (like 320 x 240 pixels); if done at high resolution like 800 x 600, the resultant files can be enormous (hundreds or thousands of megabytes in size), making them hard to transfer, or play without very large disks (tens of gigabytes), very fast processors, and often special image compression and encoding hardware. The standard way to save and present an animation is in some form of video, analog or digital. The "QuickTime" format and QuickTime movie player are common standards for animation on the web and on CD-ROM.

Figure 6.15

Two standard applications for playing animations from CD-ROM or over the web:
a. Windows Media Player;
b. Apple's Quicktime Player.

6.3.2.6 Video

Video format at the time of this writing is evolving from an analog low-resolution format to a predominantly digital, much higher-resolution format. If destined for analog television, for example on a videocassette for a VCR, the normal standard is *NTSC/VHS*, which has a limited resolution of around 512 x 380, so creating 640 x 480 is usually more than adequate (and still creates enormous files). Special video-editing software is required to match frame rates and format for NTSC video exactly. The additional technological requirements of producing television "broadcast-quality" imagery is beyond the scope of this book, and a suitable reference should be consulted.

Digital video is much more flexible, and can support multiple, different resolutions. The *QuickTime* format is commonly used to encode digital video for delivery over the web, or on DVD, CD-ROM, etc.

The new standards for HDTV include much higher resolution, and a 16:9 image proportion, better suited to landscape images. Video formats, compression techniques, and related technologies are rapidly evolving, and continually improving in resolution and quality.

6.3.2.7 QTVR

One useful format for landscapes is the panoramic view, or animation (including the *QuickTime Virtual Reality* or *QTVR* format). This provides 360° viewing around a fixed viewpoint. These can be constructed by stitching together a series of photographs, taken in a 360° circle, using special-purpose software, and some modeling systems can directly export QTVR format. QTVR also allows for embedded "hyper-links" so that portions of one scene can be linked to another QTVR scene, much like rooms connected by doors.

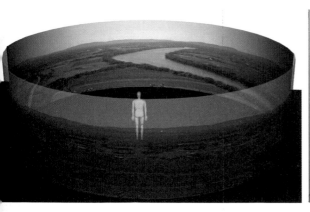

Figure 6.16
a. The QTVR format encodes a 360° image in a single file;
b. A QTVR viewer, such as Apple's QuickTime player, allows the viewer to scroll completely around, and to zoom in and out to a limited extent.

6.3.2.8 VRML

Other *Virtual Reality* (VR) display systems use a special head-mounted display to create a stereo view by projecting two synchronized images directly in front of each eye of the viewer, and use motion tracking hardware and software to change the viewpoint of the scene as the viewer's head moves, from side to side or up and down. This can give the illusion of being inside a virtual landscape. These systems must create real-time imagery, at up to about 30 frames per second, and so usually have very simple, and highly stylized contents. Very expensive, high-tech, military systems, such as flight training simulators, use similar technology but with much more detailed images.

6.3.2.9 Immersion

For the most "realistic" presentation of landscape visualizations, some form of fully immersive projection or display is the best, albeit most expensive and complicated. In these environments, an image is displayed on a screen or series of screens completely encircling the viewer, 360° around, so that wherever the eye is looking, the peripheral vision, outside of our normal 60° cone of vision but very important to our perceptual sense of context and continuity, is engaged. This requires between 6 and 24 individual projectors, each projecting an overlapping, carefully synchronized image. Another variation is the so-called "CAVE" visualization environment, in which a cubic volume of space has images projected, usually from the rear, on at least four surfaces, and up to all six surfaces including floor and ceiling. Both of these systems require special expensive, hardware, software, and presentation spaces, as well as special model formats.

Figure 6.17
A 3-screen, immersive, panoramic display environment, requiring 3 projectors. Rear-projection avoids shadows of viewers on the screen.

Figure 6.18
3-screen, immersive, display environment at the Unversity of British Columbia, Landscape Visualization Laboratory. Courtesy of Stephen Sheppard.

6.4 Data Sources

When creating a purely imaginative landscape model, with no context or constraints, you may be able to start with a blank screen and create the landscape de novo, using the tools and techniques described in previous chapters. But when you are modeling a landscape in the real world, you are ordinarily dependent upon data from a number of sources to set the context and fill in the details. These can include contours and planting plans from landscape architects, site photographs and satellite images. Acquiring and managing the necessary data for any project is an essential first step in any digital modeling undertaking.

6.4.1 USGS, GIS Agencies

The United States Geological Survey (USGS) is the federal agency responsible for mapping the national landscape, and has a huge inventory of cartographic resources including the 1:25,000 topographic map series, color and black and white aerial photographs, thematic maps such as land use and transportation, and others. Since the early 1990s the USGS has been at the forefront of developing standards and means for distributing digital maps. Their web site offers a range of options for acquiring digital data, some of which can be downloaded for free, some of which can be ordered for a small cost. For basic contextual digital maps, especially relatively large areas, the USGS maps are an obvious first start. Many of their products are derived from the 1:25,000 mapping series and so are not particularly reliable at the detailed site scale, for which higher resolution and more precise data are necessary.

Digital elevation data are most commonly available at 30 m resolution. The USGS DEM files, and their newer successor, DSTD files, are available at this resolution for most of the United States, Alaska, and Hawaii. Much more information about USGS cartographic products can be found on the web at http://mapping.usgs.gov .

For other parts of the world, coverage is more spotty and variable. Many countries have equally advanced national GIS coverage; some have none. The most common recourse when no national data is available is to look for data from one of the earth-orbiting satellites, such as the US LANDSAT or the French SPOT satellites. Often, multi-spectral images of any place in the world can be acquired at 30 m resolution, although sometimes at a substantial price (thousands of dollars per scene). Sometimes from these scenes digital elevation models can be generated at the same resolution.

The most common form of higher-resolution data now comes from ortho-

Figure 6.19

Digital Ortho Photo Quad sheet image (DOQ) from the USGS. This black and white air photo has pixels equivalent to 5 meters on the ground, and has been ortho-rectified to match perfectly the scale of USGS 1:25000 topo maps.

rectified aerial photographs, some of which offer 1 m resolution (or finer!), in which one pixel in the image represents one square meter on the ground. Modern stereo-photo interpretation can generate terrain models from these, also with 1 m resolution. An increasing number of sources can be used to acquire such imagery, often at low cost. Many state governments in the United States have GIS agencies which make the USGS 1:25,000 *digital ortho quadrangles* (or DOQ) data available, and supplement that with 1 m or 5 m DOQs. This technology is rapidly changing due to developments in remote sensing.

A new sensor of potential value to landscape sensing and modeling is LIDAR (Light Intensity Detection and Ranging), a laser-based scanner that can be used at close distances and also from an airplane or satellite. LIDAR is capable of very-high-resolution sensing of elevation, so that canopies of vegetation, as well as underlying terrain, can be digitally recorded in 3D.

Figure 6.20
LIDAR image, showing trees and vegetation as well as buildings and infrastructure.
Courtesy of the Houston Advanced Research Center (HARC).

6.4.2 Surveyors

For more detailed surveys of specific areas, a commercial contractor is usually required. Surveyors, engineers, aerial photographers, and remote sensing specialists all offer services to produce detailed digital surveys, often to within one centimeter precision if required. Increasingly, these are accomplished with the use of *Global Positioning System* (GPS) survey equipment, which depend upon a network of high-altitude satellites to achieve high-precision, three-dimensional readings of location. Coupled with laser-based survey equipment, and new techniques for "3D image capture," devices which actually measure three-dimensional coordinates of large objects such as buildings, or sites, digital models in a variety of formats can be produced.

Many times, when a landscape architect, architect, or engineer is involved, the creation of digital base data is a first step to a project, so that the data can be used for producing digital models throughout the design and construction process.

6.4.3 Digitizing

Sometimes, when sufficiently accurate paper maps or plans are available, the fastest and most direct method of getting digital data is to digitize or scan the paper maps. Large-format digitizing tablets can be used to trace lines – contours, roads and streams, parcels, etc. – directly into a 2D CAD system. In this process, human judgment is often required to set the resolution of digitizing (for example, when tracing a curved line into several short, straight, line segments, how

Figure 6.21
a. A field unit for performing automatic 3D digitizing surveys. This laser device captures "point clouds" in the field with up to 1" accuracy.
b. 3D "point cloud" scans of terrain.
c. 3D "point cloud" scans of trees.
Courtesy of Cyrax Corp.

many segments, and how long?) and to extract important features. It is important to remember when digitizing from paper maps to set the coordinate systems and units according to the standards required for the project, otherwise the result may be unusable with other information, such as a USGS site map. Especially with contour lines, it is important to set the required attributes, including elevation, during the digitizing process, or else the 3D information may be hard to extract.

Scanning is similar to digitizing, except that it produces a raster image, rather than vector data. This raster image can be used as a background image, or texture, and can also be used as a basis for *vectorizing*, extracting linear data from the pixels. This process can be automated with "raster-to-vector" software, and when the scan is high quality and high-resolution, the results can be excellent.

A relatively recent development is the introduction of high-resolution 3D scanners, which collect "point cloud" data of buildings, trees, forests, whole building sites, or other complex 3D structures. Relatively expensive, these sophisticated devices can be used for very-high-accuracy field surveys, and the data converted to faces or polylines for use with ordinary CAD modeling and rendering software.

6.5 Ethical and Representational Concerns

Making landscape models, like engaging in any other representational activity, is not always a value-free activity. When you are just expressing yourself, or making art, you have no particular obligation except to yourself in making your choices. When you are making a model that you or others will use as a basis for decision making, however, the responsibilities are greater.

In the design process, designers make models all the time, to test their ideas, to explore and evaluate alternatives, to form the basis for a next round of models and explorations. In this role, digital models and other representations have an ambivalent status: they need not be realistic, but they must be informative and appropriate. Choosing an angle of view, for example, is an implicit act of choosing between possible experiences of a landscape, for example between the omniscient but almost-never-experienced aerial perspective, or the ubiquitous eye-level view. Making these choices is a part of any design process. A power of digital models is that from a single model, multiple views can be rendered, at will (assuming that no view-dependent simplifications have been made, of course, such as rendering a grove of trees as an image, rather than 3D objects, in which case the view from within the grove would not be possible).

Not only can various different perspective viewpoints be tried out, but also different drawings altogether: plans, sections, axonometrics, as well as non-graphical views like parts lists or cost estimates can be produced. Totally integrated modeling systems that actually enable cost estimates as well as plan views from a single database are still under development, but increasingly more information of different types can be made available from a single model, so that when changes are made they can be proliferated to all appropriate views.

Designers use a variety of conventions, abstractions, and personal idiosyncratic representations, which may not be comprehensible to others. When you share your model, you need to try to make sure that you are not coloring others' perceptions with your own conventions. This is the reason that conventional representations are developed, and a reason why "photo-realism" is a goal in some modeling and rendering, so that conventional misreadings are minimized, and views are presented as if they were photographs of a finished project. Recognizing that all representations, even photographs, are abstractions from reality can help to determine an appropriate level of abstraction and realism in modeling and rendering. For many design decisions, photographic realism can be counter-productive, tending to overemphasize the details of the photographic images, at the expense of the design conception.

At the same time, especially when non-designers are asked to judge or decide from models and renderings, the responsibility of the modeler is to make sure that real-world implications are not too overshadowed or even hidden by the modeling and rendering approaches. Choosing a photogenic view is a natural human tendency, but omitting or distorting real elements is usually inappropriate, and even unethical, in a public decision-making process.

Many landscape models and renderings are made for the purpose of evaluating "looks" and often visibility; in these cases, a fine road must be walked between abstraction and realism. Questions of visibility may hinge on correct perspective and accurate terrain data, including the curvature of the earth. Questions of appearance may have everything to do with choices of colors and tonal resolution. In the end, making a digital landscape model and rendering depends on personal technical skill and aesthetic judgment, both of which are best gained with time and experience, coupled with critical self-evaluation and the opportunity to experiment and invent.

Figure 6.22
*Four slightly different images showing visual simulation of cell-phone tower installation.
a. Initial proposal;
b. tower painted brown;
c. building at base painted brown;
d. screened with evergreens.
These kinds of visualizations depend on a high degree of accuracy in geometry and color, in order to help effectively evaluate alternatives.*
Courtesy of Curt Westergard.

6.6 Final Thoughts; Next Steps

The techniques discussed in this text have been, and are, under constant development. In general there have been experiments and prototypes in research labs and academic settings that have developed one feature or another, sometimes in the specific context of landscape visualization as part of a landscape architecture or planning department, or sometimes geography or computer science, which have then been taken over and turned into features of commercial off-the-shelf software. Military and aerospace visualization systems for flight simulators and "virtual battlefields" provided some of the early development of computational techniques; more recently the motion picture special-effects industry has also played a substantial role in the development of techniques for creating digital environments for feature films, as has the entertainment/games industry in the development of backgrounds for video games. The annual SIGGRAPH meetings of the ACM (*Association for Computing Machinery, Special Interest Group in Computer Graphics*) have provided both an impetus and a showcase for new techniques in the field, and the proceedings of those meetings from the 1980s and 1990s are rich in detailed techniques for many aspects of landscape visualization.

Though there is a certain maturity to some of the techniques for modeling and rendering, there are still many developments to come and substantial challenges remaining. In general, the tension between realistic "acts-like" models and more superficial "looks-like" models remains a driving force. Many natural systems such as light, gravity, and wind which shape the natural environment are deceptively complex in their real behavior, especially in their dynamnics and in their interactions. Although techniques for simulating each of them have been developed in the context of computer modeling systems, these are all still approximations at best, and tend to be limited in their practical application, often requiring substantial computer resources such as memory, processing power, and time. Compromises for the sake of expediency or even tractability are found throughout all techniques for computer modeling and rendering, and landscape modeling because of the size and complexity of the subject matter is a prime example.

As of this writing, there are still some notable shortcomings in commercial software, and a number of developments which are still to come that will make a big difference to digital landscape modelers.

"Snapping" to a terrain model is one: the simple desire to place objects such as trees, buildings, and people in a 3D model and have their elevation interactively set with respect to an underlying surface is an obvious one, still not met in most software systems. Tracing paths and complex spline curves on an underlying terrain model is another example unsupported by most software (although the VRML specification for navigation of a virtual model allows for "gravity" to constrain the viewer's path to the terrain surface). This is just a special example of the more general need to have *constraint-based* modeling systems in which attributes of objects are constrained by specified relationships to others. Other examples include intersection-checking to prevent objects from physically intersecting (such as the branches of a tree next to a building), or dependencies such as groundcover next to a curb; if the curb is moved, the groundcover should be resized appropriately. Such developments in CAD software are underway, both in research and in the commercial arena, and will make modeling landscapes, as well as other complex systems, more effective.

Similarly, good techniques for dealing with the problems of levels-of-detail (LOD) are imperative and still mostly missing. The forest, the trees and the leaves, the fields and the blades of grass, the crowds and the individual people are all essential constituents of the landscape. Present techniques require too much detailed hand-configuration and are too limited in their scope. More automatic, default-driven, generic techniques for managing LOD will make for far more usable landscape models.

As a last example, the whole field of modeling dynamics is still in its infancy. Particle systems are useful but still limited, and procedural techniques and scripting languages are awkward at best, especially when powerful. More robust dynamic modeling will depend partly on the development of the constraint-based systems described above, and on the convergence of the best features of numerous different special-purpose dynamic modeling languages and techniques, many of which are still non-spatial. The field of landscape ecology for example has given great insights into processes such as animal movement, soil erosion and vegetative succession, but good visual models of these processes have yet to be developed outside of special-purpose research labs.

Gravity-constrained, level-of-detail savvy, ecologically aware dynamic landscape models are still some way off, but the trajectory toward them is clear. And it is important to remember that we will never have "perfect" models, for there is no such thing. Rather, landscape modelers will tinker and tailor models to suit various purposes, for some of which physical-based realism is important, but for many of which it is not. Making representations will always be an art guided by science. The science has many pathways still unexplored, and so has the art of landscape modeling.

6.7 Summary

Managing digital projects requires considerable attention to detail, from file naming conventions to data conversion parameters. Landscape modeling further requires attention to the sequence of elements, usually starting with landform, then water, then buildings, infrastructure, vegetation, and often animals, including people; followed by decisions about atmospheric effects, lighting, and rendering and output options. Making these decisions is sometimes a matter of personal artistic expression, but often is bound up in a professional design process, with communication required between team members, and serious responsibilities to colleagues, clients, or the public. In these cases, ethical concerns about making representations must be integrated with the many technical considerations. The next developments in computer graphics and dynamic modeling will add to the technical repertoire, but only practice will perfect the art of landscape modeling.

1. 3D Digital Model of Highbrook Estates, New Zealand, Peter Walker and Partners. [Courtesy Peter Walker and Partners.]

2. "Moon Lake." 3D Model created with World Construction Set Copyright 2000 Adam Hauldren, N-Light, LTD. [Courtesy of Adam Hauldren.]

3. 3D Model of HUD Plaza Improvements, Washington D.C., Martha Schwartz, Inc. [Courtesy of Martha Schwartz, Inc.]

References

Brinkman, Ron. *The Art and Scien... ...positing.* San Diego, CA: Academic Press, 1999.

Ching, Frank. *Architectural Grap... ...* New York: Van Nostrand Reinhold Company, 1975

Ebert, David S., Kenton Musgra... ...achey, Ken Perlin, Steven Worley. *Texturing and Modeling, 2nd ...* ...ego, CA: Academic Press, 1998.

Flake, Gary W. *The Computational ... ...ture: Computer Explorations of Fractals, Chaos, Complex Systems and A...* ...Cambridge, MA: MIT Press, 1999.

Fleming, Bill. *3D Photorealism Toolki...* ...rk, NY: John Wiley and Sons, 1998.

Fleming, Bill. *Advanced 3D Photorealism Techniques.* New York, NY: John Wiley and Sons, 1999.

Sheppard, Stephen. *Visual Simulation: A User's Guide for Architects, Engineers and Planners.* New York, NY: Van Nostrand Reinhold, 1989.

Figure 6.23
Image of a synthetic landscape. Modeled and rendered in Animatek World Builder. Courtesy of Igor Borovikov.

Software

The text of this book has largely avoided reference to specific computer software, except by way of identification of the technology used to create images. Both research and commercial software evolves too fast to make any reliable reference in print to specific software's existence, capabilities, or limitations. Insights from the fields of computer science and computer graphics, allied disciplines such as civil engineering and illustration, and developments in computer hardware and storage all contribute to the constant evolution of new and valuable software capabilities.

Nonetheless, at the time of this writing (summer 2000) some of the available software resources can be catalogued. The following list is surely not exhaustive, but represents the best knowledge of the authors at the time of writing. For an up-to-date listing and other Web links be sure to visit the companion on-line site on the Web at: http://www.landscapemodeling.com .

The commercial programs listed below in alphabetic order are selected from a large body of software for 2D and 3D modeling, rendering, animation, GIS analysis, and image processing. Presence on this list constitutes no special endorsement, these are just the software known to the authors to be available and useful; similarly, omission from this list is no pejorative judgment. There are also numerous research-only and "share-ware" programs which are valuable and contain many of the functions of the software below, but are not listed here. (In parentheses is noted the software compatibility with four major operating systems, Windows, Macintosh, UNIX, and IRIX; these notes too may be out-of-date, so be sure to check the manufacturer's Web site for accurate information!)

This list, with live Internet links to manufacturers' Web sites, is also included on the attached CD-ROM.

Landscape Modeling Software (in alphabetic order)

3DStudioMax by Autodesk (www.autodesk.com) 3D modeling, rendering, and animation with robust functions; with scripting language and numerous add-ons, some landscape-specific. (Windows)

3DStudioMax Plug-Ins by Digimation (www.digimation.com) adds various procedural effects including particle systems and others, for many natural phenomena such as water, smoke, fire, etc., to 3DStudiomax. (Windows)

AMAP by JMGGraphics (wwww.jmg-graphics.com) creates 3D trees and other plants from parametric variation; includes terrain and other site-related tools. (Windows)

ArcInfo by ESRI (www.esri.com) robust GIS functions, raster and vector-based, includes more functions and Internet server connectivity than related ArcView. (Windows, UNIX)

ArcView by ESRI (www.esri.com) desktop GIS functions, raster and vector-based, includes scripting language and many add-ons for topographic and hydrologic analysis. (Windows, UNIX)

AutoCAD by Autodesk (www.autodesk.com) 2D and 3D modeling and rendering; with add-on modules such as "Land Development Desktop" includes landscape-specific functions. (Windows)

Bryce3D by Corel (www.corel.com) combines fractal terrain, procedural textures, lighting, and atmospheric effects for creating fantastic landscape models and renderings. (Macintosh, Windows)

DigArts by GardenHose (www.gardenhose.com) foliage and tree visualization software for 2D and 3D modeling and rendering. (Macintosh, Windows)

ElectricImage by ElectricImage (www.electricimage.com) 3D modeling and rendering. (Macintosh)

FormZ by Auto-des-sys (www.autodessys.com) 2D and 3D modeling and rendering. (Windows and Macintosh)

Genesis by Geomantics (www.geomantics.com) combines GIS data and image processing functions to create realistic 3D visualizations. (Windows, Macintosh)

Maya by Alias (www.alias.com) advanced 3D modeling and rendering; particular strength for procedural modeling. (SGI/Irix and Windows; slated for MacOSX in 2001)

MFWorks by ThinkSpace (www.thinkspace.com) desktop GIS functions, raster and vector-based. (Windows and Macintosh)

Natural Scene Designer by Natural Graphics (www.naturalgfx.com) combines GIS data and image processing functions to create realistic 3D visualizations. (Windows, Macintosh)

Panorama Tools by Helmut Dersch (www.fh-furtwangen.de/~dersch) combines individual photographs into 360° panoramas for visualization.

Photoshop by Adobe Systems (www.adobe.com) image processing with multiple features and add-ons. (Windows, Macintosh)

Premiere by Adobe Systems (www.adobe.com) multimedia and video editing with multiple features and add-ons. (Windows, Macintosh)

RapidSite by Evans & Sutherland (www.es.com) combines GIS data, 3D modeling and image processing functions to create realistic 3D visualizations. (Windows)

RenderMan by Pixar (www.pixar.com) high performance rendering with many procedural controls. (Windows, UNIX, IRIX)

Rhino by Robert MacNeel Associates (www.rhino3d.com) NURBS-based 3D modeling and rendering. (Windows)

SoftImage by SoftImage (www.softimage.com) 3D modeling and rendering. (SGI/IRIX and Windows)

TerraVista by Terrain Experts, Inc. (www.terrex.com) terrain generation and scene visualization. (Windows)

Tree Pro by Onyx Computing (www.onyxtree.com) creates 2D and 3D trees from parametric variation. (Windows, Macintosh)

VectorWorks by Nemetschek (www.nemetschek.com) 2D and 3D modeling and rendering. (Windows and Macintosh)

VistaPro by Andromeda Software (www.andromedasoftware.com) combines GIS data and image processing functions to create realistic 3D visualizations. (Windows and Macintosh)

World Builder by Animatek (www.animatek.com) combines GIS data and image processing functions to create realistic 3D visualizations. (Windows, Macintosh)

World Construction Set by 3DNature (www.3dnature.com) combines GIS data and image processing functions to create realistic 3D visualizations. (Windows, Macintosh)

Glossary

This list contains terms from a variety of distinct disciplines – including computer graphics, modeling and rendering, image processing, landscape architecture, and geographical analysis – all of which may be encountered in the process of landscape modeling and creating digital visualizations. Many terms common in those disciplines have been omitted; this selective list contains terms used throughout (or at least once, in) this book and the sense(s) in which they are used.

2.5D surface: a simple 3D surface with no overhangs or holes (specifically, for each (x,y) location there is only a single z value); includes many 3D terrain surfaces, but not all

2D: having two-dimensional geometry, flat, characterized by Cartesian (x,y) coordinates

3D: having three dimensions, characterized by Cartesian (x,y,z) coordinates

3D digitizer: a device used to capture and record 3D coordinates from real-life objects

aerial oblique: a view taken from above looking down at an angle, as from an airplane

airlight: the lightening of the atmosphere with distance caused by particles reflecting sunlight

albedo: a measure of the brightness of a reflective object or surface

algorithm: a formula or s[...] out by an agent such as a person or computer

allee: a linear arrangemen[...]ing a street, canal, or other feature

alpha channel: a separate [...]dded within a raster image file format, used to carry additio[...] pixel; often used for transparency information

ambient light: surroundi[...] light that is everywhere equally intense and has no directiona[...]

amplitude: intensity or he[...]een peak and trough

analog: continuous, real, [...]led; contrast with digital

and: logical or boolean op[...]he intersection set

angle of repose: the maxi[...] at which a pile of loose material is stable

anti-aliasing: a technique [...]ics of adding in pixels of intermediate values at high-contrast ed[...] "jagged" appearance of diagonal lines

array: a repetitive arrangem[...]r, rectangular, or circular/concentric

aspect: the direction a surfa[...]ch as east or southeast; also called orientation

aspect ratio: of a rectangle, [...]bject such as an image or pixel, the ratio of width (*x*-axis) to height [...]

atmospheric haze: the phen[...]eing and lightening of the atmosphere at a distance, caused by airlig[...]ular matter or water vapor

AVI: Audio Video Interleave; a [...]t for multimedia and animations developed by Microsoft Corporation

base data: the original source data, such as maps or other measurements or plans, on which a project (landscape, architectural, or geographic) is based, and from which other data (e.g. slope, or intermediate layers) are derived

berm: a mound of earth, often linear

billboard: a transparent rectangular plane, used in computer graphics rendering to carry a 2D image used to represent a 3D object such as a tree in the landscape

bitmap: in general, a digital raster image; sometimes limited to a raster image with only two color values (monochrome), typically black and white

boolean: a logical system or algebra using set theory and operators such as *and*, *or*, and *not*, the basis of binary computers and some solid modeling operations, described by and named after the mathematician George Boole

bosque: a rectangular or circular grove of trees in a regular planting arrangement

bump map: a 2D image used in computer rendering to produce the appearance of depth, or bumps, in a multichannel texture-mapped image

CAD: Computer Aided Design or Computer Aided Drawing software, designed for creating digital representations of 2D and 3D objects and space; typically contains modeling and/or rendering functions, as well as import, export, and others

caustic: the characteristic sinuous, curved, shiny light rays seen on underwater surfaces, caused by refraction through the rippled top surface of water

CAVE: Computer Augmented Visualization Environment, a room or chamber with multiple displays (often six or more projectors or rear-projection screens) used to create an immersive "virtual reality" environment

cell: in a raster representation, a pixel or repeated regular element

cell size: the typical width, height, or sometimes area of a cell in a raster grid

cirrus: kind of cloud

CLUT: Color LookUp Table, a data structure used in indexed color images to correspond color values to numeric values

CMYK: Cyan, Magenta, Yellow, and Black color system, used when printing with inks; contrast with RGB

contour interval: in a contour plan, the typical vertical distance between contour lines

contour line: an imaginary line, or isoline, connecting points of equal elevation above some fixed level, or datum; used to represent 3D curved surfaces such as terrain

contour plan: a representation of a smooth 3D or 2.5D surface, using contour lines

contrast: in an image or scene, the amount of difference between the lightest and darkest areas

cumulous: kind of cloud

cut: dirt, or other earth material, removed in a grading operation; or to the act of removing, or to the area where material has been removed

cut and fill: the process of removing earth material from some locations and adding it to others by grading; the process of computing total volumes of material moved

datum: a fixed or established point of reference, usually with a fixed elevation

decal: a 2D image or texture map applied to an object in a computer rendering, like a label on a bottle

deLauney triangulation: a method of connecting an arbitrary set of points together in a network of triangles which meet certain mathematical criteria (specifically, the circle described by the three points in any triangle contains no other point in the set), used in creating a TIN

DEM: Digital Elevation Model, any digital representation of the earth's surface, but also a particular raster grid format used by the USGS and others

depth of field: the zone in which an image seen through a lens is in perfect focus

diffuse: light which is indirect, and has no reflections or highlights, similar to ambient

digital: encoded in binary integers (bits), discretized or sampled, typically on or for a computer; contrast with analog

digital ortho quadrangle: (DOQ or "digital ortho quad") a computer generated image of an aerial photograph, ortho-rectified and geo-referenced to match a typical USGS "quad sheet" map,

digitizing: generally the process of making digital, but also specifically using a "digitizer" to trace coordinates, 2D or 3D, of an object and create a digital representation

directional light: light which has a location and direction; contrast with ambient light

DLG: Digital Line Graph, a digital format used by the USGS for vector data

DOQ: see digital ortho quadrangle

DPI: dots per inch, used to measure the resolution of images either on screen or on paper

drape: to project an image, or 3D vector features, onto a 3D surface such as a digital model of terrain, to create a realistic representation, much as a flexible sheet can be draped over an irregular surface, conforming to it

SDTS: Spatial Data Transfer Standard, a conventional standard format for transferring geographic data used by the USGS

DTM: Digital Terrain Model; synonym for DEM

DV: Digital Video; a format for storing digital moving images, equivalent to, but with higher image resolution than, analog video, usually with 16:9 aspect ratio

DVD: Digital Versatile Disc, a format and optical medium for storing large amounts (2 – 5 GB) of digital data, commonly used for storing digital video

DXF: Data Exchange Format, a proprietary but widely used digital file format for describing 2D and 3D spatial data, developed by Autodesk Corporation

edge: in computer graphics, a line segment between two end points, or vertices; three or more edges combine to make faces or polygons

elevation: usually, referring to terrain data, meaning height above sea level; but also a paraline drawing of an object or scene as seen from the side

face: in computer graphics, a flat 2D bounded area or polygon, formed by at least three connected edges; at least four faces are required to make up a solid polyhedron

field of view: (FOV) the angle of the cone of vision of a lens; the usual human FOV is approximately 150°

fill: dirt, or other earth material, added in a grading operation; or to the act of adding, or to the area where material has been added

floating point: a digital representation of a number with a specified number decimal places, or fractional part, used to represent real numbers; contrast with integer

flow accumulation: a measurement of the amount of water accumulated in overland flow over a surface

flyover: an animation made from an aerial point-of-view, such as from an airplane

FOV: see field of view

fractal: an algorithm, or shape, characterized by self-similarity and produced by recursive subdivision; more generally the branch of mathematics named and explored by Benoit Mandelbrot

geo-reference: to assign accurate real-world coordinates in some map projection to the geometric representation of some object(s), or to at least the corners, and usually all points or contents, of a map, image, or photograph

geospecific: computer renderings created using photographs or other images (satellite, e.g.) which are geo-referenced and so can be used to drape over digital terrain models for realistic visualizations

geo-TIFF: a file format for images, which contains geo-referencing information

geotypical: visualizations which are created by inserting "typical" elements such as generic houses, trees, etc., in appropriate locations, determined by geographic data, so as to make realistic but nonspecific visualizations

GIS: Geographic Information System; software designed to store, manipulate, and display geographic and spatial data such as maps

God rays: visible rays of light, caused by particles in the atmosphere or underwater, sometimes called "crepuscular rays" at sunset

GPS: Global Positioning System or Satellite, a satellite-based system for determining precise geographic locations in the field

grading: the process of moving earth material for functional or aesthetic purposes; also the process of designing or creating a grading plan

grading plan: a document, often a contour plan, which directs a grading process

grid mesh: a representation of raster data produced by drawing lines between successive grid cell centers or corners; also called a "fish-net"

hard shadows: shadows created by light from a single source, causing shadows with a solid interior and sharp distinct edges, cast by the umbra; contrast with soft shadows

HDTV: High Definition Television; a format for video images characterized by a 16:9 image aspect ratio and high resolution imagery

heads-up digitizing: the process of tracing outlines from a raster image, on-screen

height field: a raster elevation model

hypsography: description of underwater surfaces using contour lines

IGES: Initial Graphics Exchange Standard, a proposed standard digital file format for computer graphics and spatial data

image-map: a digital raster image, used in rendering to give color or texture to 3D objects

immersion: a method for projecting images such that the viewer's peripheral vision is engaged, either by using head mounted displays or CAVE techniques

indexed color: a data structure for representing color images using a Color Lookup Table, capable of a smaller number of total colors than the RGB system

integer: a numeric value with no decimal places, used to represent whole numbers

intersection: the set-theoretic operation yielding only those elements that are contained in each of two operand sets, equivalent to the logical *and*

inverse kinematics: a technique for creating models of mechanical linkages of connected parts, such that motion is transmitted in a predictable way through the parts.

JAVA: an object-oriented programming language developed by Sun Microsystems

JPEG (or **JPG**): a file format for image data enabling "lossy compression," i.e., which may lose some detail when decompressed

level of detail: a name for the phenomenon that real-world objects may need to be represented with varying amounts of detail – typically less in the distance, and more in the foreground or nearby – for reasons of computational efficiency

LIDAR: Light Intensity Detection and Ranging a laser-based technique for sensing distances, analogous to RADAR, but allowing very high precision measurements, useful for scanning terrain and vegetation from airborne or hand-held instruments

LOD: see level of detail

L-systems: Lindenmeyer systems, an algorithmic method of generating branched forms and structures such as plants

lux: lumens per square meter, a measurement of light intensity

map: in computer graphics, a 2D raster image which serves as an image or texture in rendering, particularly in a multichannel texture

map projection: a mathematical formula for converting points on a sphere, such as the earth onto a plane, such as a flat map

mask: in computer graphics, an image with only two values (black and white) used in conjunction with another more detailed image to mask out, or clip, parts of the image, so as to indicate areas of transparency, or edges of the image, etc.

Mercator projection: a particular early map projection in common use especially for navigational maps

mesh: a digital representation of a surface or solid consisting of multiple, possibly curved, line segments whose intersections form a regular grid

meta-balls: a digital modeling technique for representing "blobby" shapes as aggregations of spheres and an interpolated smoothly curved surface covering them

metadata: data about data, such as the source, date, accuracy and other attributes

MIP-map: from "Multi in Parvo," a digital data format that stores images at multiple different representations, in hierarchically nested scales such as 4 x 4, 16 x 16, and 256 x 256 pixels, so that different resolutions can be displayed at different distances from the viewer

model: a representation used as a surrogate for some real thing, for the purpose of testing, modifying, presenting, etc.

modeling: in computer visualization, the processes of creating the data structures used to represent objects and scenes, usually using special-purpose software; distinct from the process of "rendering" to create images

morph: to transform a shape image or object smoothly from an initial state to a different final state; also called "tweening" (from the presence of "in-between" states)

MOV: a file format for Quicktime movies and animations, developed by Apple Computer Co.

MPEG (or **MPG**): a file format for compressed video

multichannel: in computer graphics, refers to textures composed of multiple "maps" or channels which describe different aspects of the optical properties of the texture, such as diffuse color, reflectivity, transparency, bump, etc.

NTSC: National Televison System Committee; a common format for video signals, with a 4:3 aspect ratio and lower resolution than the newer HDTV

NURB: Non-Uniform Rational B-spline, a mathematical technique for representing smooth curved surfaces

or: logical or boolean operator that creates the union set

orientation: synonym for aspect

ortho-photo: an aerial photograph that has been ortho-rectified and geo-referenced

ortho-rectify: the process of adjusting a photograph (typically aerial) to account for distortions introduced by camera, lens, and the topography of the earth's surface to create an image with a constant horizontal scale

paraline: a form of drawing projection which preserves distances and angles in the projection; includes plan, section, axonometric, and isometric drawings but not perspective projection

parametric: characterized by having one or more variables, or parameters, which can be varied for different results or effects

patch: a curved surface with a rectangular border, or outline; patches may be combined together to create compound curved surfaces

penumbra: that portion of a shadow in semi-shade between the darkest, or umbra, and the un-shadowed zone

perspective: a drawing projection that portrays the convergence of parallel lines in the visual field and the apparent reduction in size of distant objects; the closest drawing projection to what the human eye experiences

photo-realism: the effort to create synthetic images such as computer renderings, indistinguishable from photographs of real objects or scenes

phototropism: the tendency of plans to move or grow towards light

pixel: a "picture element" or single point of color in a raster image

planting plan: a document, often a drawing superimposed upon a grading plan, showing locations, sizes, and species of new plants in a proposed planting design

point cloud: a set of 3D points describing the outlines or surface features of an object, such as produced by a 3D digitizer

polyline: a line created by a series of shorter straight line segments

procedural: synonym for algorithmic

procedural texture: an image, used as a texture map, generated "on the fly" by a procedure, or algorithm

projection: the process of transforming 3D points into 2D points, to create a drawing or image; see also map projection

QTVR: QuickTime Virtual Reality, a file format developed by Apple Computer Co. to represent 360° panoramic views, animations, and hypertext links in a single file

QuickTime: a digital technology and file format for animations, developed by Apple Computer Co.

radiosity: a technique for simulating lighting effects by considering the inter-reflections between surfaces in a 3D model, more computationally demanding than ray-tracing

raster: a rectangular array of values, or cells, or pixels; a common data format for representing and displaying maps and images

ray-tracing: a technique for simulating lighting effects in a rendering by mathematically casting light-rays into a 3D model, and computing reflection, refraction, and other effects

rectification: the process of transforming a map or an image by systematically moving individual elements, such as pixels or lines, to align with some other reference image or map; sometimes called "rubber-sheeting"

recursive: characterized by processes which can be indefinitely repeatedly applied to their own output, such as algorithms which create branching and subdivision

rendering: the process of creating an image meant to portray an object or scene, especially using computer graphics software; also the image so produced; distinct from the "modeling" operations which create the input for the rendering operations

RGB: Red, Green, Blue; a method for representing colors as mixtures of the three primary colors of light, especially for display on a computer screen or projector; contrast with CMYK

rubber-sheeting: see rectification

ruled surface: a faceted curved surface created by adjoining flat faces between two curved lines, created by subdividing each line into an equal number of short segments and connecting between them

scotopic vision: the low-resolution, monochromatic vision of humans at night

self-similarity: the characteristic of certain natural and mathematically produced forms (fractals, e.g.) that they exhibit features which appear identical or similar at different scales of magnification

shadow map: a faster and less accurate alternative to ray-traced shadows for creating simulated shadows in a computer rendering

slope: measurement of the steepness of terrain, the ratio of vertical rise to horizontal distance expressed as a percentage or as degrees of angle

soft shadows: shadows created by light from multiple sources, causing multiple overlapping shadows and a region of intermediate gray values with fuzzy edges, cast by the penumbra; contrast with hard shadows

solid model: a digital representation of 3D objects which may have such attributes such as inside/outside, mass, volume, and others; contrast with surface model

specular: reflective, especially light from materials with glossy surfaces

spline: a curved line formed by two or more vertices, or "control points," and a mathematical formula describing the curve(s) between them

spot elevation: a specified 3D point with location and elevation, used to describe terrain, paving, or other fixed floor elevations

State Plane projection: a map projection used by state governments in the United States

stratus: kind of cloud

surface model: a digital representation of 3D objects which have two sides and surface area, but no thickness, and so no attributes as inside/outside, mass, or volume; contrast with solid model

surface normal: the vector perpendicular to a surface or face at any point

SVGA: a standard dimension for computer graphics hardware: 800 x 600 pixels

swale: a ditch or valley in the earth

SXGA: a standard dimension for computer graphics hardware: 1200 x 1024 pixels

texture map: a 2D raster image used in computer rendering to give color and other apparent surface characteristics ("textures") to 3D objects

TIFF (or **TIF**): a file format for color image data, which enables "loss-less compression"

tiling: regular repeated placement of a single small element covering a larger area or surface; especially an image or texture map used to cover a surface in rendering

TIN: Triangulated Irregular Network; a data format for representing surfaces as a connected network of triangles

transparency map: a 2D image or map, usually used in conjunction with other images in a multichannel texture, to indicate transparency of an object in computer rendering; see alpha channel

tweaking: the process of moving individual vertices of a 3D geometric object, such as a mesh or a TIN

umbra: the darkest central portion of a shadow

union: the set-theoretic operation yielding all those elements that are contained in either of two operand sets, equivalent to the logical *or*

USGS: United States Geological Survey, the federal agency responsible for creating and disseminating detailed maps including topographic and land-use maps of the United States

UTM: Universal Transverse Mercator, a common map projection used for geographic data

vector: a mathematical line segment with direction and magnitude; but more generally, any data representation that contains points, lines, and polygons; contrast with raster

vertex: in computer graphics, a 2D or 3D point; two vertices may be connected together by a line, or edge

VGA: a standard dimension for computer graphics hardware: 640 x 480 pixels

VHS: Video Home System; a common low-resolution format for recording video images; superceded by HDTV

virtual reality: simulated environments and the methods used to create them

visualization: the process of creating images using computers, also called "rendering" when applied to landscape or architectural material, instead of abstract scientific data; an image or images so produced

volume light: (sometimes "volumetric light") light which is itself visible, usually in the form of rays emanating from the light source (e.g., sun, window, or lamp), especially when an opaque object is in front of the light source; the effect in nature caused by particles in the atmosphere and obstructing objects such as clouds or mountains; see also "God rays"

VR: see virtual reality

VRML: Virtual Reality Modeling Language; a file format standard for representing 3D scenes especially for creating VR environments

walk-through: an animation of a 3D scene made as if from a human eye level

watershed: that area of land from which all water drains to a single specified "outfall" point

wire frame: a computer graphics representation of a 3D scene or object made only by colored lines representing the outlines, or edges of objects, with no solid faces

WWW: World Wide Web, or simply "Web," the common interface and conventions for navigation and communication over the Internet

X3D: a proposed standard for representing 3D objects and scenes combining aspects of the VRML specification with the XML standard

XGA: a standard dimension for computer graphics hardware: 1024 x 768 pixels

XML: a standard format for representing information, especially for transmission over the WWW

Index

About the CD-ROM

Landscape Modeling CD-ROM

Attached to this book is a CD-ROM, containing digital versions of some of the book's text and many of the illustrations from the book's chapters, as well as some examples of those things that cannot be fully conveyed on a printed page, such as animations and JAVA applications. All of the tutorials are also included, as PDF files.

In addition, a listing of relevant on-line links to Internet sites of interest is included, and a number of commercial vendors of landscape modeling software have provided samples and other material on the CD-ROM.

The CD's structure is similar to a WWW web site, and can be found in its most current version at **http://www.landscapemodeling.org.** The CD-ROM can be read in its entirety without being connected to the Internet; however some of the links, especially from software vendors and others, will lead to Web sites on the Internet, and so you will need to have a live Internet connection to make the most of them.

To read the CD on your computer, find and double-click on the top-level file entitled **index.htm**, or open it with a Web browser such as Netscape Navigator, Internet Explorer, Amaya, or any other standard Web browser. This will link you to a hypertext version of the book, organized in the same chapters as in the text. Most of the contents are plain HTML and require no special procedures to read. The animations naturally require software for playing QuickTime movies, and

287

the JAVA applications require a JAVA applet interpreter.

Note: All text and digital images on the CD-ROM are copyrighted and protected by digital watermark, and should not be used commercially or reproduced without permission.

CD-ROM Table of Contents

CD-ROM Table of Contents (continued)

III. JAVA Applets

JavaMountain
JavaTree

IV. Vendor Contributions
(material provided by vendors and others, on the CD-ROM)

Animatek, makers of World Builder
DigArts, makers of foliage and tree visualization products
Onyx Tree Software, makers of Tree-Pro
3DNature, makers of World Construction Set
JMG-Graphics, distributors of AMAP software
Evans & Sutherland, makers of RapidSite software
Helmut Dersch, developer of Panorama Tools
   open-source software

V. Web Links

LINKS, Pages from various sites on the web
TUTORIALS, GLOSSARIES, etc.
GALLERIES of Images, etc.
TEXTURES, SAMPLES, etc.
TERRAIN DATA, DEMs, etc.
RESEARCH PROJECTS, Academic Institutions, others
SOFTWARE VENDORS, Product-related sites

CD-ROM WARRANTY

This software is protected by both United States copyright law and international copyright treaty provision. You must treat this software just like a book. By saying "just like a book," McGraw-Hill means, for example, that this software may be used by any number of people and may be freely moved from one computer location to another, so long as there is no possibility of its being used at one location or on one computer while it also is being used at another. Just as a book cannot be read by two different people in two different places at the same time, neither can the software be used by two different people in two different places at the same time (unless, of course, McGraw-Hill's copyright is being violated).

LIMITED WARRANTY

McGraw-Hill takes great care to provide you with top-quality software, thoroughly checked to prevent virus infections. McGraw-Hill warrants the physical CD-ROM contained herein to be free of defects in materials and workmanship for a period of sixty days from the purchase date. If McGraw-Hill receives written notification within the warranty period of defects in materials or workmanship, and such notification is determined by McGraw-Hill to be correct, McGraw-Hill will replace the defective CD-ROM. Send requests to:

> McGraw-Hill
> Customer Services
> P.O. Box 545
> Blacklick, OH 43004-0545

The entire and exclusive liability and remedy for breach of this Limited Warranty shall be limited to replacement of a defective CD-ROM and shall not include or extend to any claim for or right to cover any other damages, including but not limited to, loss of profit, data, or use of the software, or special, incidental, or consequential damages or other similar claims, even if McGraw-Hill has been specifically advised of the possibility of such damages. In no event will McGraw-Hill's liability for any damages to you or any other person ever exceed the lower of suggested list price or actual price paid for the license to use the software, regardless of any form of the claim.

McGRAW-HILL SPECIFICALLY DISCLAIMS ALL OTHER WARRANTIES, EXPRESS OR IMPLIED, INCLUDING, BUT NOT LIMITED TO, ANY IMPLIED WARRANTY OF MERCHANTABILITY OR FITNESS FOR A PARTICULAR PURPOSE.

Specifically, McGraw-Hill makes no representation or warranty that the software is fit for any particular purpose and any implied warranty of merchantability is limited to the sixty-day duration of the Limited Warranty covering the physical CD-ROM only (and not the software) and is otherwise expressly and specifically disclaimed.

This limited warranty gives you specific legal rights; you may have others which may vary from state to state. Some states do not allow the exclusion of incidental or consequential damages, or the limitation on how long an implied warranty lasts, so some of the above may not apply to you.